Landscaping with
Native Plants of Michigan

Text and photography by
Lynn M. Steiner

Voyageur Press

First published in 2006 by Voyageur Press, an imprint of MBI Publishing Company, Galtier Plaza, Suite 200, 380 Jackson Street, St. Paul, MN 55101-3885 USA

Voyageur Press titles are also available at discounts in bulk quantity for industrial or sales-promotional use. For details write to Special Sales Manager at MBI Publishing Company, Galtier Plaza, Suite 200, 380 Jackson Street, St. Paul, MN 55101-3885 USA.

Library of Congress Cataloging-in-Publication Data
Steiner, Lynn M.
    Landscaping with native plants of Michigan / by Lynn M. Steiner.
        p. cm.
    Includes bibliographical references and index.
    ISBN-13: 978-0-7603-2538-4 (pbk. : alk. paper)
    ISBN-10: 0-7603-2538-3 (pbk.)
    1. Native plant gardening—Michigan. 2. Native plants for cultivation—Michigan. 3. Landscape gardening—Michigan. I. Title.
    SB439.24.M5S74 2006
    635.9'51774—dc22

On the front cover: Asters, goldenrods, and grasses add color and excitement to this native-plant landscape, which belongs to Elizabeth and Paul McKenney of Huntington Woods, Michigan. *Paul L. B. McKenney*

On the title page: The hot colors of *Asclepias tuberosa* (butterfly weed) and *Phlox pilosa* (prairie phlox) dispel any misconceptions about native plants being drab and colorless in the landscape.

On the contents page: Sanguinaria canadensis (bloodroot) is just one of many Michigan native forest flowers that adapts well to landscape use.

Editor: Michael Dregni
Designer: LeAnn Kuhlmann

Printed in China

Dedication

This book is dedicated to the entire native-plant community of Michigan, including the advocates and organizations; designers, nurseries, and garden centers; and home gardeners. Thank you for all you do to preserve and promote the state's native treasures.

Acknowledgments

There are many people who have generously offered their help and shared their expertise and landscapes, without whom this book would not have been possible.

I'd especially like to thank Robert Domm for providing several photographs for chapter 2 and Steven Nikkila for contributing photos to the Plant Profiles section. A special thank you to Elizabeth and Paul L.B. McKenney for the fabulous cover shot of their native-plant landscape.

David Michael Appel of Appel Environmental Design assisted me in finding resources and offering suggestions on content. Mike Penskar, program botanist Michigan Natural Features Inventory, and Tony Reznicek, University of Michigan Herbarium, helped me access the Floristic Quality Assessment System for Michigan. Thanks also to Eric Hofley, publisher of *Michigan Gardener*, for his support.

For help locating Michigan gardens and native plants, I'd like to thank Susan Damon, Nancy Rose, and the presidents of the Michigan chapters of Wild Ones.

Thanks to the following people and who allowed me to photograph their gardens and homes: Barbara and Don Pederson, Pat and Bob Angleson, Peggy and Wayne Willenberg, Robert and Marlene Olsen, Mary and Dick Stanley, Phil Friedlund and Lisa Isenberg, Diane Hilscher, Barb Staub and Don Mitchell, Claire Olsen, Marge Hols, Sue Price, Deb Revier, Paul and Susan Damon, Carla Henry, Richard and Olive Zoller, Outback Nursery, and Landscape Alternatives.

Lastly, I'd like to thank my family and friends for their support of this project.

Contents

PART TWO

PART ONE

Introduction

Landscaping with
Native Plants of Michigan

Michigan has a rich and diverse native-plant community, ranging from the mat-forming plants of the Great Lakes dunes to the towering conifers of the northern forests, with a wide array of grassland, wetland, and deciduous forest plants in between. The purpose of this book is to identify Michigan's native plants and plant communities and demonstrate how to use them effectively in a typical home landscape. There are several good field guides and reference books for identifying and learning about native plants. There are also good books about gardening in Michigan. My goal is to combine these two approaches in an easy-to-use format that respects the state's natural plant heritage while addressing the practicalities of modern-day landscaping.

I hope to dispel the many misconceptions people have about native plants, such as their being weedy, hard to grow, difficult to purchase, and generally inappropriate for landscape situations. I also hope to show you the many possibilities available in Michigan's native flora, so you can choose plants that are appealing, well adapted to the climate and soils of your landscape, and well suited to your lifestyle.

My first task was determining which plants are "native." I followed the distinction used by many experts and based my selections on what was growing here naturally before European settlement. For this information, I referred to the "Floristic Quality Assessment for Michigan," compiled by M. R. Penskar, A. A. Reznicek, W. W. Brodovich, G. S. Wilhelm, L. A. Masters, K. D. Herman, and K. P. Gardiner, as well as Edward G. Voss's three-volume *Michigan Flora*. I have not included plants that have become naturalized—often labeled "wildflowers"—and are not indigenous to any part of the state.

The initial list of native plants was far too long, so I had to make difficult choices about which plants to leave out. I based my final decision on each plant's ability to adapt to cultivation, its suitability for various landscape situations, and its availability at local nurseries or through mail-order sources. One of the true joys of working with native plants is observing how they match the rhythms of the seasons, so I looked for plants that provide a succession of interest year-round. I also tried to include a good variety of sun and shade plants and a cross section of plants native to the state's major biomes. I eliminated plants that are difficult to bring into the landscape because of demanding soil or cultural requirements or those that are difficult to find. To the many wonderful plants that didn't make the cut, I apologize.

Space limitations also prevented me from including detailed propagation information for each species. There are many good references on native-plant propagation—especially for wildflowers. If you are interested in this fascinating aspect of gardening with native plants, I encourage you to read *Restoring the Tallgrass Prairie: An Illustrated Manual for Iowa and the Upper Midwest* by Shirley Shirley, *The New England Wild Flower Society Guide to Growing and Propagating Wildflowers of the United States and Canada* by William Cullina, or *Native Trees, Shrubs, and Vines: A Guide to Using, Growing, and Propagating North American Woody Plants* by William Cullina.

What else is included in this book? You'll find an overview of Michigan's natural heritage, an understanding of which is crucial before attempting any type of native landscaping. You'll be inspired by photographs of what your fellow gardeners have done with native plants in their own landscapes.

You'll also find basic gardening information tailored to native plants. You'll learn what level of native-plant landscaping is right for you and you'll get valuable information on the process of designing a natural landscape that fits your lifestyle. You'll also find lots of plant lists for specific styles of gardens.

The Native Plant Profiles section includes comprehensive descriptions of over 380 species of flowers and groundcovers, trees, shrubs, vines, evergreens, grasses, and ferns native to Michigan, as well as information on planting, maintenance, and landscape uses for each plant.

Above all, I encourage you to learn from nature itself: be sure to take lots of walks in Michigan's many parks and natural areas for inspiration.

Above: Late July color comes from *Heliopsis helianthoides* (oxeye), *Monarda fistulosa* (wild bergamot), *Verbena stricta* (hoary vervain), and *Amtemisia ludoviciana* (prairie sage).

Facing page: In landscapes with large shade trees, a mixture of shade-loving native woodland flowers, such as this one featuring *Phlox divaricata* (blue phlox), is a much better choice than nonnative lawn grasses.

Chapter 1

Understanding Native Plants

What They Are and How to Use Them

Just what defines a native plant has been debated for many years by many people. A widely accepted definition—and the one used in this book—classifies native plants as those species that grew in an area before European settlement—about the mid-1800s in the Midwest. By and large, Native Americans lived in harmony with the plants and animals of an area without endangering the natural ecosystems. European settlers, on the other hand, had a major impact on the landscape as they cut down large stands of trees, plowed up acres of prairies, suppressed natural fires, and introduced plants from their homelands and other parts of this new continent.

Unlike most introduced plants, a native plant fully integrates itself into a biotic community, establishing complex relationships with other local plants and animals. Not only does a native plant depend on the organisms with which it has evolved, but the other organisms also depend on it, creating a true web of life. This natural system of checks and balances ensures that native plants seldom grow out of control in their natural habitats.

"Wildflower" is a commonly used term, but it does not necessarily mean a native plant, since not all wildflowers are native to an area. Wildflowers include introduced plants that have escaped cultivation and grow wild in areas. Examples are Queen Anne's lace (*Daucus carota*) and chicory (*Chicorium intybus*), two common roadside plants, neither of which is native to any area of the United States.

Introducing new plants is not always a bad thing. Where would we be without tomatoes, potatoes, and wheat? And it's hard to find fault with introduced plants as charming and well behaved as lilacs and hostas. However, experience has taught us that the introduction of nonnative plants into an ecosystem is a delicate operation that should be undertaken with care. More and more, we are finding that plants that evolved in other countries, or even other areas of this country, can become too comfortable in landscape situations and threaten native flora. A prime example is purple loosestrife, a European native propagated by nurseries and grown in gardens for years before people realized that it aggressively invades natural wetlands, crowding out native plants. Buckthorn is another European native that has been widely used as a hedge. Today, it is the bane of any homeowner with a wooded plot, and it is running rampant through native woodlands.

Classifying Native Plants

Before you can know and effectively use native plants, you must have a simple knowledge of plant taxonomy. The fundamental category in this book is the species, a group of genetically similar plants within a genus, a larger botanical division. Genus and species names are commonly Latin and italicized; the genus name is capitalized and comes first followed by the species in lower case. Learning Latin names can be frustrating, but it is important. Too many plants share the same or similar common names, and it's easy to end up with the wrong plant—one that may not even be native to your area. Latin names also offer clues on how to identify a plant. For example, knowing that *tomentosus* means "downy" and *laevis* means "smooth" will help you identify and remember what a plant looks like.

Within a species, there are also subspecies (abbreviated as "ssp.") and varieties ("var."). A subspecies has a characteristic that isn't quite different enough to make it a separate species. This characteristic may occur over a wide range or in a geographically isolated area.

Varieties have minor recognizable variations from the species, such as flower size or leaf color, but are not distinct enough to be labeled subspecies. An example is found in *Cypripedium calceolus* (yellow lady's slipper), which is further differentiated into var. *pubescens* (large yellow lady's slipper) and var. *parviflorum* (small yellow lady's slipper). The latter variety is shorter and has a slightly different flower shape and color than the other, but without seeing the two side by side, it can be difficult to tell which one you are looking at.

As native plants become more popular, many horticulturally selected cultivated varieties are being introduced. These "cultivars" are usually chosen for certain characteristics, such as larger or double flowers, leaf color, compact growth, or flower color, and are propagated by nurseries to maintain the trait. In most cases, these cultivars retain most of the characteristics of the native species and are fine choices for most landscape use. However, if you are doing restoration work, you will want to stick with the species, or even the subspecies or variety, native to your area to maintain the true genetic diversity you'll only get from the native species.

While the native *Physostegia virginiana* (obedient plant) is a beautiful flower suitable for naturalizing and prairie plantings, it can be too aggressive for many landscapes. 'Miss Manners', a white cultivar, is less aggressive and better suited to garden use.

For most plants, species is the final classification. However, some plants are divided further into varieties. When you see them side by side, you can see that the *Cypripedium calceolus* var. *pubescens* (large yellow lady's slipper) at left and var. *parviflorum* (small yellow lady's-slipper) at right have minor size and color differences, thus the further differentiation into varieties. Some botanists feel that the differences are distinct enough to classify *C. pubescens* as a separate species.

The Bad Guys: Invasive and Weedy Introduced Plants

While many introduced plants are well-behaved, beautiful additions to gardens, some become harmful invaders of local habitats. You may be surprised by how many common landscape plants have the potential to become invasive and weedy when grown in conditions that promote rampant growth, such as tended garden beds or abandoned and neglected sites where native plants are no longer prevalent. Here are some of the many plants that have been turning up on invasive-plant lists in recent years:

Acer ginnala (Amur maple)
Acer platanoides (Norway maple)
Aegopodium podagraria (goutweed)
Ailanthus altissima (tree of heaven)
Ampelopsis brevipedunculata
    (porcelain berry)
Berberis thunbergii (Japanese barberry)
Berberis vulgaris (common barberry)
Butomus umbellatus (flowering rush)
Campanula rapunculoides
    (creeping bellflower)
Caragana arborescens (Siberian
    peashrub)
Celastrus orbiculatus (bittersweet)
Coronilla varia (crown vetch)
Daucus carota (Queen Anne's lace)
Elaeagnus angustifolia (Russian olive)

Euonymus alatus (winged euonymus)
Euonymus europaeus
    (European euonymus)
Euonymus fortunei (winter creeper
    euonymus)
Euphorbia esula (leafy spurge)
Glechoma hederacea (creeping Charlie)
Hesperis matronalis (dame's rocket)
Hieracium aurantiacum [*Pilosella
    aurantiaca*] (orange hawkweed)
Iris pseudacorus (yellow flag)
Leucanthemum vulgare (oxeye daisy)
Ligustrum vulgare (common privet)
Lonicera japonica (Japanese
    honeysuckle)
Lonicera tatarica (Tatarian honeysuckle)
Lotus corniculatus (bird's foot trefoil)

Lythrum salicaria (purple loosestrife)
Miscanthus sinensis (maiden grass)
Phalaris arundinacea (reed canary grass)
Polygonum japonicum [*P. cuspidatum*]
    (Japanese knotweed)
Rhamnus cathartica
    (common buckthorn)
Robinia pseudoacacia (black locust)
Rosa multiflora (multiflora rose)
Saponaria officinalis
    (soapwort, bouncing bet)
Sorbus aucuparia (European
    mountain ash)
Tanacetum vulgare (common tansy)
Ulmus pumila (Siberian elm)
Vinca minor (common periwinkle)

Source: Plant Conservation Alliance's Alien Plant Working Group: http://www.nps.gov/plants/alien

Many aggressive nonnative plants are introduced as garden plants because they are showy and easy to grow. *Campanula rapunculoides* (creeping bellflower) is an example of a European native that has become a prolific garden weed. Its thick, tuber-like rhizome makes it difficult to eradicate once it becomes established.

The term "wildflower" can be a misnomer when referring to native plants, as not all plants that grow well in a region are native there. If you see a proliferation of one species—such as the oxeye daisy (*Chrysanthemum vulgare*), a European native—taking over lawns and roadsides, chances are it's an introduced plant displacing native species.

Benefits of Native Plants

There are many reasons to use native plants, some more tangible than others. For many gardeners, the initial attraction comes from native plants' reputation of being lower maintenance than a manicured lawn and exotic shrubs. For the most part this is true—provided native plants are given landscape situations that match their cultural requirements. Because they have evolved and adapted to their surroundings, native plants tend to be tolerant of tough conditions such as drought and poor soil. Native plants are better adapted to local climatic conditions and better able to resist the effects of native insects and diseases. Their reduced maintenance results in less dependence on fossil fuels and reduced noise pollution from lawn mowers and other types of equipment.

The less tangible—but possibly more important—side of using native plants is the connection you make with nature. Gardening with natives instills an understanding of our natural world—its cycles, changes, and history. Communing with nature has a positive, healing effect on human beings. Learning how to work with instead of against nature will do wonders for your spiritual health. By observing native plants throughout the year, a gardener gains insight into seasonal rhythms and life cycles. You will experience intellectual rewards that are somehow missing if you only grow petunias or marigolds.

Gardening with native plants will help you create a sense of place rather than just a cookie-cutter landscape. Your yard will be unique among the long line of mown grass and clipped shrubs in your neighborhood. A native-plant landscape will blend into the natural surroundings better that those planted with introduced species, and you will get an enormous sense of satisfaction from helping reestablish what once grew naturally in your area. You will see an increase in wildlife, including birds, butterflies, and pollinating insects, making your garden a livelier place.

On a broader scale, using native plants helps preserve the natural heritage of an area. Genetic diversity promotes the mixing of genes to form new combinations, the key to adaptability and survival of all life. Once a species becomes extinct, it is gone forever, as are its genes and any future contribution that it might have made.

Misconceptions About Native Plants

Despite the increased interest and promotion of native plants, many people still hesitate to use them for one reason or another. Here are some of the common misconceptions about using native plants.

Native plants are colorless and dull

The belief that native plants are drab or uninteresting is based in ignorance. Once you learn about the wide variety of natives and how to use them properly, you will discover that they have much to offer, not only colorful flowers but also interesting textures, colorful fruits, and year-round interest. They may not all be as bright and showy as a lot of introduced plants, but their subtle beauty can be just as effective in landscaping.

Native plants are sources of pollens that cause allergies

The truth is, most native plants are insect pollinated rather than wind pollinated. Kentucky blue grass has the potential to produce more allergens than any native plant.

Native plants are invasive

Most aggressively invasive plants are imported from other countries or another part of the United States. Keep in mind that any plant can become invasive if it is given the right conditions—a site more conducive to rampant growth than its preferred habitat.

Native plants are hard to grow

The misconception that native plants are hard to grow comes from the fact that many of them have evolved in a rather specific habitat. Once you learn about the different plant communities and their soil and sunlight requirements and determine which plants are best for your conditions, you will find that most native plants are easier to grow than their cultivated counterparts.

Native plants are messy

Nature is "messy." It's full of fallen logs, recycling plant parts, and plants that weave together rather than lay out in straight lines. Once you understand and appreciate this, native plants will no longer appear unattractive. When given proper conditions and room to grow, most native plants produce larger and better flowers than their wild counterparts. There are many things you can do to make a native landscape look neater, such as incorporating small patches of lawn grasses, creating paths and neat edges, and cutting back certain plants when they are done blooming.

Native plants are hard to find

Once you learn which plants are native, you will be surprised how many are available at local nurseries. In every part of the country, you will find nurseries that specialize in native plants, and many of them offer mail order.

Native Plants in the Landscape

Basically there are three ways to use native plants in a landscape: restoration, integration, and habitat gardening.

On the extreme side, you can grow only plants that were found in your area before European settlement. This is a wonderful way to preserve and enjoy the beauty of individual plants and also to preserve entire ecosystems or plant communities. Restoring a tall-grass prairie or creating an authentic deciduous woodland garden are wonderful ways to create pure stands of native plants.

For most people, however, using only native plants is not practical. Because our landscapes have been altered so much by human activity, it is difficult to go back to the point where you can successfully grow only native plants without investing quite a bit of time and effort in plant eradication and site preparation. If you truly want to establish a pure stand of plants that once grew naturally in your area, you should get help from a professional specializing in native-plant restorations.

For most gardeners, the most practical way to use native plants is to integrate natives with nonnative, more traditional landscape plants that have proven to be nonaggressive and adaptable to your area. You may already be doing this without realizing it. If your mixed border includes liatris, butterfly weed, and black-eyed Susans, or if your shade garden is home to wild ginger, pagoda dogwood, and maidenhair ferns, you are already well on your way to using native plants. You don't have to give up some of the well-behaved nonnative plants you love, such as spring bulbs, hostas, and rhododendrons. Most natives are adaptable and willing to coexist with nonnatives. Be warned, however; once you have discovered the subtle beauty that natives bring to your landscape, you may well become one of the many gardeners choosing to grow more and more of these fascinating plants.

People who have a strong interest in growing native plants will get immense pleasure from the creation of habitat gardens within their landscape. The goal here is to re-create a natural habitat that would have once been found in or around your area. Start by assessing the specific site conditions in an area of your landscape and determining which native habitat would be best suited to the conditions. If you have a shady area under large deciduous trees, look to the plants of the southern forests; an area in full sun would be an ideal area for a grassland habitat garden. By establishing large areas of native-plant communities, you will help preserve natural ecosystems that once flourished in your area and end up with an attractive, easy-to-tend garden filled with plants with similar cultural requirements. You will also get to experience first hand the intricacies of a natural plant community.

The bottom line is that there is really no right or wrong way to use native plants, as long as it brings you pleasure. As with any type of gardening, your landscape should reflect your own preferences for color, style, and plants. If you have a Colonial-style house in the suburbs and prefer a formal entryway with clipped hedges, there are native plants that will fit the bill. If you're a plant lover who can't resist the hodgepodge of a collector's garden, that's fine too. No matter how many natives you use or in which way you use them, you will be helping to counteract the tragedy of habitat destruction and the reduction in native-plant populations occurring around the world. And, on a more personal note, you won't have to leave home to enjoy nature. It will be right at your doorstep.

No single gardener can solve all the environmental problems of the world, but by growing native plants, you can help preserve and promote the natural ecosystem of your small patch of the globe. Like many native plants, *Geranium maculatum* (wild geranium) may not be as ostentatious as its cultivated cousins, but its subtle beautiful, adaptability, and low maintenance make it easy to use in landscaping.

Although it takes several years to establish, if you have the space and resources, a prairie restoration is a wonderful way to experience the wonders of a natural plant community.

Native Plant Conservation

Once you've been convinced of the benefits of growing native plants, it's time to temper that recommendation by saying it's important to use them properly and responsibly.

Wildflower gardeners face moral and ethical considerations that most gardeners do not. You must be sure that the native plants you buy are propagated by a nursery and not collected in the wild. You want to purchase plants that were "nursery propagated," not just "nursery grown." Reputable nurseries will readily volunteer information on the origin of their plants, so evasiveness or ambiguous answers from nursery owners should trigger caution.

Plants growing in their native habitats should never be dug up for garden use unless the plants are facing imminent destruction from development. It is always preferable to try to preserve or restore a natural habitat rather than destroy it, but sometimes this just isn't possible. If you have permission to collect seeds from a stand of native plants, take only what you need. Collect only a few seeds from several plants in the stand; never take all of the seeds from one plant. Do not collect underground plant parts. Collecting must never endanger a plant population.

The rapid destruction of native habitats in the last century means many native plants and animals are threatened with extinction. You should become aware of these plants, since in many states it is illegal to gather, take, buy, or sell plants listed as endangered or threatened. A safeguard for endangered native species is the Federal Endangered Species Act of 1973. This law applies only to federal lands, however. Protection of endangered plants on other public and private lands is left up to individual states, and each state has its own list of endangered, threatened, and special-concern plants.

A complete habitat restoration is not practical for most homeowners. Luckily, many native plants adapt readily to traditional landscape use. Here *Echinacea purpurea* (purple coneflower), *Ratibida pinnata* (gray-headed coneflower), *Eupatorium purpureum* (Joe-Pye weed), *Liatris pycnostachya* (great blazing star), and native grasses help make the transition from the water's edge to a more formal part of this landscape.

How to Select Propagated Over Collected Native Plants

For the conservation of native plant species, it's important the native plants you purchase at a nursery are propagated rather than collected from the wild. Despite assurances from nursery owners, you should trust your own eyes as well. Here are some signs that plants may be collected instead of propagated legitimately by a nursery:

- Poor or abnormal color
- Sparse foliage
- Weak stems or wilted leaves
- Legginess
- Large size or obvious maturity, especially in slow-growing plants

- Off-centered potting
- More than one species in the same pot
- Large stones in the soil
- Different soil types in the same pot
- Compacted clay rather than uniformly textured potting soil

Hydrastis canadensis (goldenseal) is a fascinating native plant with interesting leaves and showy flowers and fruits. Unfortunately, its reputed medicinal qualities have lead to over-collecting in the wild, and it is now classified as a threatened or endangered species in several states. Be sure to only purchase nursery-propagated plants if you want to include this gem in your landscape

Plant collecting can be devastating to native plant communities. Always ask the nursery or supplier where they got their plants. If they are hesitant or evasive about their sources, take your business elsewhere.

Chapter 2

Michigan's Natural
Plant Life
Learning from the Natural World

The key to creating a successful home landscape using native plants is to understand the natural plant communities in your area. Nature is truly the best garden designer, and you will never go wrong if you attempt to imitate it.

For gardeners in Michigan, the natural world has provided many options. Michigan is a mosaic of forests, barrens, and grasslands, and has an abundance of water features, ranging from trickling streams to the grandiose shores of the Great Lakes. The eastern deciduous forest and the northern coniferous forest, two major North American ecological regions, once covered most of Michigan, but the grasslands of the Central Plains also had a major influence on the state's natural vegetation.

Glaciation largely determined the topography and soils of Michigan. After the glaciers' final retreat about twelve thousand years ago, the climate stabilized somewhat and natural communities began to develop. The warmer climate and moist, rich soils of the southern half of the Lower Peninsula eventually fostered the growth of deciduous forests and scattered grasslands. Farther north, where the deposited glacial till resulted in a sandy outwash plain that was dry and nutrient poor and where the climate was cooler, coniferous forests became the dominant plant community.

The Michigan Natural Features Inventory recognizes 74 natural communities in the state. These communities developed along a continuum, and differences are generally determined by soil moisture, temperature extremes, and wildfire frequency. Michigan has more than 1,800 species of native plants; some of them evolved in only one or two of the communities, while some are native throughout the state. Obviously, plants do not recognize political boundaries such as state lines, and these plant communities spill over into neighboring states and provinces.

A successful native landscape starts with a good understanding of your area's ecosystems and the plants that grow in them. The shade garden, on the right, mirrors the tapestry of plants found in the native deciduous-forest understory, which is captured in the photo on the left. When you allow nature to be your guide and choose plants with similar native habitats, the result will be a landscape full of interesting textures, colors, and plant forms.

According to the Michigan Department of Natural Resource's Web site, 46 species of Michigan's native plants have been lost in recent times, and there are currently 51 endangered plants, 210 threatened plants, and 110 species listed as "special concern." About 23 percent of Michigan's native plant species are at risk. Three species that are threatened nationwide—dwarf lake iris (*Iris lacustris*), Pitcher's thistle (*Cirsium pitcheri*), and Houghton's goldenrod (*Solidago houghtonii*)—have their primary distribution in Michigan.

Major Vegetative Regions of Michigan

☐ Northern Coniferous Forest
▨ Eastern Deciduous Forest

Tension Line

Major Ecological Regions of North America

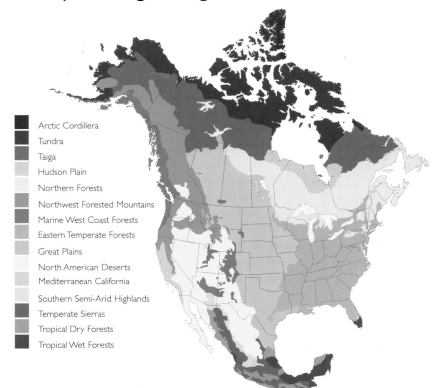

Arctic Cordillera
Tundra
Taiga
Hudson Plain
Northern Forests
Northwest Forested Mountains
Marine West Coast Forests
Eastern Temperate Forests
Great Plains
North American Deserts
Mediterranean California
Southern Semi-Arid Highlands
Temperate Sierras
Tropical Dry Forests
Tropical Wet Forests

Michigan's total area is more than 96,500 square miles, and more than 40,000 square miles are covered by water in some form. Touching on four of the five Great Lakes, the two land areas of Michigan give the state a shoreline of 3,288 miles, second only to Alaska in state shoreline length.

The mean elevation of Michigan is 900 feet above sea level. Elevations range from 572 feet above sea level along the shores of Lake Erie to 1,979 feet at Mount Arvon in the Upper Peninsula's Baraga County.

Monthly average temperatures range from a high of about 80 degrees Fahrenheit in July to a low of about 10 degrees Fahrenheit in January. The Great Lakes cool the hot winds of summer and warm the cold winds of winter, giving Michigan a milder climate than some other north-central states.

Michigan's frost-free growing season can range from fewer than 70 days to more than 170 days. The median date of the last spring freeze can be as early as late April or as late as mid-June. The first autumn freeze can occur as early as mid-August in the coldest areas and can hold off until mid-October in warmer areas.

Annual precipitation ranges from about 26 inches to 36 inches. The average seasonal snowfall varies from about 32 inches in the south-central part of the state to well over 100 inches in northern areas. The snow cover acts as a protective insulation for vegetation. About six out of every ten days are partly cloudy in summer, and seven of every ten days in winter.

Michigan Forests

Prior to European settlement, nearly all of Michigan was covered by some type of forest. These forests were part of a larger transition area that developed along the meeting point of two major North American plant biomes: the coniferous forests of Canada and the deciduous forests that stretched across most of the eastern United States. Biologists label this meeting point a "tension zone," and it roughly divides the Lower Peninsula in half. A wide variety of forest types developed along this tension zone, and several tree species reach the edges of their natural ranges in Michigan. As a result of habitat destruction and other factors, several of these species, which were somewhat rare in the state to begin with, have become endangered. Trees that have declining or relict populations include dwarf hackberry, Kentucky coffee tree, red mulberry, and Shumard's oak (*Quercus shumardii*).

Managing Michigan Wildlife: A Landowner's Guide by M. S. Sargent and K. S. Carter presents a good description of Michigan's presettlement forest communities. It describes the area south of the tension zone as having been primarily deciduous and the dominant tree species varying according to soil moisture levels. In upland areas with drier soils, common trees were black oak, white oak, red maple, and shagbark hickory. Sugar maple, American beech, basswood, and red oak were more common on mesic sites. As soil moisture increased, ashes, silver maple, red maple, swamp white oak, American elm, and cottonwood could be found. As you moved farther north in the Lower Peninsula, the shorter growing season and cooler temperatures favored the growth of American beech and sugar maple. Eastern hemlock, white pine, and yellow birch also grew in mesic soils. In the central part of Michigan, soils tended to be sandier and drier, and fires were more frequent. These factors resulted in a mosaic of pine forests, composed mainly of white and red pines and barrens, which feature jack pines. In the boggier soils of central Michigan, white cedar, black spruce, and tamarack were the main tree species.

Presettlement vegetation was similar on the Upper Peninsula, and pines dominated in the sandy, acidic soils. Cooler temperatures, especially in summer, fostered the growth of eastern hemlock, yellow birch, balsam fir, and white spruce. Sugar maples, red maples, and American beech were found on mesic sites. Farther east on the Upper Peninsula, forests gave way to large expanses of peat land, and vast marshes fronted Lakes Huron and Michigan.

Almost all of Michigan's original forests have been disturbed by human activity, such as agriculture, urban development, and logging, and well over 50 percent of the white cedar, black spruce, and tamarack swamps have been either drained or converted to other wetland types. Michigan's forest ecosystems also have been dramatically altered by the continuing invasion of nonnative trees and shrubs, such as common and glossy buckthorns and Tartarian and Maack's honeysuckles, as well as invasive insects and diseases, such as emerald ash borer and beech-bark disease.

Michigan was once covered with a mosaic of different forest types. In this area of the Pictured Rocks National Lakeshore, *Betula papyrifera* (paper birch) and *Pteridium aquilinum* (bracken fern) contrast beautifully with the background of evergreen conifers. *Robert Domm*

Conifer forests, such as this one featuring *Pinus resinosa* (red pine), found near Miner's Beach in the Upper Peninsula, once covered much of the northern half of Michigan. *Robert Domm*

Conifer Forests

Conifer forests occurred on sites that ranged widely in moisture content and topography, from very wet areas in extinct lakebeds to very dry areas, and from areas with deep loam soil to areas with thin, rocky, soil.

The driest, most acidic soils were home to a mosaic of pine-dominated communities, ranging from open barrens to pure jack-pine forests to mixed forests of jack, white, and red pines, northern pin oak, and aspen. In areas where soil moisture increased, majestic white pines became the dominant species in forests that also included oaks, red maple, eastern hemlock, and balsam fir.

In *Managing Michigan Wildlife*, Sargent and Carter estimate that mesic conifer forests once covered about 15 percent of Michigan's overall land base. They divide this habitat, which has moderate soil-moisture levels, into two subgroups: the first dominated by the tenacious eastern hemlock, and the second sometimes referred to as boreal forest. The first subgroup also included yellow birch, red maple, and white pine. Due largely to intense logging, only a few small pockets of hemlock-dominated forests still exist in Michigan, and very little eastern hemlock can be found growing in other forest types. The second subgroup, the boreal forest, was composed mainly of white

spruce, balsam fir, and white cedar. Characterized by long, cold winters; short, cool summers; and low precipitation, the boreal forest was found mainly on upland sites along the Great Lakes, on islands in the Great Lakes, and locally inward.

In areas with high soil moisture levels, such as in swamps or along streams, conifer forests were mainly composed of black spruce, white cedar, and tamarack. Eastern hemlock, white pine, and some hardwoods such as black ash appeared in transition areas between wetland and upland habitats.

The sparse middle layer of the conifer forests included seedlings and saplings of the canopy species as well as shade-tolerant small trees and shrubs such as mountain maple, mountain ashes, Canadian yew, and beaked hazelnut. The cool, deep-shade, acidic conditions of the forest floor supported mosses, ferns, and sedges, as well as the showier wild sarsaparilla, red baneberry, bluebead lily, bunchberry, twinflower, Canada mayflower, starflower, and occasionally dwarf lake iris. In drier, more open areas, bracken, wintergreen, bearberry, low-bush blueberry, trailing arbutus, sand cherry, and running serviceberry were also found. Understory shrubs in coniferous swamps included leather leaf, Labrador tea, and bog laurel.

Pine Barrens

Contrary to their name, barrens were, and still are, an intricate part of Michigan's natural vegetation. These dry-soil coniferous savannas have only a few trees per acre and little or no old growth. They were once found throughout the Upper Peninsula and on the Lower Peninsula north of the transition line. It is estimated that only about 100 acres of high-quality pine barrens remain in Michigan.

This sandy, acidic-soil ecosystem has a unique look to it, characterized by scattered small jack pines or less commonly red pines, sometimes in island-like groupings and often mixed with scrubby northern pin oaks and bur oaks. These small trees are interspersed with openings where shrubs are the dominant plant grouping, the most prevalent being low-bush blueberry. Other shrubs found on pine barrens include bearberry, wild roses, and prairie willow. The understory is home to many herbaceous plants, such as June grass, little bluestem, big bluestem, Pennsylvania sedge, sweet fern, bracken, flowering spurge, wild strawberry, wild bergamot, and wild lupine.

Without the presence of regular fires almost all pine barrens have converted to denser jack-pine forests, an unfortunate event for us as well as many types of wildlife, including Kirtland's warbler (*Dendroica kirtlandii*). This endangered bird builds its nest on the ground under dense clusters of young jack-pine trees. Fires kept Michigan's native jack-pine forests at age levels that provided an abundance of desirable nesting sites for the Kirtland's warbler, as well as providing favorable habitats for a diverse mix of other wildlife.

Northern Woodlands in the Landscape

The plant communities of the coniferous forests and pine barrens offer interesting opportunities for homeowners, but these habitats are usually difficult to re-create in most landscape situations. However, if you have what is often described as a "problem site"—an area too shady to grow lawn grasses successfully, one too acidic to grow more traditional groundcovers, or a windswept hillside too steep to mow—the plants of these habitats are just the ticket.

If your landscape includes an area with large conifers, you probably already have the necessary soil and shade requirements needed to install a shade garden featuring plants of the northern coniferous forests. If you don't have large conifers on your property but you do have shade of some sort, you can still grow many of these fascinating plants. It will just require a little more work up front. Most important is to create the necessary soil conditions. Lower the soil pH by working in lots of composted conifer needles, shredded oak leaves, or peat moss, and maintain the acidity by mulching with pine needles. The soil must also be well drained. Improve the soil with organic matter before planting, if possible, and top-dress with compost each spring.

Plant in groups of at least five to seven plants to re-create the large drifts found in nature. Include lots of ferns in your plant list, and bring in fallen logs to encourage moss growth. To truly enjoy this type of garden, you must appreciate the importance of foliage and its textural qualities, since showy blooms are less prevalent than in the other biomes. If your garden is large enough to include

Pine barrens, which are anything but barren when it comes to plant and animal life, are one of Michigan's most interesting habitats. This savanna-like habitat is home to plants found both in conifer forests and in grasslands.

paths, use pine needles or shredded bark. Wooden or stone benches will blend in nicely and offer a cool respite in summer or a spot to enjoy the evergreens and showy fruits that persist into winter. A pot of colorful shade-tolerant annuals, such as impatiens, placed on a cut stump will add summer color. Limit other embellishments to fallen logs and lichen-covered rocks.

The plants of the pine barrens tend to be hardy, tough, and drought tolerant. What they may lack in showiness, they make up for in utility. Look to this plant community for plants that will withstand harsh conditions such as those found on a steep, sandy slope. Once established, these plants form an attractive cover that helps control erosion and that is appealing to wildlife.

Iris lacustris (dwarf lake iris) and *Maianthemum canadense* (Canada mayflower) are two charming native flowers that do well in cultivation, if you can provide them with the acidic soil conditions they require.

Above: Native ferns are a good choice in deep shade areas, lending the feel of Michigan's northern forests to suburban landscape settings such as this one.

Right: This shade garden, found less than a mile inland from Lake Michigan, exemplifies the conifer forest floor. The mulch of pine needles and shredded bark gives the garden a natural look and reduces the time spent weeding and watering.

Southern Deciduous Forests

Deciduous forests originally occurred on a full range of sites in southern Michigan, from very wet places along streams and lakes, to mesic sites with deep soils, to very dry, thin soil on hills and bluffs. The most visible difference between the forested areas of southern Michigan and the northern woodlands was the lack of dominating evergreen conifers as you moved farther south.

Among the forest types in southern Michigan, the mesic hardwood forest was the most prominent, occurring in widely scattered patches in the southern and western parts of the state on sites with rich soils and moderate moisture. Sugar maple and American beech were dominant trees, along with basswood, red oak, white ash, black cherry, bitternut hickory, tulip tree, and sometimes red maple and white and bur oaks. As you moved farther north, eastern hemlock, white pine, and yellow birch replaced tulip tree, bitternut hickory, and other more southerly species. The mesic hardwood forest's understory included tree saplings and shade-tolerant shrubs such as witch hazel, maple-leaf viburnum, spicebush, American hazelnut, leatherwood, and bladdernut.

The dense canopy of the southern deciduous forest means little light reaches the forest floor during the summer. Fully leafed-out deciduous trees plunge the forest floor into shade by early summer, blocking out as much as 95 percent of the available sunlight. The forest is home to many spring ephemerals—herbaceous plants that bloom, produce seeds, and die back in May and early June, before tree leaves are fully developed. Life is a race for most of these diminutive forest denizens, and the earliest bloomers get the sunlight. Trout lilies, Dutchman's breeches, cut-leaved toothwort, false rue anemone, and wild leek have evolved to emerge before trees leaf out, and quickly convert early spring sunshine into food to be stored or used for growth and development of flowers and fruits. Other shade-tolerant wildflowers and groundcovers such as wild ginger, bloodroot, wild blue phlox, wild geranium, and trilliums usually retain their leaves after the canopy emerges, providing a green carpet throughout summer.

White and black oaks and hickories dominated drier sites in the southern Lower Peninsula. Other trees included white ash, red maple, black cherry, sassafras, and sometimes scarlet and northern pin oaks. Trees and shrubs filling in the understory included New Jersey tea, American hazelnut, witch hazel, and ironwood. Herbaceous plants that tolerated the drier soils of the oak-hardwood forests included white baneberry, yellow violet, May apple, white snakeroot, and wild strawberry. These oak-hickory forests were very dependent on fire. Without regular burning, many converted to closed-canopy oak and beech-maple forests.

The highly endangered southern floodplain forests, characterized by seasonal flooding, boast rich loamy soils that support a wide diversity of plant species. Dominant native trees include silver and red maples, green ash, and American elm. Other important species are butternut, black maple, Ohio buckeye, black ash, box elder (*Acer negundo*), black willow, and cottonwood. Understory trees and shrubs include spicebush, pagoda dogwood, hawthorns, blue beech, and bladdernut. Herbaceous plants that enjoy the moist, rich soils include wild geranium, Jack-in-the-pulpit, and twinleaf. Several native plants reach their northern limit in this habitat, including Ohio buckeye, pawpaw, sycamore, hackberry, red bud, blue ash, Kentucky coffee tree, honey locust, wild hyacinth, Virginia bluebells, red mulberry, snow trillium, and prairie trillium.

The Nan Weston Nature Preserve at Sharon Hollow in Washtenaw County is a good example of the southern floodplain forest habitat. This ecosystem supports a variety of spring ephemerals, such as the dainty *Dicentra cucullaria* (Dutchman's breeches). *Robert Domm*

Deciduous Forest in the Landscape

The key to successfully interpreting Michigan's deciduous forest is to think in terms of layers. The top layer is the tree canopy, creating dense shade by early summer. The middle layer is made up of shade-tolerant small trees and large shrubs. The last layer, formed of spring ephemerals, ferns, and shade-tolerant flowers and groundcovers, creates the green carpet that covers the forest floor.

If you are lucky enough to have a woodlot on your property, you are well on your way to having a woodland garden. Remove debris and most of the dead trees, both standing and fallen. Weed out undesirable trees and shrubs, including most hardwoods with trunks less than 6 inches or so in diameter, and buckthorn, poison ivy, and other exotics. After laying out winding paths, you can start adding shade-tolerant shrubs, groundcovers, flowers, and ferns.

If your property is devoid of large shade trees, don't despair. You can still grow these shrubs and charming herbaceous woodland plants in the shade of structures. Just be sure to create appropriate soil conditions before planting by adding lots of organic matter. And be sure to keep the soil covered with mulch. Mulch is very important in the deciduous forest garden. In nature, leaves drop to the ground each fall and their nutrients are eventually recycled back into the soil. Use organic mulch such as shredded leaves, shredded bark, or wood chips to create this look in your home landscape.

Because of the many small plants found in this ecosystem, you need to get up close and personal with woodland gardens. Be sure to include lots of paths made of crosscut logs or wood chips, and plant the smallest of the spring ephemerals near the paths where you can enjoy them. Benches of wrought iron, stone, or wood will offer pleasant places to enjoy the plants and a shady respite on hot summer days. Accent your garden with moss-covered logs, rustic stone sculptures, and planters made from cut stumps. Take advantage of the unassuming green palette and incorporate colorful sculptural pieces to add interest in summer.

Above right: *Tiarella cordifolia* (foamflower), native to Michigan's deciduous forests, is an excellent choice where you want an attractive, trouble-free groundcover.

Right: *Mertensia virginica* (Virginia bluebells) has clusters of pinkish buds that open to showy, drooping clusters of sky-blue flowers. Plant it with ferns, which will fill in after the plants go dormant.

Native Plants of Michigan Forests

A wide variety of native plants were once found in Michigan's forest communities. Here are some that adapt well to cultivation.

	Conifer Forests	Deciduous Forests	Pine Barrens
Actaea species (baneberries)	x	x	
Anemone canadensis (Canada anemone)	x	x	x
Anemone cylindrica (thimbleweed)			x
Anemone quinquefolia (wood anemone)	x	x	
Anemonella thalictroides (rue anemone)		x	
Aquilegia canadensis (wild columbine)	x	x	
Aralia racemosa (American spikenard)	x	x	
Arisaema species (jack-in-the-pulpits)		x	
Asarum canadense (wild ginger)	x	x	
Aster cordifolius (heart-leaved aster)		x	
Aster macrophyllus (large-leaved aster)	x	x	x
Campanula rotundifolia (harebell)	x	x	x
Caulophyllum thalictroides (blue cohosh)		x	
Claytonia caroliniana (Carolina spring beauty)	x	x	
Claytonia virginica (spring beauty)		x	
Clintonia borealis (bluebead lily)	x		
Cornus canadensis (bunchberry)	x	x	
Cypripedium calceolus (yellow lady's slipper)	x	x	
Dentaria diphylla (two-leaved toothwort)	x	x	
Dentaria laciniata (cut-leaved toothwort)		x	
Dicentra cucullaria (Dutchman's breeches)		x	
Erythronium species (trout lilies)		x	
Fragaria virginiana (wild strawberry)	x	x	x
Gaultheria procumbens (wintergreen)	x	x	x
Geranium maculatum (wild geranium)		x	
Helianthus occidentalis (western sunflower)			x
Hepatica acutiloba (sharp-lobed hepatica)		x	
Hepatica americana (round-lobed hepatica)	x	x	
Heuchera americana (alumroot)		x	
Hydrastis canadensis (goldenseal)		x	
Jeffersonia diphylla (twinleaf)		x	
Liatris cylindracea (cylindric blazing star)			x
Lobelia cardinalis (cardinal flower)	x	x	
Lupinus perennis (wild lupine)			x
Maianthemum canadense (Canada mayflower)	x	x	x
Mertensia virginica (Virginia bluebells)		x	
Mitella diphylla (two-leaf miterwort)		x	
Monarda fistulosa (wild bergamot)			x
Phlox divaricata (blue phlox)		x	
Podophyllum peltatum (May apple)		x	
Polemonium reptans (creeping Jacob's ladder)		x	
Polygonatum biflorum (giant Solomon's seal)		x	
Sanguinaria canadensis (bloodroot)	x	x	
Smilacina racemosa (false Solomon's seal)		x	
Smilacina stellata (starry false Solomon's seal)			x
Solidago caesia (blue-stemmed goldenrod)		x	
Solidago flexicaulis (zigzag goldenrod)	x	x	
Stylophorum diphyllum (celandine poppy)		x	
Thalictrum dioicum (early meadow rue)		x	
Tiarella cordifolia (foamflower)	x	x	
Trillium species (trilliums)		x	
Uvularia grandiflora (large-flowered bellwort)		x	
Waldsteinia fragarioides (barren strawberry)	x	x	

	Conifer Forests	Deciduous Forests	Pine Barrens
Ferns			
Adiantum pedatum (maidenhair fern)	x	x	
Asplenium platyneuron (ebony spleenwort)		x	
Athyrium filix-femina (lady fern)	x	x	
Cystopteris bulbifera (bulblet fern)	x	x	
Dryopteris species (wood ferns)	x	x	
Gymnocarpium dryopteris (oak fern)	x		
Matteuccia struthiopteris (ostrich fern)	x	x	
Onoclea sensibilis (sensitive fern)	x	x	
Osmunda species (ferns)	x	x	
Polystichum acrostichoides (Christmas fern)		x	
Pteridium aquilinum (bracken)			x
Grasses and Sedges			
Carex pensylvanica (Pennsylvania sedge)		x	x
Koeleria macrantha (June grass)			x
Schizachyrium scoparium (little bluestem)			x
Shrubs and Small Trees			
Acer spicatum (mountain maple)	x	x	
Amelanchier species (serviceberries)	x	x	
Arctostaphylos uva-ursi (bearberry)			x
Aronia prunifolia (purple chokeberry)	x		
Cercis canadensis (redbud)		x	
Comptonia peregrina (sweet fern)			x
Cornus species (dogwoods)		x	
Diervilla lonicera (bush honeysuckle)	x	x	x
Dirca palustris (leatherwood)		x	
Euonymus atropurpurea (wahoo)		x	
Hamamelis virginiana (witch hazel)		x	
Ilex verticillata (winterberry)	x	x	
Lindera benzoin (spicebush)		x	
Physocarpus opulifolius (ninebark)	x	x	
Prunus americana (wild plum)		x	
Prunus pensylvanica (pin cherry)	x	x	x
Prunus pumila (sand cherry)			x
Rhus species (sumacs)		x	x
Rosa acicularis (prickly rose)	x		
Rubus parviflorus (thimbleberry)	x		
Sambucus pubens (scarlet elderberry)	x	x	
Staphylea trifolia (bladdernut)		x	
Vaccinium angustifolium (low-bush blueberry)	x		x
Viburnum species (viburnums)	x	x	

This shady retreat, with its mix of flowers, ferns, and groundcovers, is reminiscent of a native deciduous-woodland habitat. It was once a weed patch found along the east side of a city lot.

Trillium grandiflorum (large-flowered trillium), *Phlox divaricata* (blue phlox), and *Podophyllum peltatum* (May apple) are among the native flowers in this front-yard shade garden.

The delicate nature of many native woodland flowers, such as *Claytonia virginica* (spring beauty) and *Mitella diphylla* (two-leaved miterwort), makes them good choices for the front of the shade border or along pathways in larger gardens.

Southern Grasslands

Interspersed among the deciduous forests of southern Michigan were several grassland communities, including wet meadows; oak barrens, plains, and openings; savannas; and prairies. These grasslands owed their existence to climatic conditions as well as fire. Whether caused by lightning or set purposely by Native Americans, fires perpetuated grasslands by reducing competition from weeds and by discouraging the encroachment of shrubs and trees.

These fires, along with rainfall amounts, temperatures, and other factors, created a constant state of flux between the eastern deciduous forests and the tall-grass prairie of the Central Plains, resulting in the savanna. Savannas are partially forested upland communities where tree canopies do not exceed 50 percent coverage. Bur, white, and black oaks, often with large, open-grown canopies, were dominant trees of savannas. Hickories were also sometimes present. American hazelnut and leadplant were among the occasional shrubs, and the herb layer was similar to that of dry and mesic prairies.

No one knows exactly how much of America's magnificent tall-grass prairie originally existed in Michigan, but researchers have identified thirty-nine known prairie areas, mostly in the southern Lower Peninsula. These prairies ranged in size from 80 acres to 25 square miles and totaled approximately 2.3 million acres.

Prairie subtypes ranged from wet to dry prairie according to soil moisture content. The dominant plants of rich, mesic prairies were big bluestem, little bluestem, and prairie cordgrass. Forbs included wild geranium, prairie coreopsis, pale-leaf woodland sunflower, rosinweed, hoary vervain, violets, and golden alexanders. Where soil moisture was higher, dominant grasses were big bluestem and prairie cordgrass, and there was an abundance of sedges. Thimbleweed, rattlesnake master, northern bedstraw, gray-headed coneflower, prairie rosinweed, early meadow rue, and Culver's root were characteristic forbs in these prairies.

Big and little bluestems were the dominant grasses in dry prairies. Common forbs included whorled milkweed, rough blazing star, wild lupine, spotted bee balm, hairy Solomon's seal, prairie ragwort, and cylindric blazing star. Where prairies gave way to oak openings and savannas, common plants were the bluestem grasses, Indian grass, leadplant, thimbleweed, butterfly weed, and smooth blue aster.

Oak savannas were once widespread in the southern half of Michigan. These grassland communities supported a wide array of grasses and forbs, including *Monarda fistulosa* (wild bergamot), with a few shrubby plants such as *Rhus* species (sumacs) and *Amorpha canescens* (leadplant) interspersed throughout.

Fragments of America's tall-grass prairie once covered parts of the southern Lower Peninsula of Michigan. But as in all areas of the country, this grassland habitat is almost nonexistent in the state today.

Native Plants of Southern Grasslands

Here are some plants of Michigan's native prairies and savannas that adapt well to cultivation.

Grasses

Andropogon gerardii (big bluestem)
Bouteloua curtipendula
    (side-oats grama)
Elymus species (wild ryes)
Koeleria macrantha (June grass)
Panicum virgatum (switch grass)
Schizachyrium scoparium
    (little bluestem)
Sorghastrum nutans (Indian grass)
Spartina pectinata
    (prairie cordgrass)
Sporobolus heterolepis
    (prairie dropseed)

Forbs

Allium cernuum
    (nodding wild onion)
Anemone canadensis
    (Canada anemone)
Anemone cylindrica (thimbleweed)
Antennaria neglecta
    (field pussytoes)
Aquilegia canadensis
    (wild columbine)
Asclepias species (butterfly weed,
    milkweeds)
Aster species (asters)
Baptisia lactea (white wild indigo)
Boltonia asteroides (boltonia,
    false aster)
Coreopsis species (coreopsis)
Dalea purpurea (purple prairie
    clover)
Desmodium canadense (showy tick
    trefoil)
Dodecatheon media (shooting star)
Echinacea purpurea
    (purple coneflower)
Eryngium yuccifolium
    (rattlesnake master)
Eupatorium species
    (Joe-pye weeds)
Euphorbia corollata
    (flowering spurge)
Filipendula rubra
    (queen-of-the-prairie)
Gentiana species (gentians)
Geum triflorum (prairie smoke)

Helianthus species (sunflowers)
Heliopsis helianthoides (oxeye)
Heuchera richardsonii (alumroot)
Liatris species (blazing stars)
Lupinus perennis (wild lupine)
Monarda fistulosa (wild bergamot)
Opuntia humifusa
    (eastern prickly pear)
Penstemon digitalis
    (foxglove beardtongue)
Phlox pilosa (prairie phlox)
Porteranthus trifoliatus
    (Bowman's root)
Pteridium aquilinum (bracken)
Pycnanthemum virginianum
    (Virginia mountain mint)
Ratibida pinnata (gray-headed
    coneflower)
Rudbeckia species (black-eyed
    Susans, coneflowers)
Ruellia humilis (wild petunia)
Silphium species (compass plant,
    cup plant)
Sisyrinchium angustifolium
    (blue-eyed grass)
Smilacina stellata (starry false
    Solomon's seal)
Solidago species (goldenrods)
Tradescantia ohiensis
    (Ohio spiderwort)
Verbena stricta (hoary vervain)
Veronicastrum virginicum
    (Culver's root)
Viola pedata (bird's-foot violet)
Zizia aurea (golden alexanders)

Woody Plants

Amorpha canescens (leadplant)
Ceanothus americanus
    (New Jersey tea)
Prunus species (plum, cherries)
Ptelea trifoliata (hoptree)
Rhus species (sumacs)
Rosa arkansana (prairie wild rose)
Rosa blanda (smooth wild rose)
Salix humilis (prairie willow)
Vitis riparia (frost grape,
    riverbank grape)

Michigan's native prairie plants include *Silphium laciniatum* (compass plant), a large plant with interesting cut-leaf foliage and showy yellow flowers, and *Gentiana andrewsii* (bottle gentian) and *Lupinus perennis* (wild lupine), both of which have showy purple flowers.

Savanna and Prairie in the Landscape

Of the plants in Michigan's major biomes, those of the southern grasslands are probably the most adaptable to general landscape use. Many have showy flowers and have evolved to withstand the hot, sunny conditions typical of many perennial gardens. The earliest species generally start blooming in late spring, and later species continue their show even after the first frost. Many flowers have persistent seed heads offering winter interest, and grasses remain showy until late winter.

It is possible to create the look of a prairie without doing a full-fledged restoration. Select a sunny part of your landscape with few or no large trees. (An occasional large tree will give the savanna look.) Select a mixture of prairie forbs and grasses based on your soil type. Be sure to use plenty of native grasses. Their deep roots aerate soil, improve drainage, and contribute substantial amounts of humus when they die back. Grasses also support stems of wildflowers and make your prairie or savanna look more natural.

Embellish your grassland landscape with paths, ornaments, and furniture that match its informal style. Incorporate broad and winding gravel, wood-chip, or mown paths, and place casual benches made of wood, rusted metal, or sawn logs along the paths. For ornament in prairie gardens, have fun using "junk" salvaged from farmyards, which is so popular at garden centers and gift shops. Bird and butterfly houses will provide shelter for all the fluttering friends who'll be visiting, and a birdbath or other source of water will also be appreciated.

Eupatorium species (Joe-pye weeds) and *Veronicastrum virginicum* (Culver's root) are among the tall prairie plants used for screening in this small front yard.

Clockwise, from above:
Asclepias tuberosa (butterfly weed), *Phlox pilosa* (prairie phlox), and *Amorpha canescens* (leadplant) are three grassland plants that readily make the transition to landscape use.

This backyard prairie garden is reminiscent of an English cottage garden, with its wide array of colorful blooming plants and absence of grasses.

Heliopsis helianthoides (oxeye), *Rudbeckia hirta* (black-eyed Susan), *Liatris* species (blazing stars), *Monarda fistulosa* (wild bergamot), and *Bouteloua curtipendula* (side-oats grama) are all good choices for a large prairie garden.

Water and Shoreline Communities

While Michigan may not border an ocean, there's no denying the importance of water in the state. There are over 11,000 inland lakes, not including Lake Michigan, Lake Huron, Lake Erie, and Lake Superior; more than 36,000 miles of rivers and streams; and over 150 waterfalls. Add to these the 11 million acres of wetlands—the collective term referring to wet meadows, sedge meadows, wet prairies, marshes, swamps, bogs, peat lands, and fens—that once covered the state. These areas had mostly wet soil, saturated with water either above or just below the surface, and were home to plants that adapted to having "wet feet" for part or all of the growing season.

Michigan is also home to approximately 3,200 miles of Great Lakes shoreline, which includes 275,000 acres of sand dunes—the largest collection of freshwater dunes in the world. Dune formation is dependent on perennial vegetation, wind, and sand. Because dune plants act as barriers to sand movement and hold migrating sand, they play a critical role in the formation and stabilization of dunes.

The dominant plant in these semi-stabilized open dunes is usually the sand-binding beach grass, along with sand reed grass. Once stabilized, these grasses create habitat for wildflowers and shrubs such as hairy puccoon (*Lithospermum caroliniense*), common milkweed, beach pea (*Lathyrus japonicus*), sand cress (*Arabis lyrata*), smooth wild rose, bearberry, creeping juniper, poison ivy (*Toxicodendron radicans*), wild grape, and sand cherry.

Where dunes are protected from intense wind erosion, dune forests will eventually form. In southern Michigan, oak-hickory forests are common. Northern dune forests are dominated by beech, maple, and hemlock. Though thin and slow to accumulate, the topsoil of dune forests supports a variety of spring wildflowers and woodland plants, such as Jack-in-the-pulpit and showy trillium.

As sturdy as they seem, dune plants are especially sensitive to human disturbance. Walking or driving all-terrain vehicles on them destroys surface vegetation and causes root die-off. This exposes a dune to wind erosion, allowing the sand to move or to open up channels. Without sand-dune plants, the integrity and preservation of a stable dune complex cannot exist. Recognizing this threat, the Sand Dunes Protection and Management Program was enacted in 1989 to protect sand dunes from indiscriminate development.

In the eastern part of the state, marshes and swamps are more common than beaches along the Great Lakes. Water-tolerant trees such as silver maple, cottonwood, black ash, and tamarack dominate these swamps. Shrubs that grow in swamps include buttonbush, alder, willows, and red-osier dogwood. Marshes are covered periodically by standing or slow-moving water. Soft-stemmed plants such as cattails, sedges, and rushes dominate a marsh's nutrient-rich soils.

The showy wild blue flag (*Iris versicolor*) is at home among spike rushes (*Eleocharis* species) and bulrushes (*Scirpus* species) in wet prairies, ponds, shallow marshes, and bogs throughout much of Michigan. *Robert Domm*

Ammophila breviligulata (beach grass) is an important part of the Great Lakes shoreline dune communities, holding the sand in place so other plants can become established.

Water in the Landscape

Homeowners who have a wetland, lake, pond, or stream on their property certainly have a leg up when it comes to re-creating natural water features. Fortunately, it's well within the reach of most homeowners to install an artificial pond, stream, or bog. Many good references are available if your project is simple enough to fall into the do-it-yourself category. For larger projects, it is a good idea to bring in a landscape company specializing in water features. See chapter 4 for information on creating water features in the landscape.

Homeowners who are fortunate enough to live along Great Lakes shoreline have a responsibility to preserve and protect the fragile beach and dune communities. By choosing an appropriate mix of native plants and planting them correctly, you can reduce beach erosion, stabilize dunes, and still enjoy the amenities of lakeshore living.

Caltha palustris (marsh marigold) grows in wet woods, swamps, and the shallow water of ponds throughout Michigan. It does well in landscape situations such as bog gardens, where the soil is wet and high in humus.

Native Plants of Sand Dunes

These Great Lakes dune plants are suitable for restoration and landscape use.

Flowers and Grasses
Ammophila breviligulata (beach grass)
Anaphalis margaritacea (pearly everlasting)
Anemone multifida (cut-leaved anemone)
Asclepias syriaca (common milkweed)
Asclepias viridiflora (green milkweed)
Calamovilfa longifolia (sand reed grass)
Coreopsis lanceolata (sand coreopsis, tickseed)
Elymus canadensis (nodding wild rye)
Equisetum hyemale (tall scouring rush)
Koeleria macrantha (June grass)
Oenothera biennis (common evening primrose)
Potentilla anserina (silverweed)
Schizachyrium scoparius (little bluestem)
Smilacina stellata (starry false Solomon's seal)

Trees, Shrubs, and Vines
Arctostaphylos uva-ursi (bearberry)
Betula papyrifera (paper birch)
Hypericum kalmianum (Kalm's St. John's wort)
Juniperus communis (common juniper)
Juniperus horizontalis (creeping juniper)
Pinus strobus (white pine)
Pinus banksiana (jack pine)
Prunus pumila (sand cherry)
Ptelea trifoliata (hoptree)
Rosa species (wild roses)
Salix exigua (sandbar willow)
Shepherdia canadensis (buffaloberry)
Vitis riparia (wild grape)

Lilium michiganense (Michigan lily) is one of Michigan's few native bulbs. Plant it in low areas in perennial borders, along ponds and streams, or in bog gardens, and wait for the hummingbirds to arrive.

Chapter 3

Gardening with
Native Plants

Understanding Your Climate and Soil and Mastering Basic Skills

To be successful with native plants, it is essential that you understand the basics of gardening in your climate. You should have knowledge of your hardiness zone, frost dates, rainfall amounts, and existing soil conditions. You should also be aware of the basic maintenance needs of your plants and be prepared to perform them at the appropriate times.

Hardiness Zones and Frost Dates

Hardiness zones indicate the severity of winter temperatures. The lower the number, the more severe the winter climate. This book uses the most common system, the United States Department of Agriculture (USDA) Hardiness Zones, which is based on average annual minimum winter temperatures.

While it is important to know your hardiness zone, don't live and die by it. Use it as a guideline. A plant's ability to survive winter is affected by many factors, such as snow cover, soil moisture, the plant's age, and winter mulching. Keep in mind that just because a plant is native in your state, it doesn't mean it will be hardy where you live. Remember, plants adapt to ecological conditions, which rarely follow state boundaries.

The growing season is the average length of time between the last killing frost in spring and the first frost in autumn. It generally increases from north to south, but it is affected by large bodies of water and other factors. Frost dates are more of a factor with tender annuals than they are with native plants. However, you should be aware of your last spring frost date, because it is used as a guide for spring planting.

Soils and Soil Preparation
Soil Texture

Good soil is the most important factor in any type of gardening, but especially with native plants. If you provide your plants with suitable soil, the rest is a piece of cake. Native plants will soon establish themselves and become almost maintenance free.

It's definitely worth taking some time up front to get to know your soil. A good place to start is to have your soil tested by a soil-testing laboratory; check with your local university extension office for labs in your area. A soil test will provide you with information on existing soil texture and fertility, along with recommendations on what to add to improve it.

Soils typically have four components—sand, silt, clay, and organic matter. The proportions of these ingredients largely determine the soil texture, which in turn determines other soil properties such as fertility, porosity, and water retention. Heavier soils hold more moisture; sandy soils drain faster.

Sand and silt are the chief source of minerals required by plants, such as potassium, calcium, and phosphorous. Silt particles are smaller and yield their minerals more

USDA Plant Hardiness Zones

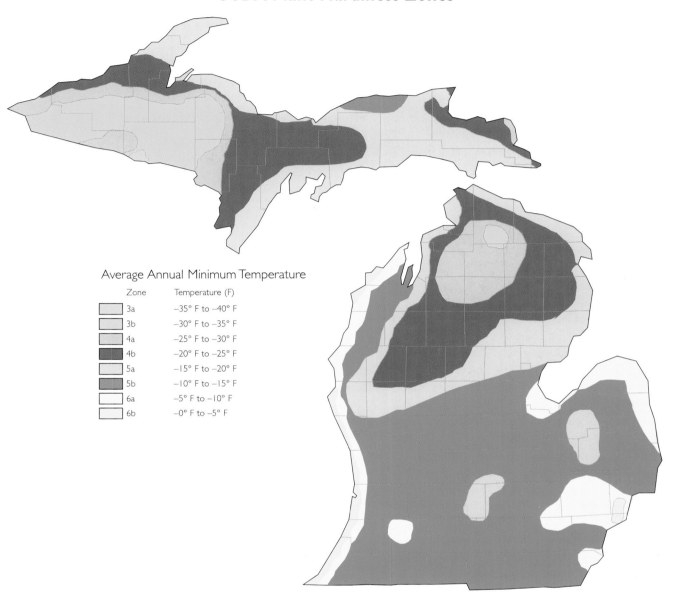

Average Annual Minimum Temperature

Zone	Temperature (F)
3a	−35° F to −40° F
3b	−30° F to −35° F
4a	−25° F to −30° F
4b	−20° F to −25° F
5a	−15° F to −20° F
5b	−10° F to −15° F
6a	−5° F to −10° F
6b	−0° F to −5° F

Approximate Low Temperatures and Frost Dates

Zone	Low Temperature	Last Frost Date	First Frost Date
3	−30° F to −40° F	May 15	September 15
4	−30° F to −20° F	May 10	September 20
5	−20° F to −10° F	May 1	October 10
6	−10° F to −0° F	April 20	October 15

readily than sand, making silt soils more fertile than sandy soils. Clay particles are the finest in size, and a heavy clay soil has reduced pore spaces between the particles. These smaller spaces make it difficult for water, air, and plant roots to penetrate effectively. Clay soils generally create the greatest problem for gardeners.

Organic matter, also known as humus, is decomposing plant or animal material. It is an important component of soils and must not be overlooked in native landscapes. Organic matter determines a soil's capacity to produce nitrogen, supports the community of soil microorganisms crucial to plant life, and retains bacterial byproducts such as water and carbon dioxide. It also creates a moist, slightly acidic environment critical for the transfer of minerals from soil particles to plants.

Soil Fertility

Plants require fifteen or so nutrients for growth and survival. Carbon, hydrogen, and oxygen are involved in photosynthesis. Nitrogen, phosphorous, and potassium—each required in substantial quantities—are called macronutrients and are used to generally define soil fertility.

Nitrogen ensures normal vegetative growth and a healthy green color. Deficiencies result in stunted plants with a yellowish green color. Excess nitrogen causes rank vegetative growth. Soil nitrogen comes mainly from decaying organic matter. Some plants also fix nitrogen on their roots. Nitrogen leaches out of soil easily, and as plants grow and remove nitrogen, more needs to be added to soil.

Phosphorus, important to flowering and fruiting, is more stable in soils than nitrogen and doesn't have to be added unless soil tests indicate a deficiency.

Potassium is essential for healthy development of roots and stems. It may need to be added to soils where plants are grown continuously.

Micronutrients necessary for healthy plants include magnesium, manganese, calcium, zinc, copper, iron, sulfur, cobalt, sodium, boron, and iodine. Since these nutrients are used in small quantities, most soils have enough for normal plant growth. Deficiencies do occur, however.

One of the great benefits of a native-plant landscape is that if you choose your plants carefully and improve your soil regularly with organic matter, artificial fertilizers will not be necessary. In fact, they may actually be harmful, encouraging growth of exotic weeds at the expense of native plants. If your soil test indicates a need to improve soil fertility, there are several organic products you can use, including compost, rotted manure, peat moss, bone meal, blood meal, fish emulsion, soybean meal, and rock phosphate. After the initial application, yearly addition of finished compost to the surface should be enough to maintain adequate fertility.

Soil pH

Soil acidity and alkalinity are measured in terms of pH on a scale from 1 to 14. A 7 on the scale indicates the soil is neutral in pH. Lower than 7, the soil is increasingly acidic; higher than 7, it is increasingly alkaline. Soil pH is important because it affects the availability of nutrients necessary for plant growth. Most nutrients are most soluble at a pH between 6 and 7. That is why most plants grow best in "slightly acidic soil." Iron chlorosis, a yellowing of foliage caused by lack of available iron, can be a problem on alkaline soils.

Most native plants tolerate a range of soil pH, but some survive only within a narrow window. It is important to know which plants these are and to change the soil pH before planting them, if possible. It is possible to change soil pH after planting, but it's not as easy. As you become familiar with the native-plant communities in your area, you'll see that the plants of a community have all evolved to grow best with a similar soil pH. By growing these native plants together in a certain area of your garden, you'll be able to base your mulch choices and soil amendments on the pH needs of the entire group. It is possible to change the soil pH around just one or two plants, however, by regularly working in the appropriate pH-altering soil amendments.

Iron chlorosis sometimes shows up on native plants grown in soils that are too alkaline. Symptoms include a light green to yellow coloring between the leaf veins. The problem is often due to a soil pH over 6.5, which can make iron unavailable to the plants. Correct this problem by acidifying the soil to lower the pH.

Improving Soil

In general, it is best to choose plants adapted to your soil texture, pH, and moisture conditions. However, if your soil has been drastically changed by construction or other factors, you will want to do all you can to improve it before planting.

Native plants generally grow better in less-fertile soil than traditional garden plants do; however, that doesn't mean native plants like poor soil. Most woodland plants require at least 40 percent organic matter in the soil. Most grassland plants thrive in leaner, drier soils; if the soil is too rich, plants may grow too lushly and flop over. However, some—especially those native to wetter prairies—do require richer soil.

Adding organic matter is the key to improving soil texture, fertility, and pH. It is difficult to add too much organic matter, especially if it is partly decomposed. Organic matter increases the aeration of clay soils and improves the moisture and nutrient retention of sandy soils. It adds valuable nutrients at a slow and steady pace, and it has a buffering effect on soil pH.

In the natural world, native plants recycle themselves, creating abundant organic matter. If you can follow this principle in your own landscape, that's great. However, for city and suburban gardeners it's not always practical to allow all fallen leaves to stay on the ground and all plants to remain without cutting back.

In most situations, you will need to add organic matter on a regular basis. The best source of organic matter for gardeners is compost. Composting materials such as cow or horse manure, peat moss, grass clippings, and leaves ensures they will be in optimum condition to work into the soil. Other good sources of organic matter are chopped straw and hay.

As with other amendments, the easiest time to add organic matter is before planting a bed. Loosen the soil with a spade or digging fork to a depth of at least 10 to 12 inches—more if possible. Spread a layer of compost or well-rotted manure 2 to 4 inches deep over the entire bed. Use a fork to mix it thoroughly into the soil. If your soil is very heavy (high in clay), you will want to add 2 inches of sharp builder's sand along with the compost or manure. Sand alone will only make matters worse, but when it is added with organic matter to heavy clay, it does help loosen the soil.

Organic Soil Amendments

Improve overall soil fertility by adding:
- Compost
- Well-rotted manure
- Fish emulsion
- Milorganite

Improve soil nitrogen content by adding:
- Soybean meal
- Alfalfa meal
- Compost

Improve soil phosphorus content by adding:
- Bone meal
- Rock phosphate

Improve soil potassium content by adding:
- Granite dust
- Greensand
- Seaweed
- Wood ashes

Raise soil pH by adding:
- Agricultural lime
- Calcium
- Wood ashes (in moderation)

Lower soil pH by adding:
- Pine-needle or oak-leaf mulch
- Organic matter, peat moss, or ground oak leaves
- Gypsum or sulfur (in moderation)

Improve soil drainage by:
- Adding compost
- Adding horticultural grit
- Adding coarse builder's sand with organic matter
- Making raised beds

Improve water-retention by adding:
- Compost
- Well-rotted manure

Composting Basics

Composting is essential to successful native-plant landscaping. Compost not only adds valuable nutrients to the soil at a slow pace, it improves soil texture—both in sandy and clay soils—and makes a great mulch. It also provides a way for you to recycle your yard waste into a useful product.

Compost is created by mixing high-carbon and high-nitrogen materials proportionately with air and moisture. High-carbon materials include straw, hay, leaves, sawdust, shredded newspaper, and pine needles. High-nitrogen materials are generally succulent green plant parts such as grass clippings, weeds, perennial prunings, and vegetables. If you aren't able to provide enough of the high-nitrogen materials from your garden, you may need to add animal manure, blood meal, or cottonseed meal. Kitchen scraps such as eggshells, vegetables and fruits, and coffee grounds can also be added to the compost pile. Do not add meat scraps, bones, or grease, which attract rodents and other pests.

There is debate about whether or not you should add diseased plants or weeds with seed heads to the compost pile. Some experts feel the heat of a properly working compost pile will be enough to kill off the diseases and seeds. Others don't think it's worth the risk. To be on the safe side, you should probably avoid both.

You will need some way to contain your compost. Most people build or purchase some type of bin, but you can compost by simply piling the debris up. An ideal location for a compost bin is one hidden from view but close enough for you to easily bring stuff to it and haul the finished compost away. It is also nice to have the compost near a water source so you can add water during dry spells, but it's not necessary.

Build your compost pile as materials become available, layering carbon materials alternately with nitrogen materials. If you have an abundance of carbon materials, put some of them on the side until more nitrogen materials become available. Too many green grass clippings can mat down and prohibit the composting process. Mix them with looser materials such as straw or shredded newspaper or allow them to dry in the sun before adding them to the pile. It's also a good idea to add thin layers of topsoil or finished compost to a new pile to introduce the decay organisms that create compost. Ideally, you will have several piles going at the same time so you will always have some finished compost available.

Once your pile is built, you'll need to do a little regular maintenance. Add water as needed to keep the pile moist but not soggy. Turn your compost regularly—once a week if possible—to get air into the pile. If you don't turn your pile, you'll still get compost, but it will take a lot longer. If you want to speed up the composting process, turn the pile more often, add more nitrogen-rich materials, and shred or chop the carbon materials before adding them to the pile so they break down quicker. You'll know your compost is ready for the garden when it is dark, crumbly, and most of the plant parts are decomposed.

The best way to improve soil conditions and encourage healthy plants is to apply an annual application of organic matter, such as shredded leaves and/or compost. The easiest time to apply organic matter is early spring, before the plants have fully expanded.

If possible, find a place to compost yard waste on site. Compost is an excellent soil conditioner and source of nutrients, and it provides a practical way to recycle leaves, grass clippings, and plant trimmings.

Starting a New Garden

Some people believe that native plants are so tough that all you have to do is scatter seeds or plant an abundance of plants and they will take over an area and thrive. This misconception couldn't be farther from the truth. Native plants establish themselves in an area over hundreds of years; they can't simply be planted and expected to grow in landscapes—especially when the soil in many landscapes is far from its natural state and covered with aggressive nonnative plants (i.e., weeds).

Proper site preparation is key to success with native plants. If you are starting a new bed, take the time to get rid of existing vegetation and improve the soil before you start putting plants in the ground. This preparation will pay significant dividends in the end.

There are several ways to get rid of existing vegetation. A lot depends on how much time you have and how you feel about using herbicides. If your garden bed is not too large, you can dig it up manually. Just be sure to get rid of all the existing plant roots. Even tiny pieces of tough perennial-weed roots can grow into big bad weeds in no time. A major disadvantage with this method is that you lose substantial amounts of topsoil. To avoid this, if you have the time, you can simply turn the sod over and allow it to decay on site.

There are several alternatives that are easier on your back, but they take up to a year to be effective. You can smother the existing vegetation with about 6 inches of organic mulch, such as straw, shredded bark, or compost. Mow closely in spring, cover with a thick layer of newspaper (ten sheets or so) and the organic mulch, and let it stand all summer. Replenish the mulch in fall, and by the next spring your garden should be ready for planting. This method works best on lawn areas rather than areas with lots of deep-rooted perennial weeds.

If you don't have a year to prepare the soil or the manual method doesn't appeal to you, you can use a nonselective glycophosphate-based herbicide, such as Monsanto's Roundup, which kills tops and roots of herbaceous plants. Products based on a glycophosphate formula do not linger in the environment in a toxic form. If you follow directions exactly, aim carefully, and use only when necessary, these products should kill invading plants without causing undue harm to the environment. Once the existing vegetation is dead (usually ten days to two weeks after spraying), you can turn the soil by hand or use a mechanical tiller to turn the dead vegetation into the soil.

Avoid using a mechanical tiller without killing all existing vegetation first. While it may look like you've created a bare planting area, all you've done is ground the roots into smaller pieces, which in turn sprout into many more plants than you started with. Even after multiple tillings spaced weeks apart, you'll be haunted by these root pieces.

Whatever method you use, be careful if your garden is under large trees. Disturb soil as little as possible because digging can damage the trees' active surface roots. If you will be installing a garden right under a tree's canopy, it is best to dig individual planting holes and add organic matter to holes as needed, rather than till or dig up the entire area.

Planting

The best time to plant most plants is spring, which gives them ample time to become established before they have to endure their first winter in the ground. Summer- and fall-blooming flowers and most woody plants can be planted in spring or fall—actually, all season long if they are container grown. However, planting in the high temperatures of midsummer means you will have to be diligent about providing adequate water. You may also need to provide shelter from the sun for a few weeks. Plant or transplant early blooming and spring-ephemeral species after they flower, usually in late spring.

Container-grown plants can be planted at almost anytime during the growing season. Be sure to dig a hole large enough to accommodate the entire root system and water well after planting. If planting in the heat of summer, provide some type of protection from the hot sun for a few days after planting.

Bare-root plants should be planted only in spring. To plant bare root, dig the hole wider and deeper than the largest roots. Make a cone of soil in the bottom of the hole, and spread the roots out over the cone. Add soil as needed to keep the plant's crown at the right level. Right after planting, water the new plants well.

Potted plants need to be carefully removed from their containers before planting. If grown in a loose soilless mix, shake off the excess and plant them like bare-root plants. If roots are circling, disentangle them to encourage outward growth. If the root ball is dense, use a sharp knife to cut through some of the roots. Cutting may sound harsh, but the roots must be free to move into the surrounding soil.

Seeds take longer to produce a showy end product, but they are less expensive and there are often more choices available than with grown plants. Many woodland plants have specific moisture and temperature requirements for germination and are difficult for beginners to grow from seeds. Most grassland plants, however, are relatively easy to start from seeds. If you will be seeding a large area, you may want to consider a seed mixture. However, be sure to purchase one from a reputable native-plant propagator in your area. Avoid the nationally available "meadows in a can."

Mulching

There are so many good things about mulching, it's hard to know where to start. Organic mulch keeps down weeds, holds water in the soil, and improves fertility. It cools the soil in woodland gardens and replenishes the rich soil that woodland plants need. It also sets the plants off nicer than nondescript bare soil. Mulch around lawn trees keeps the lawn mower and weed whipper away from trunks. Keep the mulch a few inches away from the base of trees to discourage mice from hiding there in winter.

There are several good organic mulches. Select one based on your plants and garden type. Shredded leaves are good in almost any situation, but they are not always available. Shredded bark or wood chips are good in shrub borders or woodland gardens, but they can be too coarse for flowerbeds. Chopped straw is good in flowerbeds but it's not as attractive as leaves. Avoid using peat moss as mulch. It tends to form a nonpermeable crust that makes it difficult for water to penetrate the soil. Mulch prairie gardens at planting time with a light layer of chopped, weed-free straw 1 to 2 inches deep. Once prairie gardens are established, they can be left unmulched, but it is still a good idea to top-dress them annually with compost.

Winter mulch offers added protection from the freezing and thawing that can result in frost heaving of plants. It should be laid down after the ground has frozen to keep

Meadow-in-a-Can Seed Mixtures

Dame's rocket (*Hesperis matronalis*) is a nonnative plant often included in seed mixtures that has escaped from gardens to become a roadside weed.

Beware of meadows-in-a-can. These seed mixtures often contain many annuals that give a quick burst of color in their first year but don't reseed. Many include weedy, nonnative species that may become aggressive. If you do go this route, get the seeds from a reputable local dealer or mix your own.

Here are some plants commonly found in seed mixes that you should avoid using in any area of your landscape. All are native outside the United States and can get out of control in garden settings.

baby's breath (*Gypsophila paniculata*)
bouncing bet (*Saponaria officinalis*)
chicory (*Cichorium intybus*)
cornflower (*Centaurea cyanus*)
dame's rocket (*Hesperis matronalis*)
four o'clock (*Mirabilis jalapa*)
oxeye daisy (*Leucanthemum vulgare*)
purple loosestrife (*Lythrum salicaria*)
Queen Anne's lace (*Daucus carota*)
St. John's wort (*Hypericum perforatum*)

Nature's mulch is the fallen layer of leaves or needles that carpet the ground each fall. Imitate nature by surrounding landscape plants with a 2- to 4-inch layer of organic mulch such as shredded bark, pine needles, or shredded leaves.

the cold in. If you put it down too early, it acts as an insulator, and the ground can remain warm too long. Winter mulch should be removed in early spring just as the plants begin poking above ground.

Weed Control

A walk in the woods or through a restored grassland may lead to the mistaken idea that native landscapes don't need weeding. While it's true that a dense planting of native plants does tend to reduce weed problems, most home landscapes are a long way from their natural state, and these changes frequently invite unwelcome pests. Weeds come in from many sources, including neighbors' yards, surrounding fields, visiting birds, and even the wind. Most weeds have their origins in Europe or Asia, but not all. Certain species of *Helianthus*, *Eupatorium*, *Heliopsis*, *Viola*, and *Solidago* can become weedy in landscape situations.

Mulching is a good way to keep weeds out of your garden. However, mulch is only effective when placed on soil where the existing weeds have been removed.

Once your garden is planted and mulched, you'll still need to invest a small amount of time in weed control. Weeds are easiest to pull when they are young and the soil is moist. By taking a weekly walk through your garden after a rain, you should be able to keep weeds under control. Be sure to remove the entire plant root. Use a weeding tool to get leverage if needed.

The invasive common buckthorn (*Rhamnus cathartica*) was introduced to North America as an ornamental shrub, but it has now become a troublesome weed. Once established, this species aggressively invades natural areas and forms dense thickets, crowding and shading out native plants, often completely obliterating them.

If you have persistent perennial weeds such as thistle or quack grass in an established garden and hand pulling has not been effective, you may want to consider spot treatments with a nonselective herbicide such as Roundup. To apply it without harming yourself or nearby desirable plants, choose a calm day; protect yourself with long sleeves, safety glasses, and gloves; and carefully but thoroughly spot-spray individual weeds.

In woodland gardens, where woody plants such as buckthorn, poison ivy, and raspberries can become weedy, weed control will require a little more effort. You can pull or dig up smaller specimens by hand, but larger plants may require the use of a nonselective herbicide. Cut the woody trunk low to the ground and use a disposable foam paintbrush to immediately apply a triclopyr-based herbicide labeled for woody plants such as poison ivy (e.g., Ortho's Brush-B-Gon) on the fresh cut. The herbicide will work its way into the trunk, destroying the plant and any plants that grow from the same root system. If you are careful and selective about using these herbicides and do not use them near water, they can effectively control weeds in the garden while causing little harm to the environment.

If you're concerned about the potential hazards of using chemical herbicides, there are alternative herbicides such as those made from potassium salts of fatty acids. You can also use straight vinegar, boiling water, or a butane torch.

Watering

One of the main attractions of using native plants is to reduce or even eliminate the need for supplemental watering. If you've chosen plants correctly, improved the water-holding capacity of sandy soils by adding organic matter, and have added organic mulch, established native plants rarely need supplemental watering.

Almost all plants—drought-tolerant natives included—need supplemental water while becoming established. Keep soil adequately moist until new plants have a full year of new growth on them. All trees, shrubs, and vines need to be watered regularly for at least the first full year after planting. In hot weather, they may need supplemental water once or twice a week. If the autumn is dry, continue watering until the first hard frost. Once fully established—after three to four years—most native woody plants should be self-sufficient as far as watering.

Encourage deep rooting by watering less often and more deeply. The most efficient way to water is to water the soil and not the plants. Avoid overhead sprinklers. Not only are they inefficient, but also the wet foliage can lead to disease problems on plants. Drip-irrigation systems and soaker hoses are good choices for effective watering.

Xeriscaping: Water-Wise Gardening

Xeriscaping promotes water conservation by using drought-tolerant, well-adapted plants within a landscape carefully designed for maximum use of rainfall runoff and minimum care. It is more common in western and southern states where rainfall is lower and water use is more regulated, but the principles behind water-wise gardening directly apply to native-plant landscaping.

Xeriscaped landscapes are not all cactus and rock gardens. They can be green, cool landscapes full of beautiful plants maintained with water-efficient practices. Xeriscape gardening recognizes that indigenous plants are not only visually and aesthetically pleasing, they are naturally accustomed to local climates and therefore good choices for water- and waste-efficient landscapes.

Water-wise landscaping incorporates these seven basic principles, which closely match the philosophy behind native-plant landscaping:

Planning and design
Select plants based on their cultural requirements and group plants with similar water needs.

Soil analysis and improvement
Determine whether soil improvement is needed for better water absorption and improved water-holding capacity. Mix compost or peat moss into soil before planting to help retain water. Reduce water runoff by building terraces and retaining walls.

Limited lawn area
Use turf grasses as a planned element in the landscape and limit their use. Avoid impractical turf use, such as in long, narrow areas, and use turf only in areas where it provides functional benefits. Plant groundcovers and add hard-surface areas like patios, decks, and walkways where practical.

Plant selection
Keep your landscape more in tune with the natural environment. Select plants that have lower water requirements or those that only need water in the first year or so after planting.

Efficient irrigation
You can save 30 to 50 percent on your water bill by installing drip or trickle irrigation systems for those areas that need watering. Install timers and water-control devices to increase their efficiency even more.

Mulch
Apply organic mulch to reduce water loss from the soil through evaporation and to increase water penetration during irrigation.

Regular appropriate maintenance
Properly timed pruning, weeding, pest control, and irrigation all conserve water. Raise mower blades to get a higher cut. Higher grass encourages grass roots to grow deeper, making stronger, more drought-resistant plants.

Grooming

Grooming is not about making the outdoors immaculate. It's about caring for plants and removing flowers and foliage that are past their prime in order to keep plants healthy and the garden looking pleasantly kempt. One advantage of native plants is that they require less grooming than nonnatives. However, some tasks will help plants grow better and others keep your landscape looking more tended, which is especially important if you have a front-yard garden in the city.

Pruning

Almost every tree and shrub in your landscape will need pruning at one time or another, and the better job you do, the healthier your plants will be. Proper pruning not only encourages healthier plants, it also helps native plants, which often have a habit of irregular growth, look neater and tidier in the landscape.

The keys to successful pruning are appropriate timing and the right tools. Most native trees and shrubs are best pruned in their dormant period, reducing the chance of infection from insects and diseases. You can also see a deciduous plant's silhouette when the leaves are off. Evergreen conifers should be pruned in late spring and early summer just after you see new growth. Spring-blooming shrubs begin setting their flower buds soon after flowering and should be pruned as soon as possible after flowering. If you prune them in winter or spring, you will be cutting off their flower buds; this won't kill them, it will just mean you won't have flowers for one season. Summer-flowering shrubs are best pruned in early spring. Don't wait too long, however, or you may cut off flower buds, which start to form in spring.

Pruning tools must be sharp and clean. The basic pruning tool is a handheld bypass pruner. Larger shrubs and small trees will require loppers and a pruning saw. If you have large trees in need of major pruning, you should have it done by a professional tree trimmer.

Pruning is somewhat of a subjective activity, but there are some basic rules to follow. Always remove dead wood and branches that rub against each other. It is usually best to try to maintain the natural shape of a tree, especially evergreens. In general, do not remove more than one-third of the branches in one pruning. However, overgrown deciduous shrubs may need renewal pruning; cut them all the way back to the ground in early spring.

Pruning large trees is a way to alter available light. Don't be afraid to limb up large shade trees by removing some of the lower branches. This change will allow more light to penetrate the garden underneath and allow you to grow a wider variety of plants.

Staking

Even with proper plant selection, taller perennials often need assistance. In a closely planted prairie garden, grasses create natural support. For the flower border, many systems using hoops and sticks of wood or metal are available from nurseries. Use small tomato cages for bushy plants. Long-stemmed plants will need a stake for every blooming stem. Get stakes in the ground as early as possible to avoid root damage, and loosely tie plants to the stake with inconspicuous green or brown twine.

Deadheading

Removing spent flower buds stimulates prolonged and repeated blooming on many perennials. Cut back to the next set of leaves to encourage new buds to open. Think twice before deadheading plants that provide bird food and winter interest, however.

Pinching and Disbudding

Gently removing some of a plant's new growth in spring will encourage more compact growth. This new-growth removal is effective on some of the taller grassland plants, such as *Boltonia*, *Eupatorium*, and *Monarda* species. Pinching back will delay bloom somewhat. Do not do any pinching back after early June.

Thinning and Dividing

If you are growing perennials, ferns, and grasses in mixed borders or foundation plantings, they will benefit from being divided every three or four years. Dividing prevents overcrowding and keeps the plants healthy, vigorous, and more prone to flower production.

The best time to divide most plants is early spring, so they have a full growing season to recover. However, early spring-flowering plants are best divided in fall so as not to interfere with flower and seed production. To divide herbaceous plants, simply unearth the plant with a spade or trowel, wash excess soil from roots, pull or cut apart rooted sections, and replant.

Tall perennials such as *Aster novae-angliae* (New England aster) may need staking when grown in gardens. Make it easier on yourself and the plant by getting the stake in the ground early in the season while plants are still young and easy to work with.

Pest Management

Here is where native plants have a definite advantage over nonnatives. If you've spent some time preparing your site and matching plants to your site, your pest problems should be few and not serious.

The key in pest management is to really get to know your gardens and the plants in them. Keep your eyes open on daily walks. The earlier you spot problems, the easier they are to control. If you spot a problem, identify it correctly (get help from a local expert, if needed), find out what is causing it, and decide if it is serious enough to warrant attention. Most pest problems are purely cosmetic and won't do any lasting damage to your plants. You have to decide what your level of tolerance is and determine whether you want to take action or live with the problem.

Keep in mind that many problems are due to cultural conditions, not pests. Yellowing or browning foliage, stunted growth, and buds that rot before opening could be signs that you have poor soil drainage or your plants are overcrowded. Once again, making sure you have the right plant for the site and the appropriate soil conditions is the best way to avoid such problems.

Native plants are by no means free of pest problems. However, many problems, such as the leaf miner damage on this columbine, are purely cosmetic and do not threaten the life of a plant. By learning to live with a few tattered leaves and less-than-perfect flowers, you'll free yourself from the need for pesticides and excessive maintenance.

Diseases and Viruses

Because native plants are adapted to a particular region, diseases and viruses are rare. If they do occur, they are rarely serious and can usually be prevented the next year by altering cultural practices, such as changing watering habits or thinning out branches. Prevention in the form of good site selection and proper planting distance is the best way to avoid disease problems. If disease problems become severe, you'll need to pull up the infected plants and choose another plant for that site.

Powdery mildew is often seen on native plants, both in the wild and in gardens. To reduce chances of infection, increase air circulation by pruning out inside branches and removing some nearby plants. Cornell University has developed a baking-soda-based spray for fighting black spot and powdery mildew. Mix 1 tablespoon baking soda and 1 tablespoon horticultural oil with 1 gallon of water. Spray each plant completely about once a week before infections appear. It's a good idea to test the spray on a few leaves before spraying the entire plant to make sure the spray won't do more damage than the disease.

Insects

Puckered foliage could indicate sucking insects, and sticky leaves often point to aphids. Do you see tiny webs on your plants? Turn over the leaves and use a magnifying glass to look for spider mites. If you catch these problems early, you can get rid of many of the pests by spraying the plants with a strong blast from your garden hose or using an insecticidal soap.

With slugs and Japanese beetles, hand picking (with gloves) and dropping them in soapy water is a good place to start. Slugs can also be killed using beer traps or diatomaceous earth placed around plants.

If any of your trees or shrubs has severely infested branches, prune the branches off well beyond the problem and dispose of them off site. Insects may chew and tatter leaves by the season's end; this is usually not a serious problem for most plants. Revive plants by adding compost or fish emulsion to the soil.

Natural predators keep things in check, and it is important to learn the difference between good and bad bugs. Even if you know which the bad guys are, it's still never worth it to use insecticides. Not only are they toxic to you and your garden guests, they destroy too many beneficial insects. If an insect problem becomes so bad that the health of your plant is questionable, you should consider replacing the plant with something better suited to the conditions. It's cruel to lure wildlife to your landscape and then use herbicides, insecticides, and other pesticides that can poison and destroy them.

Other Animal Pests

Insects aren't the only pests you'll find in your garden. Deer and rabbits are often more serious and difficult to control. There are many repellents available; however, all of them are only temporary solutions, and they require a lot of time and effort to be effective, especially against deer.

Rabbits are repelled by blood meal, which can be regularly sprinkled around plants, or hot-pepper spray, which needs to be applied after every rain.

Owning a large dog can be effective in deterring deer. But the best long-term solution for a serious deer problem is to install some type of fencing, which must be at least 8 feet tall to be effective.

You can also make plant choices based on deer feeding. For starters, plant a wide variety of plants so an entire section of your landscape won't be eliminated in one meal. Although no plant can really be considered "deer proof" under all conditions, deer generally do not like plants with thorns, aromatic plants, and plants with leathery, fuzzy, or hairy foliage. Once deciduous trees reach 6 feet in height and their bark has become corky, they are out of reach of deer browsing. Young trees can be protected with a wire cage.

Planting patterns can deter deer as well. Deer do not like to cross hedges or solid fences where they can't see what's on the other side. They do not like to force their way through dense shrubs or shrubs with thorns and firm branches. By massing plants, you will discourage deer from feeding in the center of the planting, where you can plant more-susceptible plants.

Deer-Resistant Native Plants

A plant's resistance to deer feeding is affected by fluctuations in deer populations, availability of alternative food, the time of year, environmental factors, and even individual animal preference. No plant is safe under all conditions, but here are some native plants that have consistently shown some resistance to deer feeding.

Herbaceous Plants
Actaea species (baneberries)
Allium species (wild onions)
Andropogon gerardii (big bluestem)
Aquilegia canadensis (Canada columbine)
Arisaema species (jack-in-the-pulpits)
Asclepias species (milkweeds, butterfly weed)
Asarum canadensis (wild ginger)
Aster species (asters)
Baptisia species (wild indigos)
Bouteloua curtipendula (side-oats grama)
Coreopsis species (tickseeds)
Dicentra cucullaria (Dutchman's breeches)
Echinacea purpurea (purple coneflower)
Eryngium yuccifolium (rattlesnake master)
Euphorbia corollata (flowering spurge)
Geranium maculatum (wild geranium)
Iris versicolor (northern blue flag)
Jeffersonia diphylla (twinleaf)
Liatris aspera (rough blazing star)
Lobelia species (cardinal flowers, lobelia)
Monarda species (wild bergamot, bee balm)
Opuntia humifusa (eastern prickly pear)
Penstemon species (beardtongues)
Podophyllum peltatum (May apple)
Rudbeckia species (black-eyed Susans)
Sanguinaria canadense (bloodroot)

Schizachyrium scoparium (little bluestem)
Solidago species (goldenrods)
Sporobolus heterolepis (prairie dropseed)
Tradescantia species (spiderworts)
Verbena species (vervains)
Veronicastrum virginicum (Culver's root)

Woody Plants
Acer species (maples)
Amelanchier species (juneberries, serviceberries)
Asimina triloba (pawpaw)
Betula species (birches)
Carpinus caroliniana (blue beech)
Crataegus crus-galli (cockspur hawthorn)
Dirca palustris (leatherwood)
Fraxinus species (ashes)
Gleditsia triacanthos (honey locust)
Hamamelis species (witch hazels)
Ilex verticillata (winterberry)
Juniperus species (junipers)
Larix laricina (tamarack)
Lindera benzoin (spicebush)
Picea species (spruces)
Potentilla fruticosa (shrubby cinquefoil)
Quercus species (oaks)
Tsuga canadensis (eastern hemlock)
Viburnum species (viburnums)

Deer are the bane of many gardeners. While no plant is guaranteed to be completely deer proof at all times, some have proven to be less palatable than others. This deer resistant planting includes *Carpinus caroliniana* (blue beech), *Asarum canadense* (wild ginger), and *Podophyllum peltatum* (May apple).

Chapter 4

Landscaping with
Native Plants

Choosing Garden Styles and Incorporating Plants

Landscape design is the process of creating beautiful, useful spaces that you will enjoy being in. Your landscape should be a reflection of your lifestyle, including spaces for things you and your family enjoy doing, as well as space in which to entertain and relax. Base your landscape decisions on practical considerations such as current conditions, future use, and maintenance issues, but don't forget to have fun and make it a place you'll truly enjoy.

A properly planted native-plant landscape will look natural on your property and with your house. Don't just carve out a geometric island bed in the lawn and fill it with plants. Aim for creating gardens that have the feel of a native habitat, keeping in mind limitations imposed by the site and its proximity to neighbors. Look to nature for inspiration. Take walks in parks and nature areas. Bring a notebook and camera and record things and plants you see. Bring ideas home to help you re-create these areas—literally or by suggestion. Try to base your natural landscape on your reactions to natural beauty.

If you are starting from scratch with a new home or doing a major landscape redesign of an existing home, there are many good books available to take you through the process. Consider taking a class where a landscape designer helps you develop a plan. You may want to work with a professional landscape architect who specializes in native plants.

Assessing Your Site

Even if you're the type of gardener who doesn't like to plan everything on paper, you should have some sort of overall organized approach to your landscape. Start with a rough sketch of your property. Identify everything that is on the site, including your home and garage, existing trees and shrubs, driveways, sidewalks, outbuildings, doors, windows, utilities, faucets, downspouts, air conditioners,

If your lot includes a sloped shady spot where it is difficult to grow lawn grasses, stop fighting it and install a shade garden. This one mixes native plants with well-behaved nonnatives such as *Pulmonaria* species and *Athyrium nipponicum* 'Pictum' (Japanese painted fern).

Keep the architectural style of your house in mind when designing a native landscape. This prairie-style house is perfectly suited to the informal planting that surrounds it.

and planting beds. Measure everything and mark it on a map. Don't stop at the property lines. Note changes in grade and possible drainage problems. Take photographs to help you see things you may miss.

Note sunlight patterns, slopes, and compass directions. Discover and identify microclimates—those small areas where physical or biological features cause conditions to differ from the surrounding area. These can be south-facing house walls or low areas where cold air can collect.

If you are working with a developed landscape, take note of existing plants and decide what you want to save and what you want to discard. You may be surprised at the number of native plants you already have. Note their growing conditions. Since many plants are particular about their growing requirements, you'll get clues as to what existing soil and light conditions you have.

Once you have your base drawing, it's time to determine what you want on your property. Your list should include practical needs as well as dreams. Chances are it will be way too long to be practical. You'll need to prioritize and decide just what you can add at this point and what things will have to be put on hold for a while.

Choosing a Style

Once you know what you want in your landscape and have decided where to put it, it's time to think in terms of garden styles. Traditional home landscapes usually try to mimic the look of a city park—open areas with large trees and benches placed around the outside. This style is rarely the most attractive or the most comfortable setting for

native plants. Once again, look to nature for inspiration. Nature arranges elements according to ecological principals. Beauty in nature follows usefulness and necessity, important keys to successfully reproducing that beauty in your own backyard.

There should be continuity between your house and landscape, but the style of your house doesn't have to dictate the style of your gardens. Most garden-design books will recommend formal gardens for traditional house styles and less-formal gardens for contemporary houses, at least in the front yard. While most native plants adapt best to naturalistic designs, they can be used in formal settings. You'll just have to put a little more thought into plant selection and planting design. See the sidebar on page 46 for ideas on how to make native plants work in more traditional settings.

When planning your landscape, decide what kind of habitats you want to include. Determine what indigenous plant community makes ecological sense in each spot. For best results, try to mimic a natural habitat compatible with your conditions. If your site is wooded, marshy, or otherwise undeveloped, the simplest and soundest course is simply to build on the natural habitat. Rather than fill in the wet spot, stock it with native wetland species and create a marsh, pond, or bog. If you are tired of fighting with grass under large shade trees, remove the grass and begin creating a deciduous woodland garden. If you have a large open lawn area in full sun that is just a drain on your lawn mower and your time, consider a prairie garden. There are native plants to fit most popular garden styles and landscape situations.

There are many things suburban gardeners can do to help make their native landscape more acceptable to their inexperienced neighbors, such as maintaining some turf areas, using mulch, and planting clumping plants rather than spreaders.

Placing Plants

When it comes to choosing what to grow and where to grow it, most books will overwhelm you with design lingo about form, texture, color, and so on. While you should keep these things in mind, landscaping with native plants frees you from much of this. Nature has already made these decisions for you. If you follow its lead, you'll end up with a landscape full of interesting textures, colors, and plant forms without much effort. Plants found growing together in the wild will usually combine nicely in a garden setting.

It should be clear by now that landscaping with native plants focuses more on your existing site conditions and matching plants to them rather than selecting plants first—a holistic approach, rather than thinking in terms of individual plants. By grouping plants with similar soil, water, and light requirements, you'll end up with combinations that work well together naturally.

That said, even with all the information geared toward choosing the right plant for the right place, don't be afraid to try a few things that intrigue you, even if odds are against survival. Make a point of growing something new each year. Even if it doesn't survive, you'll gain confidence and skill from the experience.

There is a misconception that natural landscapes are chaotic and lack perceptible patterns. In relatively undisturbed, naturally evolving landscapes, patterns are ever present—not in the form of orchard-like grids of trees, but in the subtle arrangements of plants. Nature tends to mass similar forms together and accent them with contrasting forms. Take a cue and use contrast sparingly to give your garden a natural look.

Avoid the neat, orderly rows of plants common in formal gardens; nature's pattern is randomness. Cluster plants in odd-numbered groupings rather than scattering them singly here and there. Plant in drifts of color rather than in

A Well-Tended Native Garden

Even with all the benefits of using native plants, there are still people who have a hard time appreciating them in the landscape. If you live in an urban area and are concerned about what the neighbors will think, here are some things you can do to make your native landscape look more tended and less wild.

❏ Maintain at least a small area of turf grass.
❏ Use a buffer of grass or mulch between planted areas and sidewalks and streets, so plants don't flop over onto the paved areas, making visitors uncomfortable.
❏ Cut back plants in fall.
❏ Prune trees and shrubs so they grow more open, like nursery-grown trees.
❏ Add embellishments such as sculpture and benches to make it look more like a garden and less like a field of weeds.
❏ Avoid planting excessively tall plants.

❏ Install some straight edges, either around garden beds or in the form of paths and fences.
❏ Plant natives in a more traditional way, putting even spacing between plants, and mulch with cocoa-bean hulls or shredded bark.
❏ Limit your number of species.
❏ Plant in clumps, as is more typical of nonnative landscapes.
❏ Use natives that are "more controllable" in their growth habit; these tend to be the clump-forming plants rather than spreaders.

straight rows. Drifts can consist of several of the same plants or, for the plant collectors among us, single plants of similar colors from several different species.

Texture comes from foliage as well as bark and stems, stone walls, and pathways. Place an emphasis on choosing plants with interesting foliage shapes and textures, since foliage is usually decorative for much longer than flowers are. Incorporate a variety of foliage colors into borders, including traditional greens in all shades, silvers, blues, chartreuse, and the occasional variegated form. Plants with light-colored flowers and silver-leaved foliage glow in the moonlight and are ideal in a garden next to a deck or patio that will be used at night.

Make sure your landscape has a wide variety of species—both within it and compared to all the other trees and shrubs on the street. Monocultures can lead to big problems in the landscape, as we saw with the American elm. Go for diversity, especially with woody plants.

Choose plants with varying bloom times, both con-current and consecutive, to ensure that there is some-thing happening in your landscape all year long. Evergreens are essential to winter landscapes, but many other woody ornaments offer interesting bark and color-ful berries or rose hips that persist through winter. Plants with showy persistent fruits include Jack-in-the-pulpit, bunchberry, wintergreen, winterberry, partridge-berry, false Solomon's seal, and highbush cranberry. Allow goldenrods, milkweeds, rattlesnake master, Joe-pye weeds, and grasses to remain through the winter so their dried flower heads can provide visual interest, as well as food for birds. Prolong the growing season by including fall-blooming perennials that survive several degrees of frost.

For a sense of unity, repeat a few specific plant group-ings or color schemes at intervals throughout the land-scape. Include some areas of visual calm where the eye can rest momentarily from stimulation. Green lawns, a small grouping of silver-leaved plants, or a simple green decid-uous or evergreen shrub all create spots of calm.

Choose plants that appeal to all the senses: plants in a variety of colors, shapes, and textures to see; fragrant blos-soms and foliage to smell; berries to eat; soft, hairy foliage, smooth bark, and silky seed heads to touch; leaves that whisper and rustle in the wind to hear. Plant fragrant species close to seating areas or under windows where they can be fully appreciated.

If space allows, let woodland flowers and groundcovers spread and seed themselves to form natural drifts like those found in nature. An occasional clump of snow-white *Trillium grandiflorum* (large-flowered trillium) provides accent and interest in this planting, which includes *Phlox divaricata* (blue phlox), *Mitella diphylla* (two-leaved miterwort), and ferns.

Allowing native grasses such as *Schizachyrium scoparium* (little bluestem) and the seed heads of *Rudbeckia hirta* (black-eyed Susan) to remain over winter not only provides birds with food and shelter, it also adds interest to the landscape.

Creating Mixed Borders

The mixed border is a plant-lover's garden. This combination of woody and herbaceous plants can include small trees, shrubs, flowers, grasses, groundcovers, ferns, and even evergreens. It is a place to experiment with colors and textures, combining plants that not only grow well together, but also complement each other.

A well-planned mixed border will have color and interest year-round. Mix heights, shapes, and textures to give depth and dimension; have taller, spikier plants generally located toward the back, and shorter, clumpier plants closer to the front of the garden or along paths. For contrast, plant one or two taller see-through plants toward the front of the border.

Many native plants combine well with nonnatives in mixed-border situations. Most of these natives are found in prairie and savanna ecosystems and require full to partial sun. In general, plant in groups of three to five; however, don't be afraid to use single plants here or there for accent and interest. If you want to create more of a prairie-garden or savanna look, avoid planting nonnatives and go heavier on the grasses, keeping in mind that natural grasslands consist of roughly 80 percent grasses and 20 percent flowers.

Geum triflorum (prairie smoke) is an excellent plant for mixed borders. Showy rosy pink flowers appear early in spring, the foliage is attractive all growing season, and the heads of feathery plumes add interest in late summer.

Black-eyed Susans (*Rudbeckia* species) may well be the most popular native plants found in home landscapes—and rightly so. They are easy to care for and bring long-lasting color to perennial beds and mixed borders.

Native Plants for Mixed Borders

Shrubs and Small Trees

Amelanchier x *grandiflora*
(apple serviceberry)
Amorpha canescens (leadplant)
Ceanothus americanus (New Jersey tea)
Cephalanthus occidentalis (buttonbush)
Cercis canadensis (redbud)
Cornus alternifolia (pagoda dogwood)
Cornus florida (flowering dogwood)
Dirca palustris (leatherwood)
Ilex verticillata (winterberry)
Lindera benzoin (spicebush)
Physocarpus opulifolius cultivars
(ninebark)
Picea cultivars (dwarf spruces)
Pinus cultivars (dwarf pines)
Potentilla fruticosa cultivars
(shrubby cinquefoil)
Prunus nigra 'Princess Kay'
(Canada plum)
Ptelea trifoliata (hoptree)
Spiraea alba (white meadowsweet)
Viburnum species (highbush cranberry,
arrow-wood)

Flowers

Allium cernuum (nodding wild onion)
Aquilegia canadensis (Canada columbine)
Asclepias tuberosa (butterfly weed)
Aster species (asters)
Baptisia species (wild indigos)
Boltonia asteroides (boltonia)
Campanula species (harebells,
bellflowers)
Coreopsis lanceolata (sand coreopsis,
lanceleaf tickseed)
Dalea purpurea (purple prairie clover)
Echinacea purpurea (purple coneflower)
Eryngium yuccifolium
(rattlesnake master)
Eupatorium species (Joe-pye weeds)
Gentiana species (gentians)
Geum triflorum (prairie smoke)
Helenium autumnale
(autumn sneezeweed)
Heliopsis helianthoides (oxeye)
Heuchera americana (alumroot)
Liatris species (blazing stars)
Lobelia species (cardinal flower, lobelias)
Lupinus perennis (wild lupine)
Mertensia virginica (Virginia bluebells)
Monarda species (wild bergamot,
bee balm)
Penstemon species (beardtongues)

Phlox species (phloxes)
Physostegia virginiana 'Miss Manners'
(obedient plant)
Polemonium reptans (spreading Jacob's
ladder)
Ratibida pinnata (gray-headed
coneflower)
Rudbeckia species (black-eyed Susans)
Ruellia humilis (wild petunia)
Senecio aureus (golden ragwort)
Sisyrinchium species
(blue-eyed grasses)
Solidago rigida, S. speciosa (goldenrods)
Tiarella cordifolia (foamflower)
Tradescantia species (spiderworts)
Verbena species (vervains)
Veronicastrum virginicum (Culver's root)
Zizia aptera (heart-leaved alexanders)

Ferns and Grasses

Adiantum pedatum (maidenhair fern)
Matteuccia struthiopteris (ostrich fern)
Panicum virgatum (switch grass)
Schizachyrium scoparium
(little bluestem)
Sorghastrum nutans (Indian grass)
Sporobolus heterolepis
(prairie dropseed)

Amelanchier 'Princess Diana' is a good small tree for mixed borders, offering year-round interest—delicate white flowers in spring, clean foliage and showy berries in summer, good fall leaf color, and smooth gray bark for winter interest.

Shade Gardening

Many gardeners consider shade to be a liability, a spot where they can't grow grass or colorful flowers. However, all landscapes should have a cool, shady retreat from the summer heat, and some of the most interesting plants grow in these areas protected from the hot sun. With a little effort, you can eliminate the struggle with lawn grasses and fill the area with the beautiful tapestry of colors and textures of native plants that thrive in shade. And a shade garden is a joy to tend. It is usually less weedy than sunny gardens and much more comfortable to work in, especially on a hot summer day.

The key to successful shade gardening is understanding the different degrees of shade, which can range from light to heavy shade and are different at different times of the growing season. "Light shade" areas receive bright to full sun for all but a few hours each day. Areas with bright light or sun for about half the day are called "partial shade." Most shade plants will do fine in either of these sites, especially if the sun is morning sun. "Full shade" areas are shaded for most of the day, and "dense shade" is for only the most shade-tolerant plants. Don't be afraid to limb up some taller trees to provide the partial shade that so many woodland wildflowers thrive under.

When it comes to plant selection, simplicity, rather than ostentation, is the key. Textures and shades of green play an important role. If possible, allow flowers and groundcovers to spread and seed themselves and to form natural drifts. You want plants that are adapted, attractive, and long-lived; you also want plants that increase, but not so rapidly that they crowd out other desirable plants. Some plants that have many desirable characteristics—such as wild ginger, baneberries, violets, and May apple—may be too much for smaller gardens.

Most woodland plants require a slightly acidic, fertile soil. Add 2 to 4 inches of organic matter when building the garden or at planting time. Watering is important, especially where large tree roots compete for available moisture. Mulch with 2 to 4 inches of shredded leaves, bark, or pine needles to conserve moisture and replenish nutrients. If your garden is large enough, include curved paths covered with wood chips or shredded bark. Create points of interest along the way—ornaments such as wagon wheels or hollow stumps filled with showier flowers, larger patches of flowers, or trees and shrubs with unique growth patterns or bark that are enhanced by pruning. Allow some branches and logs to remain after falling. To add sound, consider adding a trickling stream lined with marsh marigolds and other moist-soil plants.

Shade gardens are at their best in spring, when the delicate woodland flowers and bright green foliage are set off by the rich color of the bare ground. *Mitella diphylla* (two-leaved miterwort) and *Podophyllum peltatum* (May apple) are two good choices for light to full shade.

*Uvularia grandiflora (*large-flowered bellwort) has long-blooming, lemon yellow flowers that provide a striking contrast to the more common white, pink, and purple flowers of spring and attractive sea green foliage in summer. It likes spring sun and summer shade, conditions found under deciduous trees.

Native Plants for Shade Gardens

Woody Plants

Abies balsamea (balsam fir)
Amelanchier species (serviceberries, juneberries)
Cornus species (dogwoods)
Dirca palustris (leatherwood)
Hamamelis virginiana (witch hazel)
Lindera benzoin (spicebush)
Ostrya virginiana (ironwood)
Ptelea trifoliata (hoptree)
Tsuga canadensis (eastern hemlock)
Viburnum species (viburnums)

Ferns

Adiantum pedatum (maidenhair fern)
Athyrium filix-femina (lady fern)
Dryopteris marginalis (marginal shield fern)
Matteuccia struthiopteris (ostrich fern)
Osmunda species (ferns)
Polystichum acrostichoides (Christmas fern)

Flowers and Groundcovers

Actaea species (baneberries)
Allium tricoccum (wild leek)
Anemone species (anemones)
Anemonella thalictroides (rue anemone)
Aquilegia canadensis (Canada columbine)
Arisaema triphyllum (Jack-in-the-pulpit)
Asarum canadense (wild ginger)
Aster macrophyllus (large-leaved aster)
Carex species (woodland sedges)
Caulophyllum thalictroides (blue cohosh)

Claytonia virginica (spring beauty)
Dentaria laciniata (cut-leaved toothwort)
Dicentra cucullaria (Dutchman's breeches)
Erythronium species (trout lilies)
Hepatica species (hepaticas)
Isopyrum biternatum (false rue anemone)
Jeffersonia diphylla (twinleaf)
Lobelia cardinalis (cardinal flower)
Maianthemum canadense (Canada mayflower)
Mertensia virginica (Virginia bluebells)
Mitchella repens (partridgeberry)
Mitella diphylla (two-leaved miterwort)
Phlox divaricata (blue phlox)
Podophyllum peltatum (May apple)
Polemonium reptans (spreading Jacob's ladder)
Polygonatum species (Solomon's seals)
Sanguinaria canadensis (bloodroot)
Smilacina species (false Solomon's seals)
Solidago flexicaulis (zigzag goldenrod)
Stylophorum diphyllum (celandine poppy)
Thalictrum dioicum (early meadow rue)
Tiarella cordifolia (foamflower)
Trillium species (trilliums)
Uvularia species (bellworts)
Viola species (violets)

Nonnative Plants for Shade

Here are some shade plants not native to Michigan that combine nicely with the subtle beauty of native woodland plants and are not a threat to Michigan's native habitats.

Alchemilla mollis (lady's mantle)
Amsonia tabernaemontana (bluestar)
Asarum europaeum (European ginger)
Astilbe species and hybrids (astilbes)
Athyrium nipponicum 'Pictum' (Japanese painted fern)
Brunnera macrophylla (brunnera)
Corydalis lutea (yellow corydalis)
Dicentra species (bleeding hearts)
Epimedium species and hybrids (barrenworts)
Galium odoratum (sweet woodruff)
Helleborus niger (Christmas rose)
Helleborus orientalis (Lenten rose)
Heuchera species and hybrids (heucheras)
×*Heucherella* hybrids (heucherellas)
Hosta species and hybrids (hostas)
Lamium maculatum (lamium)
Ligularia species (ligularias)
Phlox stolonifera (creeping phlox)
Primula species (primroses)
Pulmonaria species (lungworts)
Trycertis species (toad lilies)

Attracting Butterflies

Butterflies add a wonderful dimension to the landscape, and they are one of the best side benefits of having a native-plant landscape. Your efforts at butterfly gardening can be as simple as incorporating a few nectar plants into a flower garden or as elaborate as creating an area entirely devoted to these fascinating creatures.

To become a successful butterfly gardener, you should start by learning which butterfly species are native to your area and what plants they like. Most butterflies are vagabonds on their way somewhere else when you see them in your garden. You can think of your garden as a rest stop along the way, a place where they can linger for a while to enjoy food, water, and shelter. If you want to provide a complete butterfly habitat, you will have to include the proper host plants for butterflies to lay eggs, keeping in mind that these are not always the showiest plants and that they become even less attractive when they have been eaten by the newly hatched caterpillars. These host plants are important, however, as without them, butterflies will not lay eggs.

When it comes to nectar sources, these insects are drawn to big, bold splashes of color and concentrations of fragrance. Butterflies like two kinds of flowers: clusters of nectar-filled tubular blossoms that they can probe in sequence, and large, rather flat blossoms that provide them with landing pads. Purple, red, orange, and yellow attract the most butterfly species; blue and white flowers are least popular. However, color preferences can vary from species to species, so you should plant the entire color palette. Especially valuable for butterflies are early-blooming flowers that are open when the first hatches emerge or the first returning migrants arrive, and late-blooming plants that are still in bloom after the first fall frost. Early violets are occasionally weighted down with butterflies, as are late-blooming asters and Joe-pye weeds.

In addition to host plants, butterflies need mud puddles or other wet areas, and they need shelter—shrubs, trees, and bushy flowers where they can hide from birds, find shade at midday, and rest at night. They also look for basking stones, where they can build up enough body heat to fly, and windbreaks to temper the wind.

Echinacea purpurea (purple coneflower) and *Monarda fistulosa* (wild bergamot) are two good sources of nectar for butterflies.

With its intense orange-red flowers, *Asclepias tuberosa* (butterfly weed) is one of the showiest and easily recognized of native flowers. Butterflies agree, and the flowers are covered with them in June and July.

Native Plants to Attract Butterflies

Here are some native plants that are nectar sources as well as food for caterpillars. Many of these plants can be incorporated into large sunny gardens where you can plant drifts. If you want to include several of the less-showy nectar sources, you may want to set aside a special area of your landscape specifically for a butterfly habitat. "N" indicates it is a good adult nectar source; "L" indicates a larval food source.

Trees and Shrubs
Amorpha canescens (leadplant) N
Betula species (birches) L
Ceanothus americanus (New Jersey tea) N
Celtis occidentalis (hackberry) N
Cephalanthus occidentalis (buttonbush) N
Cornus species (dogwoods) N
Ledum groenlandicum (Labrador tea) N
Populus species (poplars) L
Prunus species (plums) N
Quercus species (oaks) L
Rhus typhina (staghorn sumac) N
Rosa species (wild roses) N
Salix species (willows) L
Sambucus species (elders) N
Spiraea alba (white meadowsweet) N
Symphoricarpos albus (snowberry) L
Viburnum species (viburnums) N

Herbaceous Plants
Agastache species (giant hyssops) N
Anaphalis margaritacea
    (pearly everlasting) N
Antennaria species (pussytoes) N
Asclepias species (milkweeds, butterfly
    weed) N, L
Aster species (asters) N, L
Baptisia species (wild indigos) N
Carex species (sedges) L
Chelone species (turtleheads) N
Coreopsis species (coreopsis,
    tickseeds) N
Dalea purpurea (purple prairie clover) N
Echinacea purpurea
    (purple coneflower) N
Eupatorium species (Joe-pye weeds) N
Fragaria virginiana (wild strawberry) N
Helianthus species (sunflowers) N
Heliopsis helianthoides (oxeye) N

Liatris species (blazing stars) N
Lupinus perennis (wild lupine) L, N
Monarda species (wild bergamot,
    bee balm) N
Penstemon species (beardtongues) L
Phlox species (phloxes) N
Pycnanthemum species (mountain
    mints) N
Ratibida pinnata (gray-headed cone-
    flower) N
Rudbeckia species
    (black-eyed Susans) N, L
Schizachyrium scoparium
    (little bluestem) L
Silphium species (compass plant,
    cup plant) N
Solidago species (goldenrods) N
Verbena species (vervains)
Viola species (violets) L
Zizia species (alexanders) L

Creating a Hummingbird Habitat

Hummingbirds bring movement to a garden, mesmerizing you as they zoom from one plant to the next. There's nothing more enjoyable than a visit from these tiny, wing-flapping guests.

Because of its high rate of metabolism, a hummingbird needs to eat more than one-half its weight in food daily. A hummingbird habitat should include several types of flowers—herbaceous and woody plants of varied heights and bloom dates. Your hummingbird habitat can also include several properly maintained feeders. The most effective habitats also attract and nurture the tiny insects and spiders that hummingbirds ingest to meet their protein requirements.

Since hummingbirds, like most birds, have virtually no sense of smell, the flowers that attract them tend to have little or no fragrance, instead directing resources toward high visibility and nectar production. Note also that cultivated hybrids often make much less nectar than wild strains. Most hummingbird-attracting flowers are tubular in shape and many are red, though certainly not all. A successful hummingbird garden provides nectar sources from May through the first frost. There is a great temptation to plant acres of wild bergamot or cardinal flower, two of the hummingbird's favorite nectar sources. However, with each of these flowers, nectar is available for just a brief period in a hummingbird's life.

Your garden should also have space for hummingbirds to nest and locations where they can roost and find shelter from the elements. Have fresh water available for drinking as well as for bathing. Include shady spots where hummingbirds can perch as well as build their nests. Willows provide pliable twigs used for nesting. Hummingbirds also use bits of leaves, spider webs, moss, and lichens to build their tiny nests.

Hummingbirds are attracted to red flowers, so it's no surprise that showy *Lobelia cardinalis* (cardinal flower) is at the top of every hummingbird plant list.

Native Plants to Attract Hummingbirds

Here are some native plants that are important nectar sources for hummingbirds. You'll notice that many of them are also attractive to butterflies.

Woody Plants
Aesculus glabra (Ohio buckeye)
Ceanothus americanus (New Jersey tea)
Parthenocissus quinquefolia (woodbine)
Symphoricarpos albus (snowberry)

Herbaceous Plants
Agastache species (giant hyssops)
Aquilegia canadensis (Canada columbine)
Asclepias tuberosa (butterfly weed)
Chelone species (turtleheads)
Epilobium angustifolium (fireweed)
Liatris species (blazing stars)
Lilium species (lilies)
Lobelia cardinalis (cardinal flower)
Mertensia virginica (Virginia bluebells)
Monarda species (wild bergamot, bee balm)
Penstemon species (beardtongues)
Phlox species (phloxes)
Physostegia virginiana (obedient plant)
Silene virginica (fire pink)
Silphium perfoliatum (cup plant)

The nodding, upside-down, red and yellow flowers of *Aquilegia canadensis* (Canada columbine) are a favorite of hummingbirds.

Gardening among Rocks

True rock gardens are made up of low-growing plants that inhabit rocky areas in high elevations. However, rocks themselves are an important feature of many natural habitats, including outcrops, woodlands, and stream banks, and they can be a real asset in naturalistic landscape design. You can use a few here and there for accent, or you can create a "rock garden" where suitable plants are planted on a rock-filled hillside.

If you are starting from scratch, there are a few things you can do to make your garden look more natural. Select an indigenous type of rock and stick with it throughout the entire garden, incorporating a range of sizes. Bury the rocks at least halfway to make them look like they were positioned by nature and have been there through time. To be convincing, plant placement calls for an appreciation of how they grow naturally on rocky sites. Usually irregular drifts of low plants carpet the soil surface or occupy the spaces between rocks, running along narrow crevices or congregating in areas at the bases of miniature cliffs. A sunny rock garden is one of the few places where gravel mulch is appropriate.

Phlox pilosa (prairie phlox) is a resilient yet showy prairie native that tolerates the hot, dry conditions found in sunny rock gardens.

Native Plants for Rock Gardens

Rock-garden plants tend to be low growing and tolerant of hot, dry conditions, but there are also plants that are suitable for shadier sites among rocks edging pathways and streams. Here are some native plants to use among rocks.

Plants for Sunny Spots

Allium cernuum (nodding wild onion)
Allium stellatum (prairie wild onion)
Anaphalis margaritacea (pearly everlasting)
Antennaria species (pussytoes)
Aquilegia canadensis (Canada columbine)
Asclepias tuberosa (butterfly weed)
Aster sericeus (silky aster)
Campanula rotundifolia (harebell)
Coreopsis species (coreopsis, tickseeds)
Dalea purpurea (purple prairie clover)
Dodecatheon meadia (prairie shooting star)
Eryngium yuccifolium (rattlesnake master)
Euphorbia corollata (flowering spurge)
Fragaria species (wild strawberries)
Geum triflorum (prairie smoke)
Heuchera species (alumroots)
Hypoxis hirsuta (stargrass)
Liatris punctata (spotted blazing star)
Opuntia humifusa (eastern prickly pear)
Penstemon species (beardtongues)
Phlox bifida (sand phlox)
Phlox pilosa (prairie phlox)
Physostegia virginiana (obedient plant)
Potentilla fruticosa (shrubby cinquefoil)
Potentilla tridentata (three-toothed cinquefoil)

Ruellia humilis (wild petunia)
Silene virginica (fire pink)
Sisyrinchium species (blue-eyed grasses)
Solidago nemoralis (gray goldenrod)
Tradescantia species (spiderworts)
Viola pedata (bird's-foot violet)
Waldsteinia fragarioides (barren strawberry)

Plants for Shady Spots

Adiantum pedatum (maidenhair fern)
Anemonella thalictroides (rue anemone)
Aquilegia canadensis (Canada columbine)
Asarum canadense (wild ginger)
Asplenium platyneuron (ebony spleenwort)
Carex pensylvanica (Pennsylvania sedge)
Cystopteris bulbifera (bulblet fern)
Dodecatheon meadia (prairie shooting star)
Dryopteris marginalis (marginal shield fern)
Gaultheria procumbens (wintergreen)
Hepatica species (hepaticas)
Mitchella repens (partridgeberry)
Phlox divaricata (blue phlox)
Polypodium virginianum (rock-cap fern)
Thalictrum dioicum (early meadow rue)
Uvularia species (bellworts)
Viola sororia (common blue violet)

Rocks play an important role in native landscape design. Use them in shade gardens to add texture and interest.

Water Gardens and Bog Gardens

Water, whether moving or still, is a great addition to the landscape. A water feature offers boundless possibilities for creative design, as well as a place to grow many interesting native species that require the conditions found in water-based ecosystems.

If you have a natural wet area on your property, instead of altering the habitat by drainage or fill, work within the parameters of the existing environment to create a pond, bog garden, or marshy habitat. If you don't have a natural water feature on your property, it is fairly easy to create a pond or bog garden.

To make your water feature look natural, think about how pools of water occur in nature. The pond will look most natural in the lowest place in the yard. However, avoid areas where runoff collects. Runoff can cloud the water or fill the pond with leaves, mulch, and other debris after heavy rain. If your yard is flat, you can site the pond just about anywhere, but it should get at least five hours of sunlight a day for good bloom on water lilies and other flowering aquatics.

Also, consider the size and proportion in relationship to your yard. A 5-by-8-foot pond is a generous size even in a large backyard and can accommodate many plants. A 3-by-5-foot pond is appropriate for a small space. Shape the pond as nature would—no corners, no symmetry, nothing perfectly round. Avoid rigid pond liners that come in precast shapes.

Bog gardens are areas of permanently moist but not waterlogged soil. A bog garden can be created by excavating to a depth of 15 to 18 inches and covering the bottom with a tarp or pool lining material to retard drainage. Fill the depression with the removed soil and amend generously with peat moss or other organic matter. Make slits in the liner to allow seepage during wet weather and plan to add supplemental water during periods of low rainfall. Fill your garden with wet-soil and shallow-water plants.

Planting techniques for aquatic and wetland species are basically the same as those used with other plants. Do not allow the plants to dry out while planting, and plant them at the proper level—not only to the soil but also to the depth of the water over the crown.

Aquatics can be planted directly in a thick layer of soil at the bottom of a pond, but they are best planted in containers because many are aggressive and quickly become unmanageable if not restricted. Planting in containers also makes it easier to remove them or shift their position. You can use specially designed plastic water-lily baskets or used 3-gallon nursery containers with the sides perforated.

Aquatics should be planted in good, clean garden soil, free from organic matter and low in nutrients, both of which encourage algae growth. Do not fertilize garden pools.

To create the feel of a natural water feature, place plants in concentric rings radiating from your water feature, with the plants requiring the most soil moisture closest to the pond or stream. Emergent aquatics inhabit the margins of ponds and slow-moving streams. They are used to soften the edge of ponds and streams with contrasting growth habits and textures. Many native emergent aquatics provide additional summer color and homes for many forms of wildlife. They should be grown in shallow water or in the mucky soil bordering water features.

Many native plants adapt well to the soggy soil conditions found along streams and ponds. This planting features *Lobelia cardinalis* (cardinal flower), *Rudbeckia triloba* (three-leaved coneflower), *Eupatorium purpureum* (Joe-Pye weed), and *Chelone glabra* (white turtlehead).

Rainwater Gardens

A rainwater garden is a great way to create a useful wetland that helps control runoff from impervious surfaces and filter out pollutants before they reach streams and lakes.

Rainwater gardens are shallow—usually less than a foot deep. They can be as small as the area under your downspout to as large as several city blocks. By slowing down stormwater runoff, rainwater gardens collect water and allow it to slowly seep into the soil.

Planted with appropriate native species, rainwater gardens become attractive additions to the landscape and a haven for butterflies and birds. Any of the plants listed in the sidebar as "moist-soil" plants are suitable for use in a rainwater garden.

This successful wetland landscape includes *Nymphaea odorata* (American white water lily) and moisture-loving edging plants, which make the transition to the neighboring prairie area.

Native Plants for Water Gardens

Pond Plants
Nymphaea odorata (American white water lily)

Shallow-Water Plants
For planting in water levels less than 14 inches:
Calla palustris (wild calla)
Carex stricta (tussock sedge)
Cephalanthus occidentalis (buttonbush)
Glyceria species (manna grasses)
Pontederia cordata (pickerelweed)
Sagittaria latifolia (broad-leaved arrowhead)

Plants for Moist-Soil Areas
Grasses
Calamagrostis canadensis (blue joint)
Deschampsia caespitosa (tufted hair grass)
Hierochloe odorata (sweet grass)
Panicum virgatum (switch grass)
Spartina pectinata (prairie cordgrass)

Flowers
Acorus calamus (sweet flag)
Anemone canadensis (Canada anemone)
Arisaema triphyllum (Jack-in-the-pulpit)
Asclepias incarnata (swamp milkweed)
Aster novae-angliae (New England aster)
Caltha palustris (marsh marigold)
Camassia scilloides (wild hyacinth)
Campanula americana (tall bellflower)
Chelone species (turtleheads)
Cornus canadensis (bunchberry)
Epilobium angustifolium (fireweed)
Equisetum hyemale (tall scouring rush)
Eupatorium species (Joe-pye weeds)
Filipendula rubra (queen-of-the-prairie)
Gentiana andrewsii (bottle gentian)
Helenium autumnale (autumn sneezeweed)
Hibiscus moscheutos (swamp rose mallow)
Iris species (blue flags)
Lilium michiganense (Michigan lily)
Lobelia cardinalis (cardinal flower)
Lobelia siphilitica (great blue lobelia)
Lysimachia ciliata (fringed loosestrife)
Mertensia virginica (Virginia bluebells)
Physostegia virginiana (obedient plant)
Pycnanthemum virginianum (Virginia mountain mint)
Senecio aureus (golden ragwort)
Silphium perfoliatum (cup plant)
Thalictrum dasycarpum (tall meadow rue)
Verbena hastata (blue vervain)
Vernonia missurica (Missouri ironweed)
Veronicastrum virginicum (Culver's root)
Viola sororia (common blue violet)

Ferns
Most ferns will do well in moist soil, but these are especially well suited to planting along ponds and streams and in bogs.

Athyrium filix-femina (lady fern)
Cystopteris bulbifera (bulblet fern)
Gymnocarpium dryopteris (oak fern)
Matteuccia struthiopteris (ostrich fern)
Onoclea sensibilis (sensitive fern)
Osmunda species (ferns)
Thelypteris species (ferns)

Woody Plants
Acer rubrum (red maple)
Acer saccharinum (silver maple)
Alnus rugosa (speckled alder)
Aronia melanocarpa (black chokeberry)
Betula alleghaniensis (yellow birch)
Cephalanthus occidentalis (buttonbush)
Cornus racemosa (gray dogwood)
Cornus stolonifera (red-osier dogwood)
Fraxinus nigra (black ash)
Fraxinus pennsylvanica (green ash)
Ilex verticillata (winterberry)
Larix laricina (tamarack)
Ledum groenlandicum (Labrador tea)
Picea mariana (black spruce)
Quercus bicolor (swamp white oak)
Salix species (willows)
Sambucus canadensis (common elder)
Spiraea alba (white meadowsweet)
Thuja occidentalis (white cedar)
Viburnum trilobum (highbush cranberry)

Hardscapes and Accents

The hardscape is anything in your landscape that isn't living. It includes paths, fences, decks, patios, driveways, and all structures such as arbors, compost bins, and stairways. These structures are important parts of the landscape and should be given as much thought as the plants you choose—perhaps even more, since they are often permanent.

Hardscapes can be made up of many different materials, the most common being brick, wood, stone, and gravel. Keep your overall design in mind when choosing materials. Although no hardscape will look completely natural, certain materials will blend into a native-plant landscape better than others.

Paths and walkways allow access to inner areas of a garden while reducing the chance for delicate plants to be trampled. Some paths are meant to whisper the way to go;

Hardscapes are just as important in native landscapes as they are in traditional ones. Choose materials carefully. In most cases you want them to blend into the landscape rather than stand out from it, so stick with earth tones and natural materials when practical.

others are meant to shout it. Making a path obvious doesn't mean it has to be boring, however. Bend it around a corner so it disappears for a while, and place plants and stones to break up the site line of the path edges. Avoid edging the path with rigid rows of plants, stones, or logs, and vary the materials that form the path. Meandering paths look more natural than straight ones. Plant your smaller, more delicate flowers along paths where they can be seen and enjoyed.

Paths should blend with their surroundings, but they should always be sturdy and wide enough for safe use. Don't forget to include benches and chairs along your paths and within your gardens, so you and your guests have places to sit and enjoy your landscape.

Good walkway materials include brick, gravel, wood chips, and even bare soil. If a path runs under tall pines, use pine needles. If you have a stream or bog garden, you may need to install stepping stones, wooden bridges, or boardwalks.

Steps can be made of stone, natural-looking concrete, or logs. Think of them as terraced elevations formed naturally in the landscape, but be sure that they are safe and easy to negotiate. Wood is slippery when it is wet. Consider installing a handrail alongside your steps. Use small plants and groundcovers to tie the steps into the path and the rest of the landscape.

One of the misconceptions about native-plant landscapes is that they are boring. Unfortunately, sometimes people take native plant design a little too seriously and think they can't use funky garden accents. Not true! There's no reason you can't incorporate any of the garden accents you'd use in a regular landscape. Native-plant landscapes can include sculpture, sundials, gazing balls, fountains, and feeders, houses, and baths for birds, just like any other garden. It's your garden, and you should include things that make you happy. As with all gardens, keep in mind that these items are meant to be accents. They should be used with discretion and carefully placed rather than just plopped down in the garden.

If you are trying to re-create a truly natural habitat, you'll want to limit your accent pieces to well-placed natural materials such as rocks and logs. Take cues from nature and try to place them as if they had been left there. Moss-covered logs should look like they were once part of a tall forest tree that fell to the ground years ago. Rocks should be buried one-half to two-thirds underground, as if a glacier placed them eons ago, rather than set on the surface. Select sculptural pieces that can be nestled into the garden and surrounded by plants, as if they were growing up out of the ground rather than sitting on a concrete pedestal.

Using Native Mosses

One of the best ways to soften rocks or paving stones and make them look as though they've been in place for centuries is with patches of moss. Moss will only grow where soil is shaded and moist with high humus content and a low pH (acidic). Even if you don't have moss on your property, once you set up these conditions, moss will appear, since spores travel for miles.

If you are transplanting moss from another place in your garden, take some soil with it, and keep it moist until you are ready to put it in. Before planting moss, work up the soil between stones, freeing it of roots and weeds. Water until it is soaking wet, and allow the surface water to sink in. Then press the patches of moss into the muddy soil, making good contact. Wet the newly planted moss with very dilute fish emulsion. For good measure, pour a cup of milk into each gallon of water you're wetting the moss with to help acidify the soil. Once established in a spot with the right conditions, your moss will need no further care.

Moss will grow naturally where the soil is acidic and moist. Try to look at moss as an asset, and encourage it to grow on fallen rocks and logs to soften them.

Nature provides accents in the form of unusual textures and colors. This brightly colored fungus really stands out against the backdrop of fallen leaves in this deciduous woodland.

Don't be afraid to use nonplant items as accents in native landscapes. These stacked rusty pots are the perfect pedestal for the whimsical fish in this woodland garden.

Using Nonnative Plants

As knowledgeable as you may be about selecting and using native plants, there are still some effects that will be difficult to achieve. The lack of native bulbous plants means you can't get the early, vibrant color from spring bulbs. It will be hard to find a native plant that can give you the season-long show of tropical annuals that so many people rely on for patio containers and hanging baskets. And there are not a lot of showy vines available for covering trellises and arbors or adding that important dimension of height. If these things are important parts of your landscape design, that's fine. There are many nonnative plants that will readily adapt to the conditions found in a native-plant landscape and complement the native plants.

Most spring bulbs grow well in the same conditions native prairie plants enjoy, and some even adapt well to the conditions found in a deciduous forest garden. Most minor spring bulbs blend beautifully into spring woodland gardens, bringing colors that aren't commonly found in native plants. These smaller bulbs—such as scillas, snowdrops, dwarf iris, miniature daffodils, glory of the snow, and some species of crocuses—blend into the spring garden well. The bolder colors and exotic look of most tulips, daffodils, crocuses, and hyacinths are too strong for woodland gardens. They can, however, be used in the mixed border with prairie plants.

Bulb foliage should be allowed to die down naturally after flowers fade. Grow bulbs with plants that will mature and fill in while the foliage is still there. Good natives for camouflaging bulb foliage include prairie smoke, columbine, wild ginger, and ferns.

There's no denying the importance of containers in garden design. They bring color and interest to entryways, decks, and patios, and in some situations, are the only way to grow plants successfully. A good way to make containers of nonnative plants blend into your native landscape is to use containers made of natural materials. Make a pathside planter in a hollowed-out log or stump, or plant a batch of sun-loving annuals in a stone trough.

As a rule, few native plants adapt well to container growing. Many of them have taproots or a limited bloom time. If you do want to use native plants in containers, group several large pots of mixtures of grasses and perennials that will provide interest throughout the season, rather than individual pots containing just one plant. Native plants that adapt well to container culture include little bluestem, black-eyed Susans, blazing stars, coral bells, bird's-foot violet, nodding wild onion, and purple coneflower.

If your landscape plan includes a vine-covered arbor or trellis and you can't find a suitable vine among the list of natives, several nonnatives are well behaved and blend into native landscapes. Several nonnative types of clematis have an understated beauty. Consider *Clematis terniflora* (sweet autumn clematis), *C. texensis* 'Duchess of Albany', or *C.* 'Huldine'. Annual vines such as morning glory, black-eyed Susan vine, and nasturtium will look good with any of the sunny prairie perennials. *Campsis radicans* (trumpet creeper), native to the southeastern part of the United States, is a perennial woody vine with showy red-orange flowers that are attractive to hummingbirds.

For season-long color, it's impossible to beat tropical annuals such as petunias, impatiens, and begonias. Don't be afraid to use traditional annuals in a native-plant landscape. Shade-tolerant types are a good way to bring color into the woodland garden in summer. However, instead of planting one or two six-packs in neat rows, consider a flat or two planted in a large drift—the way nature would do it. Instead of using many different annuals, select one or two types and use them throughout your garden.

In the natural world, you'll find that rich, strong colors such as reds, oranges, and yellows have generally evolved in sunny sites. Cool blues, purples, pinks, and white tend to inhabit lightly shaded areas and woodland gardens. Keep these color schemes in mind when choosing nonnative plants to complement your native plantings and the result will be a much more natural look.

Turf Grasses and Groundcovers

A lawn is a labor-intensive, expensive way to cover the ground. It requires untold hours of mowing, raking, weeding, fertilizing, and watering. This expense and time is justified when you need a resilient groundcover for pets or play areas, but it is an extravagance when the lawn is just a decoration. Maintain only as much lawn as you really use, and replace the rest with a more environmentally friendly and interesting alternative.

There are several alternatives for covering large areas usually given to the traditional lawn. If the area is primarily used for entertaining or relaxing, consider installing a patio or deck and surrounding it with low-growing native plants. If you prefer keeping the area planted, consider a groundcover.

Groundcovers are plants that, by virtue of creeping runners, stolons, or rhizomes, form a low, self-spreading carpet of greenery that prevents erosion and do not need to be mowed. However, groundcovers do not take foot traffic. Several native-plant nurseries have started offering lower-maintenance alternatives to traditional Kentucky bluegrass lawns for situations where people don't want to fuss with a highly manicured lawn but still want some

The delicate purple of scillas is a perfect complement to early-blooming woodland plants. This minor bulb can tolerate the shade found under deciduous trees, flowering and storing the necessary energy before the trees fully leaf out.

Few native vines adapt well to use in formal landscape settings. Fortunately, there are several well-behaved exotic species, including *Clematis* 'Huldine', that combine nicely with native plants.

"Low-mow" mixes are becoming popular as alternatives to traditional lawn grasses. They are good choices in well-drained areas with minimal foot traffic and partial to full sun.

Responsible Lawn Care

In the areas where you do want to have lawn, practice responsible lawn care. Here are some tips for minimizing the negative effects of large areas of lawn grasses.

• Start with a soil test to determine which, if any, nutrients are lacking. There's no need to apply fertilizer if your soil has ample nutrients. Over-fertilized soil encourages excess growth and runoff.
• Add 1/2 inch of compost twice a year, in spring and fall, to provide necessary nutrients.
• Mow at 3 1/2 inches to 4 inches. Longer grass shades its own roots, reducing water loss. Taller grass is also better able to outcompete many annual weeds, including crabgrass.
• Don't remove more than one-third of the blade at any mowing.
• Let clippings fall to recycle nutrients. Clippings do not lead to thatch problems.
• Water wisely. Most lawns are overwatered. Allow your cool-season lawn grasses to follow their natural cycle and go dormant in mid to late summer. They will green up again once the cooler, wetter days of late summer roll around.

kind of low-growing, green play area. These are usually mixtures of slow-growing fescues that will form a soft 4- to 6-inch-tall carpet of grass. They can be mown once a month to a height of 3 to 4 inches. These mixes grow best in sun or partial shade in loamy or sandy soils; they are not recommended for wet soils, deep shade, or clay soils that exhibit standing water after a rain.

Native Groundcovers

Many native plants have a tendency to expand and fill in areas, eventually covering the ground. Typically, a groundcover plant is low growing, aggressive to the point of keeping others out, and does not require a lot of care once established. Here are some good choices:

Anemone canadensis (Canada anemone)
Antennaria species (pussytoes)
Arctostaphylos uva-ursi (bearberry)
Asarum canadense (wild ginger)
Comptonia peregrina (sweet fern)
Euphorbia corollata (leafy spurge)
Fragaria virginiana (wild strawberry)
Heuchera species (alumroots)
Juniperus species (junipers)
Maianthemum canadense (Canada mayflower)
Onoclea sensibilis (sensitive fern)
Opuntia humifusa (eastern prickly pear)
Osmunda species (ferns)
Tiarella cordifolia (foamflower)
Viola species (violets)
Waldsteinia fragarioides (barren strawberry)

Adiantum pedatum (maidenhair fern) and *Mertensia virginica* (Virginia bluebells) are good choices for more-formal landscapes in shade.

Dealing with City Laws and Neighbors

Homeowners who decide to go native are often confronted with an array of laws, regulations, requirements, and sometimes outright hostility. Most of these issues are simply due to ignorance, which is difficult to overcome, at least at first.

There are several things you can do to prepare yourself for neighborhood opposition. To begin, learn your local laws and ordinances. Chances are you will be able to stay well within them by putting some thought into your landscape before you plant.

Once your landscape is planted, be attentive and keep up with the necessary maintenance. Let your neighbors know by your presence and activities that your yard is being cared for and not neglected. Be purposeful. Talk with neighbors about your plans before you start planting, if possible. Educate. Take the time to tell your neighbors what the plants are and what butterflies and birds they attract. Share plants and seeds with them if they are interested. In the end, you may make a new convert.

Prunus nigra 'Princess Kay' has a "cultivated look" and adapts well to front-yard use.

Front-Yard Native Plants

Most native plants will stay neat and tidy if properly pruned and groomed. However, some are easier to keep looking neat than others. Here are some easy-to-establish, attractive native plants that adapt well to more-formal landscape situations without a lot of attention. Keep in mind also that cultivars, when available, often look less wild than the species.

Herbaceous Plants for Sunny Sites

Allium cernuum (nodding wild onion)
Asclepias tuberosa (butterfly weed)
Aster laevis (smooth aster)
Aster novae-angliae cultivars (New England aster)
Boltonia asteroides (boltonia)
Camassia scilloides (wild hyacinth)
Cypripedium calceolus (yellow lady's-slipper)
Echinacea purpurea (purple coneflower)
Gentiana andrewsii (bottle gentian)
Geum triflorum (prairie smoke)
Helenium autumnale (autumn sneezeweed)
Heliopsis helianthoides (oxeye)
Heuchera americana (alumroot)
Liatris species (blazing stars)
Monarda species (wild bergamot, bee balm)
Panicum virgatum (switch grass)
Penstemon species (beardtongues)
Phlox pilosa (prairie phlox)
Physostegia virginiana (obedient plant)
Ratibida pinnata (gray-headed coneflower)
Rudbeckia species (black-eyed Susans)
Schizachyrium scoparium (little bluestem)
Sporobolus heterolepis (prairie dropseed)
Verbena stricta (hoary vervain)
Waldsteinia fragarioides (barren strawberry)
Zizia aptera (heart-leaved alexanders)

Herbaceous Plants for Shady Sites

Actaea species (baneberries)
Adiantum pedatum (maidenhair fern)
Aquilegia canadensis (wild columbine)
Arisaema triphyllum (jack-in-the-pulpit)
Asarum canadense (wild ginger)
Athyrium filix-femina (lady fern)
Claytonia virginica (spring beauty)
Dicentra cucullaria (Dutchman's breeches)
Erythronium species (trout lilies)
Geranium maculatum (wild geranium)
Hepatica species (hepaticas)
Isopyrum biternatum (false rue anemone)

Lobelia cardinalis (cardinal flower)
Maianthemum canadense (Canada mayflower)
Matteuccia struthiopteris (ostrich fern)
Mertensia virginica (Virginia bluebells)
Mitella diphylla (two-leaved miterwort)
Phlox divaricata (blue phlox)
Polemonium reptans (creeping Jacob's ladder)
Polygonatum biflorum (giant Solomon's seal)
Polystichum acrostichoides (Christmas fern)
Sanguinaria canadensis (bloodroot)
Smilacina racemosa (false Solomon's seal)
Solidago flexicaulis (zigzag goldenrod)
Thalictrum dioicum (early meadow rue)
Tiarella cordifolia (foamflower)
Trillium species (trilliums)
Uvularia grandiflora (large-flowered bellwort)

Woody Plants

Abies balsamea (balsam fir)
Acer rubrum (red maple)
Acer saccharum (sugar maple)
Amelanchier x *grandiflora* (apple serviceberry)
Carpinus caroliniana (blue beech)
Cercis canadensis (redbud)
Clematis virginiana (virgin's bower)
Cornus species (dogwoods)
Dirca palustris (leatherwood)
Gymnocladus dioica (Kentucky coffee tree)
Ilex verticillata (winterberry)
Lindera benzoin (spicebush)
Juniperus species (junipers)
Ostrya virginiana (ironwood)
Physocarpus opulifolius cultivars (ninebark)
Potentilla fruticosa cultivars (shrubby cinquefoil)
Prunus nigra 'Princess Kay' (Canadian plum)
Ptelea trifoliata (hoptree)
Quercus species (oaks)
Tilia americana (basswood)
Tsuga canadensis (eastern hemlock)
Viburnum species (viburnums)

PART TWO

Native Plant Profiles

Flowers and Groundcovers

Native flowers and groundcovers are the most fun aspect of landscape design. Their showy blooms, various sizes and forms, and interesting leaves add color, interest, and texture. Many are attractive to butterflies, birds, and bees, and some are good for cutting. Others are more functional, offering erosion control on a slope, or attractive ways to deal with a low area in the lawn or dry shade under large trees.

Many native flowers are well suited to garden and landscape use. Some you may already know and grow. Monarda, butterfly weed, Joe-pye weeds, asters, and black-eyed Susan are all commonly grown in perennial beds and mixed borders, and wild ginger, bloodroot, and blue phlox are common in shade gardens. Many other native flowers adapt well to cultivation, especially if you can provide them with suitable soil and site conditions.

Groundcovers are plants that spread readily to cover the ground, usually in tough sites. Typically these are low-growing plants, but some are a foot or more tall. Most grow in shade, but some need sun. Groundcovers take a little effort to get established, but once they are set, they can be an effective way to reduce mowing and other maintenance.

When choosing flowers and groundcovers, think in terms of ecosystems instead of individual plants. If you want to put a flower garden in a sunny area with well-drained sandy soil, look to the grassland ecosystems. Choose plants that are native to these habitats and have a wide variety of bloom times, and you'll end up with a showy, low-maintenance border with interest from spring until fall. If you have an area under the canopy of large deciduous trees, look to the shade-loving plants of the deciduous forest. By planting flowers and groundcovers that have evolved together naturally, you'll end up with a group of plants that not only grow well together, but look good together, too.

Planting

There are several ways to plant flowers and groundcovers. Seeds of native plants are available from many specialty nurseries, both as individual species and as mixes. Some plants, especially woodland types, require a cold, moist period or some type of mechanical scarification to break dormancy. If you buy your seeds from a knowledgeable source, you'll get detailed germination information. Many native plants are available bare-root from mail-order nurseries and container-grown from nurseries and garden centers. New plants can also be obtained by divisions of older, established plants that you have growing in another area of your landscape, or from a friend. Never dig plants from the wild.

If you will be planting a large prairie garden, a seed mix is the most practical way to go. Seeds take longer to become established plants and to reach flowering age, but the result is a more natural look. Seeds are also more economical. Order seed mixes from a nursery specializing in wildflowers in your area. If your goal is a true grassland restoration, try to find a nursery within about two hundred miles of you to ensure an authentic genotype. Be wary of wildflower-in-a-can mixes. Many contain nonnative plants, including annuals that won't be around for more than a year or two. Grasslands can be seeded in spring or fall, but to be successful, seeds must be sown on a well-prepared seedbed, not just scattered in existing vegetation. You can augment your seeding with plants to get flowers faster.

Bare-root plants must be planted in early spring. Dig a hole slightly deeper and wider than the longest roots of your plant. Make a cone of soil in the center of the hole to set the plant on. The crown (where the stems join roots) should be level with the soil surface. Spread roots evenly and refill the hole with soil, watering well. Spring is also the best time to plant most container-grown native flowers, but they can be planted throughout the growing season if you pay close attention to watering. Choose a cloudy day to plant, and give all newly planted flowers a thorough drink of water.

Most native flowers and groundcovers can be divided in spring or early fall. Water thoroughly and keep the soil moist until plants are established. After the ground has frozen, it is a good idea to put down a winter mulch of weed-free straw or leaves, which helps ensure that the new plants will remain firmly planted in the soil through winter freeze-thaw cycles.

Space plants based on their mature sizes and their use. Perennials should be spaced roughly half their height apart. If they grow 2 feet tall, for example, place them about a foot apart. Groundcovers should be spaced a little closer than is recommended so they will fill in faster.

Although some flowers can be used as single specimen plants, most flowers look best in groups of three, five, or seven or more, as they are in nature. Repeating a plant or a grouping is an effective technique in any garden where there is sufficient room.

Many native flowers are ephemeral in nature, meaning they go dormant during summer's heat. Plant them with summer plants that will cover the bare ground when the ephemerals "disappear." Be careful not to dig up dormant clumps of spring ephemerals. If you will be cultivating that area of the garden, you may want to mark them in late spring so you don't disturb their roots in summer or fall.

Many native flowers and groundcovers readily adapt to landscape use. Two of the most popular are *Rudbeckia hirta* 'Goldsturm' and *Eupatorium purpureum* 'Gateway', growing here with *Echinacea purpurea* (purple coneflower) and *Heuchera* 'Palace Purple' in a perennial border.

Care

Sun-loving grassland plants grow in almost any average garden soil, but most shade-loving native flowers and groundcovers do best in slightly acidic, well-drained soils with at least 40 percent organic matter. Whenever possible, add organic matter to the soil before planting any native plant. Dig the garden bed as deeply as possible and incorporate 3 to 4 inches of organic matter—well-rotted manure, compost, or peat moss. Some plants require nitrogen-fixing bacteria, which can be incorporated into the soil in the form of a commercially available inoculant. Even though many native plants tolerate tough conditions, most—including dry-soil grassland plants—will grow better in a garden setting if the soil has been amended with organic matter.

Flowers and groundcovers will benefit from a 1- to 2-inch layer of organic mulch to retain moisture, to keep weeds down, and to improve the soil. Good mulches are shredded leaves, pine needles, or compost. Shredded bark can be used in woodland gardens and mixed borders, but it's usually too coarse for perennial beds.

If you've amended the soil with organic matter before planting and if you keep plants mulched, most native flowers and groundcovers will not need additional fertilizer. If you do want to fertilize, apply a layer of well-rotted compost around plants in early spring or fall. You can also use an organic fertilizer such as Milorganite, fish emulsion, or blood meal. Apply these in early spring, and water well.

As with all garden plants, water is important for establishment during the first year. Once plants are established in an appropriate site, a layer of mulch should be all that most plants need. Grassland plants especially prefer to be on the drier side. If you are incorporating new plants into an established bed, use a stake or some other type of marker to remind yourself to give them extra water.

Weeds are always a problem for gardeners, even in established landscapes. The best way to keep weeds under control is a good defense. Kill weeds before planting your garden, if possible. Once your garden is planted, keep the bare soil covered with mulch. Try to pull or cut back annual weeds before they go to seed. Avoid using pre-emergent herbicides, as they will prevent all seeds from sprouting, including the self-sown seedlings of your native plants that give your garden the natural look you want.

There are other maintenance tasks you may choose to perform on some flowers. Taller plants may need stakes or supports to keep them from flopping over. In prairie gardens, support tall flowers by placing them near stiff grasses, such as big bluestem and Indian grass. Use wooden stakes or small tomato cages to support individual plants. Most later-blooming plants can be pinched or cut back by about half in late May, keeping the plants shorter and more compact. However, if you do it too late, you run the risk of having no flowers. Deadheading is the cutting out of spent flowers to encourage more bloom. It is more important with nonnative annuals, but it does help some natives produce more flowers. However, some native flowers, such as blazing stars and coneflowers, have seed heads that are attractive to birds and also offer winter interest; these seed heads should not be removed until spring.

Possible Problems

Most native flowers and groundcovers will not be bothered by serious insect or disease problems if they are growing in appropriate sites. Keep moisture-loving plants in heavier soils and dry-soil plants out of low areas. Match plants to available sunlight conditions. Powdery mildew is a fungal disease that may show up during wet summers on some plants, but it's rarely serious. Cut back diseased plants in fall and remove the foliage. If the problem continues year after year, choose another plant for that site.

Common insect pests include slugs and leaf miners, both of which usually result in only cosmetic damage. If you want to have butterflies in your garden, you'll have to learn to live with the few holes in leaves that come from caterpillar feeding. If you find a heavily damaged plant, put in a few more plants to compensate for what you'll be sharing with the butterflies. Whatever insect problems you face, don't resort to insecticides. They kill too many beneficial insects, including bees and butterflies.

Actaea rubra
Red baneberry
Zone 2

Actaea rubra

Native Habitat Rich, neutral to acidic soils of woodland areas throughout Michigan.

Height 12 to 30 inches

Description Showy, dense clusters of fluffy white flowers rise above attractive, deeply cut compound leaves, starting in late April and continuing well into May. Shiny red berries follow flowers in late summer. Mature plants have a shrublike appearance.

Landscape Use Red baneberry is well suited to woodland or shade gardens, where it will be an attractive addition throughout the growing season. Its shrublike appearance allows it to be used in foundation plantings. Place it where the showy red fruits will be enjoyed in late summer; a backdrop of lacy ferns is nice. The berries are poisonous to people, but are a favorite food of birds.

Site Moist, humus-rich, slightly acidic soil in partial to full shade.

Culture Amend soil with organic matter before planting. Once established, red baneberry will require little care, and it has no serious insect or disease problems. It spreads slowly to form showy clumps that seldom need division. Self-sown seedlings may appear.

Good Companions Flowering plants combine nicely with other taller woodland plants such as ferns, columbines, and wild geranium. Great blue lobelia, zigzag goldenrod, and large-leaved aster are good companions for the red berries in late summer.

Other Species *A. pachypoda* (white baneberry) is native to similar conditions and locations. It is similar to red baneberry except for its berry color, which is white with a single black dot.

Actaea pachypoda

It is also called doll's eyes because the berries resemble the china eyes once used in dolls. Use and culture are the same as for red baneberry. Zone 3.

Allium cernuum
Nodding wild onion
Zone 3

Native Habitat Moist soils of open deciduous woodlands and grasslands, mainly in the far southern part of Michigan.

Height 12 to 24 inches

Description Nodding clusters of 1/4-inch purple-pink to white flowers hang from the downturned tips of erect stems in June and July. Basal leaves are grasslike and grow up to 18 inches. The plant has a pleasant onion-like scent.

Landscape Use Nodding onion adds a touch of lavender to the gardens in midsummer. The foliage is attractive all season, and the papery dried seedheads are decorative in autumn. Use it in open woodland gardens, in rock gardens, and in mixed borders. It can be grown in containers.

Site Average to rich, well-drained soil in full sun to very light shade. Soil can be neutral to slightly alkaline.

Culture Nodding onion grows from bulbs that look like miniature versions of their cultivated relatives. It adapts readily to cultivation. Divide garden clumps every third year in early spring or as they go dormant to promote better flowering. Self-sown seedlings will appear.

Good Companions Plant nodding wild onion with wild petunia, purple coneflower, prairie phlox, Culver's root, and obedient plant. Rattlesnake master and switch grass are good background plants.

Other Species *A. tricoccum* (wild leek) is native to rich deciduous woods throughout most of Michigan. It grows 6 to 16 inches tall in flower. The creamy white clusters of flowers appear on leafless stems in June and July, after the two or three 8- to 10-inch, canoe-shaped leaves have withered away. These bright green leaves are showy when they first appear in early April on the forest floor when little else is up. Wild leek prefers moist, rich soil high in organic matter. The leaves need early season sunshine to generate food for flower production, but the

Allium cernuum

Allium tricoccum

plants grow in summer shade; a site under deciduous trees is ideal. Plant wild leek with wild ginger, which will fill in when the wild leek leaves die back. Zone 3.

Anaphalis margaritacea

Anaphalis margaritacea
Pearly everlasting
Zone 2

Native Habitat Dry-soil areas, including dunes, throughout most of Michigan.

Height 1 to 3 feet

Description This bushy plant has flat-topped clusters of small, silvery white, daisylike flowers from July into September. The narrow leaves are grayish above, woolly white underneath.

Landscape Use Pearly everlasting is a tough, drought-tolerant perennial with interesting flowers. Use it in prairie gardens, butterfly gardens, and dune restorations. The flowers are attractive to butterflies, especially painted ladies. They also make long-lasting dried bouquets when picked before completely open. The silver leaves offer a nice contrast in large mixed borders.

Site Tolerant of tough, dry conditions and can be grown in poor to average soils in full sun.

Culture Pearly everlasting requires little care once established and has no insect or disease problems. This stoloniferous plant can become invasive in some landscape situations.

Good Companions Pearly everlasting is a perfect companion for other drought-tolerant plants such as prairie smoke, nodding wild onion, butterfly weed, and cinquefoils.

Anemone canadensis

Anemone cylindrica

Anemone quinquefolia

Native Habitat Cool, wet grasslands and open woodlands, in a variety of soils, throughout Michigan.

Height 12 to 24 inches

Description The long-stalked, snowy white, 2-inch flowers have numerous gold stamens. They appear in June. Leaves are deeply divided into three to seven lobes with toothed margins.

Landscape Use Canada anemone grows into large patches in moist prairies and open woods, and a large colony is quite striking in bloom. It makes a good groundcover beneath large trees and shrubs. It is good for filling in open or partially shaded areas. It tolerates moist soil and can be used in bog gardens.

Anemone canadensis
Canada anemone
Zone 2

Site Prefers moist, average to rich soil in full sun to light shade, but tolerates a wide range of soils.

Culture Canada anemone can be aggressive in formal gardens and may need to be confined by edging strips buried in the soil. Plants are less aggressive in drier soil and in partial shade. Divide crowded plants in spring to encourage better blooming.

Good Companions Combine it with other native flowers such as butterfly weed, roses, columbines, black-eyed Susan, wild geranium, and bunch grasses in naturalistic plantings. It makes a nice yellow-white spring combination when planted with *Euphorbia polychroma* (cushion spurge) or *Doronicum* (leopard's bane) in mixed borders.

Other Species *A. cylindrica* (thimbleweed) is native to barrens and dry savannas in all but the western half of the Upper Peninsula. It grows 2 feet tall and has long erect stalks topped by interesting greenish white flowers that turn into cottony seed heads. It can be grown in moist to dry soil in full sun or light shade. Zone 3.

A. multifida (cut-leaved anemone) is native on sandy soils and dunes in the northern half of Michigan. It grows 12 to 30 inches tall; it has whitish flowers and attractive, finely cut foliage. Var. *sanguinea* (red anemone) is a naturally occurring variety prevalent in northern Michigan. It has showy red or maroon flowers. Zone 2.

A. quinquefolia (wood anemone) is native to rich, moist soils throughout Michigan. It grows 3 to 8 inches tall, forming large colonies over time. The solitary flowers, which bloom from late April to June, are white above and pink to purple on their undersides. It prefers moist, slightly acidic, fertile soils in sheltered, partially shaded woodlands. It will eventually form a persistent carpet as it weaves its way among other plants. It goes dormant in early summer. Zone 3.

FLOWERS AND GROUNDCOVERS

Anemonella [Thalictrum] thalictroides
Rue anemone
Zone 4; trial in zone 3

Native Habitat Open, rocky woods and clearings, in a variety of soils, in the southern third of Michigan.

Height 4 to 8 inches

Description This delicate woodland plant has several long-stalked white, pink-tinged, or lavender-tinged flowers that radiate from a whorl of leaflets, each about 1 inch wide with three rounded lobes. The flowers dance in the slightest breeze. Rue anemone starts blooming in mid- to late April, continues into June, and goes dormant by midsummer.

Landscape Use This cheerful harbinger of spring is attractive along path edges and as a carpet in woodland or shade gardens. It grows well in rocky terrain and can be planted in shady rock gardens. Keep in mind that it disappears by midsummer.

Site Moist or dry, slightly acidic soil in filtered or partial sunlight.

Culture Keep plants blooming by watering during dry springs, since this plant survives dry spells by going dormant early. Avoid competition from larger plants that may overtake this delicate plant. Plants are best left undisturbed.

Good Companions Create a beautiful spring carpet in wildflower gardens by growing rue anemones with delicate ferns and low groundcovers such as wild ginger and hepaticas. In shade gardens, combine it with early spring bulbs, primroses, violets, pulmonarias, and epimediums.

Cultivars 'Cameo' is a vigorous grower with soft-pink double flowers. 'Green Dragon' has single green flowers. 'Green Hurricane' has interesting greenish double flowers held above wiry foliage. 'Schoaf's Double Pink' is a robust grower with deep rose-pink double flowers.

Anemonella thalictroides

'Schoaf's Double Pink'

Antennaria parlinii [A. plantaginifolia]
Smooth pussytoes
Zone 3

Native Habitat Usually dry soil on open sites but also some woodlands, throughout most of Michigan.

Height 3 to 16 inches

Description This plant is mainly grown for its grayish, woolly leaves and stems. The leaves grow only a few inches tall and plants spread by runners. Dome-shaped clusters of fuzzy white flower heads appear from late April into June on 12- to 16-inch stalks.

Landscape Use Smooth pussytoes is a good groundcover for sunny areas near hot pavement or on banks, where it helps control erosion. The flat, silvery foliage is attractive all season and is effective in twilight gardens. It can also be used in rock gardens, between paving stones, and atop stone walls.

Site Thrives in dry, poor, well-drained soil in full sun, but tolerates partial shade.

Culture Smooth pussytoes requires little care once established. Divide in spring if you want more plants.

Good Companions Grow smooth pussytoes with other drought-tolerant, sun-loving plants such as prairie smoke, nodding wild onion, and cinquefoils. When planted with spring bulbs, it will fill in after the bulb foliage has died back.

Other Species *A. neglecta* (field pussytoes) is native to dry soils and prairies in the southern part of Michigan. It is similar to *A. parlinii*, but its leaves are narrower and often more yellowish green. Plants are shorter, growing to 12 inches. Zone 3.

Antennaria plantaginifolia

69

Aquilegia canadensis

Aquilegia canadensis
Canada columbine, wild columbine
Zone 3

Native Habitat Rocky woods and savannas, in a variety of soils, throughout Michigan.

Height 12 to 24 inches

Description Canada columbine is a graceful, erect plant; it has nodding, upside-down, red-and-yellow flowers with five upward-spurred petals dangling from the tips of branching stems. The grayish leaves are compound, divided into lobed leaflets grouped in threes. It blooms from early May to early summer, and the foliage is attractive all season.

Landscape Use Grow this charming plant anywhere, from woodland borders to prairies. Include it in rock gardens or scatter it around a garden pool. It attracts hummingbirds. Allow it to self-sow and form natural drifts in wild gardens.

Site Moist to dry, average, well-drained soil in full sun to almost full shade.

Culture Canada columbine is easily cultivated. Seedlings need moisture to become established, but deep rootstocks of mature plants survive dry spells. It will self-seed, but not to the point of becoming a pest. Old rootstocks do not transplant well. Leaf miners may attack the foliage, causing tan tunnels or blotches. Remove and destroy affected leaves as soon as you see them.

Good Companions Canada columbine's delicate nature combines nicely with a wide variety of plants. In native gardens, plant it with ferns, nodding wild onion, Canada anemone, prairie smoke, wild geranium, Virginia bluebells, and bird's-foot violet. In mixed borders, plant it near late tulips, hostas, irises, pulmonarias, peonies, and perennial geraniums.

Cultivars 'Corbett' is a pale yellow selection that combines beautifully with blue forget-me-nots or blue phlox in partial shade. 'Little Lanterns' is a diminutive selection growing only 8 to 10 inches tall.

Aralia racemosa
American spikenard
Zone 3

Native Habitat Rich soils in deciduous or mixed coniferous woods throughout most of Michigan.

Height 2 to 6 feet

Description The huge, twice pinnately divided, 2½-foot leaves have heart-shaped leaflets that are 4 to 6 inches long. The small, terminal, greenish flowers that bloom from May to July turn to showy, deep purple berries in late summer.

Landscape Use Spikenard is limited by its size, which relegates it to the accent or specimen category. Although it is herbaceous, think of it more as a shrub, and use it to screen an area or as a foundation plant on the north or east side of a building. It becomes an understory plant in woodland gardens.

Site Rich, moist soil in partial to deep shade.

Culture Allow plenty of room for plants to spread. Established plants are difficult to move, so place plants in their permanent site if possible. Self-sown seedlings develop slowly and are usually not a problem.

Good Companions Combine American spikenard with other bold plants such as large ferns and hostas. Be careful about siting it next to smaller plants, which can be overtaken by this giant.

Other Species *A. nudicaulis* (wild sarsaparilla) is native in a wide variety of soils in woodlands throughout Michigan. It is a more diminutive but more aggressive relative of American spikenard, growing only 1 to 1½ feet tall. The umbrella-like, double-compound basal leaves shade three dome-shaped clusters of greenish white flowers growing on a leafless stem. Plants spread aggressively via underground rhizomes and may need to be contained by burying edging strips if you don't want them to become a groundcover. Zone 3.

Aralia racemosa

Arisaema triphyllum
Jack-in-the-pulpit
Zone 3

Native Habitat Rich, moist deciduous woodlands throughout Michigan.

Height 12 to 36 inches

Description Jack-in-the-pulpit has one or two long-stemmed, compound leaves with three leaflets that form a canopy over the unusual flower. A ridged, hooded spathe with purplish brown streaks encloses an erect, brown spadix, starting about mid-May. The bright red clusters of fruits are showy in late summer.

Landscape Use Jack-in-the-pulpit has an almost tropical look to it and catches the eye of many visitors. Use it in shady woodland gardens or mixed borders. The hooded spadix is interesting and intriguing to children. It will grow in heavily shaded, poorly drained soils.

Site Prefers a moist, rich soil in moderate to full shade.

Culture This easy-to-grow perennial adapts well to cultivation. Plants self-sow, but only to form a nice colony. When grown in drier conditions, it often goes dormant in summer.

Good Companions Jack-in-the-pulpit grows well with wild geranium, blue phlox, May apple, Canada columbine, and maidenhair fern.

Other Species *A. dracontium* (green dragon) is native to moist woods in the southern half of the Lower Peninsula. Its long spadix is covered with tiny greenish yellow flowers that protrude well beyond the pointed spathe surrounding it. The solitary basal leaf is divided into five to fifteen leaflets. It grows 12 to 42 inches tall and blooms May to June. It prefers wet, rich, high-humus soil in full sun to light shade. Showcase this unique plant along a path, near a garden pond, or against a ledge. Zone 4.

Arisaema triphyllum

Asarum canadense
Wild ginger
Zone 3

Native Habitat Deciduous and some coniferous forests, in nearly neutral or acidic soils, mainly in the southern two-thirds of the Lower Peninsula but also farther north.

Height 6 to 8 inches

Description Wild ginger is a rhizomatous creeping plant with large, textured, heart-shaped leaves up to 8 inches wide. The leaves are up early in spring, and they cover the interesting nodding, maroon flowers that appear in midspring.

Landscape Use Wild ginger is an excellent groundcover in shady areas. It forms an extensive carpet that is good for hiding empty spots left by spring ephemerals.

Site Prefers consistently moist, humus-rich soil in partial to full shade, but tolerates drier, less acidic soils.

Culture Make sure new plants receive adequate water. Wild ginger is quite drought tolerant and carefree once established. It spreads quickly via creeping rhizomes but rarely becomes invasive. Divide plants in spring or as they go dormant in fall if you want to increase your numbers.

Good Companions Wild ginger is a good plant to use among spring ephemerals such as trout lilies, false rue anemone, and prairie shooting star, which go dormant in summer. Combine it with foamflower in dappled shade to get a solid groundcover with widely differing leaf shapes and sizes.

Asarum canadense in flower

Asarum canadense

Asclepias tuberosa
Butterfly weed
Zone 3

Native Habitat Dry barrens and woodland edges and openings throughout most of the Lower Peninsula.

Height 1 to 3 feet

Description Butterfly weed has dense clumps of leafy stems topped with broad, flat clusters of fiery orange, red, or sometimes yellow flowers. The flowers bloom from late spring to late summer.

Landscape Use Butterfly weed adds a splash of summer color to gardens. It is particularly striking when planted with complementary-colored blue and purple flowers. Plant it in perennial gardens, mixed borders, or prairie gardens. As the name implies, it attracts butterflies and their larvae, as well as hummingbirds, bees, and other insects.

Site Moist or dry soils in full sun or light shade. Mature plants can take full sun and dry soil.

Culture Set out young plants in their permanent locations, as the deep taproot makes plants difficult to move. Good drainage is essential; plants may rot in overly rich or damp soil. No major insect or disease problems, but plants may die over winter from root rot if the soil is too heavy. Plants are slow to emerge in spring, so cultivate carefully until new growth appears; you may want to mark the site each fall. Plants can get a little top-heavy and may require gentle staking.

Good Companions Plant butterfly weed with other summer-blooming perennials such as purple salvias, white shasta daisy (*Leucanthemum* x *superbum*), and yellow daylilies for a showy display of contrasting shapes and colors. Good native companions include blazing stars, silky aster, leadplant, purple prairie clover, and wild bergamot.

Cultivars and Other Species 'Gay Butterflies' is a seed-grown strain of mixed yellow, red, and orange flowers.

Asarum canadense

Asclepias incarnata 'Soulmate'

A. exaltata (poke milkweed) is native to woodlands and savannas throughout most of Michigan. It grows 2 to 5 feet tall and has whitish green flowers from late spring to early summer. Being the only true woodland species, it is somewhat shade tolerant. Zone 3.

A. incarnata (swamp milkweed) is native to moist soil areas throughout Michigan. It has flat, terminal clusters of pale rose to rose-purple flowers on 3-foot plants, June to August. It grows best in constantly wet soils in full sun, such as in bog gardens, but it adapts well to the conditions of sunny perennial borders if it receives supplemental water. It is a food source for several butterflies and their larvae. 'Ice Ballet' has creamy white flowers. 'Cinderella' and 'Soulmate' have fragrant, long-lasting, rose-pink flowers. Zone 3.

A. sullivantii (Sullivant's milkweed, prairie milkweed) is native to moist to mesic grasslands in southeastern Michigan. Best used in prairie gardens, it is a rhizomatous species growing 2 to 3 feet tall and having pink flowers. It is on Michigan's list of threatened plants; be sure to only purchase nursery-propagated plants. Zone 3.

A. syriaca (common milkweed) is native to average to moist soils throughout most of Michigan. It has slightly drooping, 2-inch clusters of mauve-pink, butterfly-attracting flowers on 24- to 60-inch downy stems. The undersides of leaves are covered with woolly gray hairs. It prefers moist but well-drained soil in full sun. It is easy to grow in gardens, but can become invasive. Zone 3.

A. verticillata (whorled milkweed) is native to dry soils mainly in southern Michigan but also farther north. It has small, creamy white flowers in mid- to late summer. Plants spread from rhizomes to form large colonies. Zone 3.

A. viridiflora (green milkweed) is native to dry soils, including dunes and oak woodlands in southern Michigan. It has small greenish flowers in tight clusters. Grow it in average or sandy dry soil in full sun. Zone 3.

Aster novae-angliae [Symphyotrichum novae-angliae]
New England aster
Zone 3

Native Habitat Wet to moist soils in a wide variety of habitats, mainly in the southern half of the Lower Peninsula but also in the rest of Michigan.

Height 3 to 6 feet

Description New England aster flowers have violet or lavender petals surrounding yellow centers on heads 1 to 2 inches wide. Flowers are clustered at the ends of branches from late August into October. Mature plants have woody, fibrous root systems.

Landscape Use This fall bloomer brings purple shades to fall gardens. Use it in mixed borders, prairies, and even large rock gardens. It attracts butterflies and bees.

Site Moist, average soil in full sun to partial shade.

Culture New England aster likes consistent soil moisture. The tall stems can become top-heavy when in bloom and often need some type of support. Pinch stems back in late May to promote bushier plants. Divide plants in spring every third year to promote vigorous growth. Avoid too much nitrogen, which can result in abundant foliage and floppy plants.

Good Companions Plant New England aster with goldenrods, grasses, oxeye, obedient plant, bottle gentian, showy tick trefoil, and boltonia for an outstanding fall show.

Cultivars and Other Species 'Andenken an Alma Potschke', usually sold simply as 'Alma Potschke', is covered in bright rose-pink flowers in fall. 'Purple Dome' is a dwarf cultivar (18 to 24 inches) with semi-double, deep purple flowers showy from late summer into fall. It is naturally dense and requires no pinching or staking.

You will find *Aster* species reclassified as *Symphyotrichum* in some references.

A. cordifolius (heart-leaved aster) is native to open woods and clearings in the southern half of the Lower Peninsula. The stems grow 3 to 4 feet tall with domes of white to sky-blue flowers in late summer. Give it a moist,

humus-rich soil in light to partial shade. Zone 4.

A. ericoides (heath aster) is native to prairies and woodland edges in the southern half of the Lower Peninsula. It has hundreds of white or pale blue flowers on 1- to 3-foot plants. Plant it in average to rich, moist soil in full sun. 'Blue Star' has sky-blue flowers. Zone 3.

A. laevis (smooth blue aster) is native to dry open woods throughout the Lower Peninsula and into the Upper Peninsula. It has light blue flowers on 2- to 3-foot plants and is one of the last asters to bloom in autumn. Plant it in average to rich, moist but well-drained soil in full sun or light shade. Use it in woodland or prairie gardens where the floppy stems will be supported by nearby plants. 'Blue Bird' is a compact selection with deep sky-blue flowers. Zone 2.

A. lateriflorus (calico aster) is native to open, sandy woods throughout Michigan. This 2- to 4-foot bushy plant has especially attractive foliage in addition to bearing hundreds of small white flowers. It forms clumps but is never invasive. Grow it in average to rich, well-drained soil in full sun or light shade. 'Horizontalis', 'Prince', and 'Lady in Black' have deep plum-purple foliage to set off the flowers. Zone 4; trial in zone 3.

A. macrophyllus (large-leaved aster) is native to woodlands throughout Michigan. It has flat-topped clusters of violet or lavender flowers with yellow to reddish centers on 1- to 4-foot stems, August to September. Create a lush groundcover by planting it in moist, humus-rich soil in sun or partial shade. It tolerates dry sites and deep shade and has good fall color. Zone 3.

A. oolentangiensis (sky-blue aster, azure aster) is found on open woodlands and savannas in the southern half of the Lower Peninsula. Its light blue flowers are smaller and more open than smooth aster, and it grows 2 to 5

feet tall. Give it well-drained soil in full sun. Zone 3.

A. puniceus (swamp aster) is native to moist to wet soils throughout Michigan. It grows 2 to 6 feet tall and has white flowers beginning in August. Zone 3.

A. umbellatus (flat-topped aster) is native to moist places throughout Michigan. It has large, flattened clusters of small white flowers in late summer. It can grow up to 10 feet tall and may need support in some situations. It is a good companion for Joe-pye weeds in moist soil in full or partial shade. Zone 3.

Aster ericoides

Aster novae-angliae 'Purple Dome'

Native Habitat Open woods, prairies, and savannas, in moist or dry soils, in southern Michigan.

Height 3 to 5 feet

Description Wild white indigo has long, erect, pea-like, white flowers in late spring. The compound leaves are an attractive bluish green color. Showy gray or brown seedpods rattle in the wind when they are ripe.

Landscape Use White wild indigo adapts well to cultivation. Use it in prairie gardens or in the middle to back of mixed borders, where the blue-green foliage provides a nice backdrop for smaller perennials. It forms a large clump, so leave plenty of space around it. The seedpods add interest in fall and winter and are often used in dried arrangements.

Site Well-drained soil in full sun or light shade.

Culture This long-lived perennial starts out slowly but eventually forms huge clumps that are difficult to transplant. Choose a site carefully, and space plants at least 3 feet apart to allow for growth. Plants rarely need dividing and resent disturbance. White wild indigo is drought tolerant once established. It is on Michigan's special

Baptisia lactea [B. alba, B. leucantha]
White wild indigo
Zone 4

Baptisia lactea

concern list and should be protected in the wild.

Good Companions Use white wild indigo as an accent plant for yarrows, artemisias, asters, and phloxes. Plant low, bushy plants such as geraniums around the base of clumps to hide the bare lower stalks. In prairie gardens, plant it with purple coneflower, prairie phlox, butterfly weed, and prairie clover.

Other Species *B. leucophaea* (cream wild indigo) is native to dry soil in only one documented location in southern Michigan. It grows to about 2 feet tall and has cream-colored flowers. It needs well-drained soil and full sun. It is on Michigan's endangered species list. Zone 4.

B. tinctoria (wild indigo) is native to dry soils in the southern part of Michigan. It grows 2 to 3 feet tall and has bright yellow flowers in summer. Zone 3.

Boltonia asteroides

Boltonia asteroides var. recognita
Boltonia, false aster
Zone 4

Native Habitat Wet prairies and marshes, only in the far southeastern corner of Michigan.

Height 3 to 5 feet

Description Boltonia has small heads of white, aster-like flowers, which have yellow centers. It starts blooming in late July and continues through September. It is an erect plant with narrow, gray-green leaves.

Landscape Use This summer bloomer provides much-needed white color in late summer, when yellows dominate perennial borders and prairie gardens.

Site Tolerates a wide variety of soils, from wet to dry, in full sun.

Culture Plants may need support to keep them from flopping over. They can be pinched back in late May to encourage compact growth. Overgrown clumps are easily divided every three to five years in spring.

Good Companions Plant boltonia with other late-summer perennials, such as asters, goldenrods, fireweed, Joe-pye weeds, and grasses.

Cultivars 'Snowbank' is more compact and has sturdy stems smothered in white flowers in September. 'Pink Beauty' flowers a littler earlier than 'Snowbank' and has attractive pale lavender-pink flowers.

Caltha palustris
Marsh marigold
Zone 2

Native Habitat Wet woods, swamps, and the shallow water of ponds, throughout Michigan.

Height 12 to 24 inches

Description Marsh marigold has thick, branching stems bearing lustrous, dark green, heart- or kidney-shaped leaves with lightly scalloped margins. The bright yellow flowers cover the plants for a long time, starting in mid- to late April and continuing well into May.

Landscape Use Plant marsh marigold along stream banks, in bogs, or near water gardens in small clumps or large patches that can be seen from a distance.

Site Requires a wet soil high in humus and full sun to light shade. It is readily grown in shallow water or in the wet soil of bog gardens.

Culture Amend soil with organic matter before planting. Marsh marigolds can be grown in containers of rich potting soil and covered with 2 inches of pea gravel before submerging in water. Plants go dormant about a month after flowering. Divide overgrown clumps as they go into dormancy.

Good Companions Pair with white-flowering wild calla to extend the season of color after marsh marigold goes dormant in midsummer. Other moisture-loving companions include pickerelweed, arrowhead, primroses, irises, and ferns.

Cultivated Varieties Var. *alba* has pure white flowers. 'Flore Pleno' has fully double, long-lasting flowers.

Caltha palustris

Campanula rotundifolia
Harebell, bluebell
Zone 2

Native Habitat Sandy shores, dunes, dry woodlands, and barrens, throughout Michigan.

Height 6 to 18 inches

Description Harebell has violet-blue, bell-shaped, nodding flowers that appear on slender stalks at ends of branched stems. It blooms from June to September.

Landscape Use Plant harebell where the delicate flower won't be overpowered by nearby plants. It does well in rock walls, in rock gardens, and between pavers on a terrace, where it will bloom all summer.

Site Needs a well-drained soil in full sun.

Culture Add sand and organic matter to improve soil drainage if necessary. Avoid overly rich soils, which can encourage vigorous growth on nearby plants that can overtake harebell. In the right setting, the underground stems of harebell will spread.

Good Companions Plant harebell with other diminutive dry-soil plants such as creeping thymes, pussytoes, alliums, columbines, prairie smoke, and beardtongues.

Other Species *C. americana* (tall bell-flower, American bellflower) is native to open deciduous woodlands in the southern third of Michigan. It is an annual or biennial that will self-sow. The light blue flowers grow in clusters atop 4- to 6-foot stems. The blooms progress up the stem and appear spring to summer. Plant it in moist, average soil in full sun to partial shade. It is sometimes listed as *Campanulastrum americana*. Zone 3.

Campanula rotundifolia

Cassia hebecarpa [Senna hebecarpa]
Wild senna
Zone 3

Cassia hebecarpa

Native Habitat Moist, fertile soils in the southern third of Michigan.
Height 3 to 7 feet
Description Wild senna is a large, stately plant with pea-like leaves held perpendicular to stems. Golden yellow flower clusters grow from axils in upper leaves in summer. Flowers turn into long, thick bean pods that offer fall and winter interest.
Landscape Use The tiered leaf arrangement, along with its height, give wild senna a strong vertical presence in the landscape. Use it at the back of a large perennial border or as a transition plant at the edge of a wood-land. It is a good choice for naturaliz-ing in heavy clay soil. The fruits are attractive to wildlife.
Site Moist to moderately dry soil in sun to partial shade; will grow in heavy clay.
Culture Wild senna won't get as tall in drier soils. Plants are difficult to move once established so choose a site care-fully. The ornamental but heavy seed-pods can cause tall plants to bend after wind or heavy rain. Cut off spent flow-ers to keep plants from falling over.
Good Companions Match wild senna's stature with other tall moisture lovers such as Joe-pye weeds, boltonia, and sneezeweed.

Caulophyllum thalictroides
Blue cohosh
Zone 3

Caulophyllum thalictroides

C. thalictroides fruits

Native Habitat Rich, damp, deciduous woods throughout most of Michigan.
Height 1 to 3 feet
Description This handsome, erect plant has a thrice-compound leaf with an attractive sea-green color. Stems have a purplish tint when they emerge in spring. The yellowish green or pur-plish flowers, which bloom in May, are rather small and are followed by showy, berrylike midnight-blue fruits borne in a loose cluster.

Landscape Use Use blue cohosh in shade or woodland gardens. Be sure to place it where you can enjoy the strik-ing purple stems in early spring and the bright blue fruits in late summer.
Site Prefers partial to full shade and a moist, well-drained soil with abundant organic matter.
Culture Plants form multistemmed clumps over time. Divide in early fall and cut apart crowns, leaving at least one eye per division.
Good Companions Plant blue cohosh with early spring ephemerals, which will set off the purple emerging stems. It will fill in when Dutchman's breeches, spring beauty, false rue anemone, trout lilies, and other ephemerals go dormant. It grows natu-rally with two-leaved miterwort, which also makes a good garden companion. The fall berries combine nicely with zigzag goldenrod and white snakeroot.

Chelone glabra
White turtlehead
Zone 3

Chelone glabra

Native Habitat Wet soil of woodlands and openings throughout Michigan.
Height 1 to 3 feet
Description White turtlehead has terminal clusters of white, inflated, arching, two-lipped flowers that are often tinged with pink or lavender. They appear in late summer and early fall and are followed by attractive dried seed heads. Plants have an upright to slightly vase-shape form and dark green leaves.
Landscape Use Plant white turtlehead in flower borders, wet prairies, and alongside water features. The flowers attract bees and hummingbirds.
Site Evenly moist to wet, rich soil in full sun to light shade.
Culture Mulch plants well to conserve soil moisture. Plants will tolerate brief dry spells once they are established. Plants spread by rhizomes but do not become invasive.
Good Companions In flower borders, white turtlehead combines nicely with asters, prairie phlox, goldenrods, Joe-pye weeds, and grasses. Near ponds, grow it with irises, cardinal flower, ferns, and obedient plant.
Other Species *C. obliqua* (purple turtlehead) is rare in Michigan, found naturally only along the Huron River near Ann Arbor. It grows 1 to 3 feet tall and has rich pink to rose-red flowers on upright to arching stems. Grow it in moist to wet, humus-rich soil in full sun to partial shade, in the same places as white turtlehead. It is on Michigan's endangered species list. Zone 4.

Claytonia virginica
Spring beauty, Virginia spring beauty
Zone 3

Claytonia virginica

Native Habitat Moist woods and stream banks in deciduous forests, in the southern half of Michigan.
Height 6 to 8 inches
Description This dainty spring ephemeral has loose clusters of charming white or white-and-pink candy-striped flowers in April and early May. The narrow leaves appear in basal clumps 4 to 6 inches tall.
Landscape Use Spring beauty makes a beautiful but short-lived spring groundcover in woodland gardens. Plant it in masses to intermingle with other early wildflowers and bulbs, or showcase a group of three to five plants at the base of a tree. It disappears soon after flowering, so interplant it with ferns and other summer flowers. It can be naturalized in lawns; plant a few plants, let them reseed, and do not mow the grass until they go dormant.
Site Prefers moist, rich soil in light shade or spring sun.
Culture Spring beauty grows from a small, tuberlike corm that is easily divided after flowering. It also self-sows. Be careful not to disturb the dormant clumps in summer. Plants can take considerable drought in summer, but need consistent soil moisture in spring and fall.
Good Companions Plant spring beauty with other ephemerals such as trout lilies, cut-leaved toothwort, and Virginia bluebells, along with persistent plantings such as wild ginger, ferns, and baneberries. Mix it with spring bulbs such as snowdrops, species crocus, and glory-of-the-snow under flowering shrubs and trees.
Other Species *C. caroliniana* (Carolina spring beauty) is native in deciduous and coniferous woods in the northern half of Michigan. It has shorter, broader leaf blades and fewer leaves and flowers, which are white to pale pink. It spreads slower than Virginia spring beauty but will eventually form a dense carpet. Zone 3.

Clintonia borealis

Clintonia borealis
Bluebead lily
Zone 2

Native Habitat Rich, acidic, mixed coniferous woods, in the northern two-thirds of Michigan.

Height 6 to 15 inches

Description The steel blue berries that adorn this plant in late summer are more distinctive than its loose cluster of greenish yellow, nodding, bell-shaped flowers that appear in late May to mid-June. The shiny, oblong basal leaves are 5 to 8 inches long and resemble flattened tulip leaves.

Landscape Use Bluebead lily's bold texture brings interest to shade or woodland gardens. Plant it in masses as a groundcover, or mix scattered clumps with other finer-textured plants. Children should be discouraged from eating the mildly poisonous berries.

Site Moist, high-humus soil in partial to deep shade.

Culture Bluebead lily is somewhat difficult to grow in cultivated settings. It requires cool, shady, moist sites and prefers temperatures below 75 degrees.

Good Companions Grow bluebead lily with other northern wildflowers such as twinflower (*Linnaea borealis*), starflower (*Trientalis borealis*), trilliums, and ferns.

Coreopsis tripteris

Coreopsis palmata

Coreopsis lanceolata
Sand coreopsis, tickseed
Zone 3

Native Habitat Sand dunes, open grasslands, and open woodlands, mainly along Lake Michigan but also farther inland.

Height 1 to 2 feet

Description Plants have thick clumps of mostly basal leaves and smaller stem leaves. Golden yellow, daisylike flowers with ragged petals and yellow centers appear in early summer.

Landscape Use Sand coreopsis is a tough, vigorous plant often found in wildflower seed mixtures. It is a good choice for naturalizing, dune restoration, and wild gardens. It attracts butterflies.

Site Average sandy or loamy, well-drained soil in full sun or light shade.

Culture Sand coreopsis is a tough, low-maintenance plant. Plants will reseed, often prolifically.

Good Companions Plant sand coreopsis with other summer-blooming grassland plants such as butterfly weed, wild bergamot, flowering spurge, and purple prairie clover.

Cultivars and Other Species 'Sterntaler' is a long-flowering selection with red-brown bicolored flowers.

C. palmata (bird's-foot coreopsis) is native to dry prairies in the far southwestern corner of Michigan. It grows 2 to 3 feet tall and flowers from June through August. Mature plants tolerate summer drought. Plants may flop over if the soil is too rich. Regular deadheading will prolong flowering. It spreads rapidly by underground rhizomes to form a dense mat. It is a good choice for stabilizing dry, sunny slopes, but it is probably too aggressive for most landscape situations. Grow it in moist or dry soils in full sun or light shade. It is on Michigan's threatened species list. Zone 4.

C. tripteris (tall coreopsis) is native on dry to wet prairies and in oak woodlands in the southern part of Michigan. It grows 3 to 6 feet tall and starts blooming in mid- to late summer and continues into late fall. Use it at the back of a large border or with tall grasses in a prairie garden. It is another prolific reseeder. Zone 3.

Cornus canadensis
Bunchberry
Zone I

Native Habitat Moist, acidic wood-lands and bogs throughout most of Michigan.

Height 4 to 8 inches

Description Bunchberry has a whorl of satiny, oval, evergreen leaves 2 to 3 inches long. What appears to be a single flower atop the stem is actually a cluster of small, greenish yellow flowers surrounded by four creamy white, petal-like bracts, blooming from late May into June. Clusters of bright orange-red berries appear in summer. This subshrub grows from creeping, wiry stems to form extensive colonies.

Landscape Use Bunchberry makes an effective groundcover under acid-loving plants such as azaleas. The showy flowers and berries brighten shady recesses in wild gardens. Plant it in colonies for best effect.

Site Requires moist, acidic, high-humus soil in light shade.

C. canadensis fruits

Culture If necessary, acidify soil to a pH of 4 to 5 before planting, and work in ample organic matter. Conifer needles are a good acidic mulch. Soil should be constantly moist but not waterlogged. It will not tolerate summer heat or drought. It is difficult to keep as a garden plant under less-than-optimum conditions.

Good Companions Plant bunchberry with other northern wildflowers and shrubs such as wintergreen, starflower, Canada mayflower, bluebead lily, low-bush blueberry, leather leaf, and ferns.

Cornus canadensis

Cypripedium calceolus var. pubescens
Large yellow lady's slipper
Zone 3

Native Habitat Almost any moist soil, from shaded bogs to moist woods, throughout most of Michigan.

Height 12 to 24 inches

Description Yellow lady's slipper has leafy stems bearing one or two flowers, each consisting of a pale yellow pouch 2 inches long flanked by two petals and two greenish brown, twisted sepals. It blooms in May. Leaves are 6 to 8 inches long and have parallel veins and smooth margins.

Landscape Use This showy plant should be used as a specimen or massed in moist shade or woodland gardens in a spot where it can be enjoyed while in bloom. It is long lived and resents transplanting, so choose a site carefully.

Site Wet, high-humus soil in light shade.

Culture Yellow lady's slipper is the easiest native orchid to grow. Prepare the soil well before planting it 12 inches apart in groups of three or randomly. Maintain a 1- to 2-inch mulch layer to keep the soil moist. It will form large clumps that can be carefully divided in spring. Exercise caution when obtaining plants: all lady's slipper are difficult to propagate, and many commercially available plants were probably collected in the wild.

Good Companions Grow this showy plant with background plants that will complement rather than compete with it, such as low-growing ferns and small-flowered wildflowers such as wood anemone.

Variety Var. *parviflorum* (small yellow lady's slipper) is native to bogs and low woods in the southern half of the

Cypripedium calceolus var. pubescens

Lower Peninsula. It grows 10 to 14 inches tall and has two to four 1 1/2-inch flowers per spike. It blooms a week or two later than the large yellow lady's slipper, and its lip is a darker yellow. Zone 3.

Dalea purpurea

Dalea purpurea [*Petalostemum purpureum*]
Purple prairie clover
Zone 3

Native Habitat Occasionally found on dry prairies and savannas in the southern part of Michigan. It is believed that all of Michigan's native populations of purple prairie clover have been extirpated.

Height 2 to 3 feet

Description Purple prairie clover has unique, densely packed, $1/2$- to 2-inch, rose-purple to crimson flowers in June and July. The flowers bloom in a ring around the flower head, starting at the bottom and working up to the top. The foliage is pinnate and finely textured. Seed heads are attractive in winter.

Landscape Use This prairie denizen is attractive to bees and butterflies. Plant it in groups of three to five in perennial beds, prairie gardens, and xeriscaped beds. A single plant can be used as an accent in rock gardens.

Site Moist to dry soils in full sun.

Culture Purple prairie clover is a tough, low-maintenance garden plant. It fixes soil nitrogen so it doesn't need additional fertilizer. You may need to use an inoculant to help plants become established in some soils. Mature plants tolerate summer drought, and clumps seldom need dividing. Allow seed heads to remain for winter interest.

Good Companions Plant purple prairie clover with other summer-blooming flowers, such as monarda, leadplant, butterfly weed, coreopsis, mountain mint, ornamental onions, and with smaller grasses such as little bluestem and prairie dropseed.

Dentaria laciniata

Dentaria laciniata [*Cardamine concatenata*]
Cut-leaved toothwort
Zone 3

Native Habitat Moist, deciduous woods, bottomlands, and stream banks throughout the state but mainly in the south.

Height 4 to 12 inches

Description Drooping, white to pink flowers appear in loose terminal clusters from April to June. Midway up the stem is a whorl of three deeply divided, toothed leaves.

Landscape Use This beautiful plant will eventually form large colonies that weave through other plants in woodland gardens, but it is not as vigorous in spreading as some other ephemerals.

Site Moist, high-humus soil; tolerates fairly dense shade and drier soils in summer, but needs some direct sun in spring.

Culture Weed out aggressive neighbors before planting and as they appear. Plants go dormant in early summer but may appear again in fall.

Good Companions Plant cut-leaved toothwort with other spring wildflowers such as Virginia bluebells, Dutchman's breeches, false rue anemone, and spring beauties. Be sure to include some persistent plants such as ferns and wild ginger to fill the void when these ephemerals go dormant.

Other Species *D. diphylla* (two-leaved toothwort) is native in moist woodlands throughout Michigan. It grows 4 to 6 inches tall, has a similar flower, and has broader, fatter leaves that are opposite on the flower stem. It fills in faster than cut-leaved toothwort. Zone 3.

Desmodium canadense
Canada tick trefoil
Zone 3

Native Habitat Dry and moist soils in grasslands and wood edges, mainly in the southern half of Michigan but sometimes also farther north.

Height 2 to 4 feet

Description This well-branched, bushy plant has trefoil-shaped leaves and elongated terminal clusters of bright purple, pea-like flowers. It blooms from July to early September.

Landscape Use Plant Canada tick trefoil in prairie gardens or at the back of perennial borders, keeping in mind its somewhat aggressive nature. The seeds are eaten by a variety of birds and other wildlife.

Site Does well in clay soil, but will grow in any moderately rich, well-drained or slightly damp soil; needs sun to light shade.

Culture Canada tick trefoil may be difficult to establish because of its deep taproot, but it is drought tolerant once established. A member of the legume family, it improves the soil by adding nitrogen. Plant it with a commercial soil inoculant to provide the root nodules with the necessary nitrogen-fixing bacteria. It can become large and aggressive, so plant it where there is growing room.

Good Companions Combine Canada tick trefoil with other summer-blooming prairie natives such as leadplant, bird's-foot coreopsis, butterfly weed, Culver's root, and bottle gentian.

Desmodium canadense

Dicentra cucullaria
Dutchman's breeches
Zone 3

Native Habitat Rich deciduous woods throughout Michigan.

Height 6 to 12 inches

Description Dutchman's breeches has delicate, fernlike, blue-green basal foliage and unique blooms that resemble white pantaloons hanging upside down along arched stems. Flowers are white with traces of yellow. Blooms first appear in mid- to late April and last for about two weeks. Plants go dormant in mid- to late May.

Landscape Use Use this dainty ephemeral in woodland or shade gardens. In the wild, it is often found growing tucked into root flares of large trees; it tolerates the shallow soil found around mature tree roots because plants go dormant before it becomes too dry.

Site Needs spring sun and moist soil to bloom well, but can grow in shade and dry soil once plants are dormant.

Culture Dutchman's breeches grows from tuberous rhizomes. You may need to cover dormant plants with hardware cloth to discourage rodents from stealing the tubers. Colonies often form a dense carpet of foliage punctuated by clusters of flowers. Plants disappear soon after flowering. Self-sown seedlings will appear.

Good Companions Plant Dutchman's breeches with other spring ephemerals as well as plants that will fill in blank spots, such as ferns and wild ginger.

Other Species *D. canadensis* (squirrel corn) occurs naturally in moist deciduous forests in all but the far northwestern part of Michigan. It has white heart-shaped flowers that are 1/2 to 3/4 inch long, which dangle from 6- to 12-inch stems above compound, finely cut foliage that resembles Dutchman's breeches. It blooms from mid-April to June, about a week later than Dutchman's breeches. Plant it in moist, high-humus soil in direct or filtered spring sun. Zone 4.

Dicentra cucullaria

Dodecatheon meadia

Dodecatheon meadia
Shooting star
Zone 4

Native Habitat Fertile, moist woods and prairies in the far southwestern and southeastern corners of Michigan, plus one location in Menominee County.

Height 10 to 20 inches

Description The flowers have delicate, white to pink, strongly reflexed petals surrounding a yellow-and-red cone-like center, giving the appearance of shooting stars. The lush, green, basal foliage has reddish tints at the base.

Plants bloom for a long time, from late April to June.

Landscape Use Shooting star has somewhat of a split personality, being both a prairie and a woodland flower. A spring bloomer, it's at its best when most other prairie flowers are just appearing. Showcase this interesting plant along walkways, in rock gardens, or in perennial borders. It can also be grown in partial-shade areas of woodland or shade gardens. Plant it in groups of at least three, and do not crowd it with other species.

Site Any good soil, in sun or light shade, but does best in rich garden soil. Requires direct sun in spring, but shade is okay in summer.

Culture The ideal soil pH is 6 to 7; add limestone before planting if necessary. Plants need moisture while blooming but are drought tolerant after that. Plants develop slowly and take several years to bloom from seeds. Fall transplanting is recommended, but planting in early spring is also fine. The basal rosette of leaves disappears after flowering, by early August, to make way for summer- and fall-blooming flowers. Shooting star is on Michigan's endangered species list; be sure to purchase only nursery-propagated plants.

Good Companions In shadier spots, plant shooting star with Canada columbine, hostas, ferns, and primroses. In sunnier sites and prairie gardens, it combines nicely with golden alexanders, prairie smoke, prairie phlox, wild geranium, and violets.

Cultivars 'Album' is a white selection. 'Goliath' is several inches taller than the species and has large, lavender-rose blooms.

Echinacea purpurea

Echinacea purpurea
Purple coneflower
Zone 3

Native Habitat Once found in prairies in the southwestern corner of Michigan. It is believed that there are no longer any native occurrences of purple coneflower in Michigan, and it is considered extirpated.

Height 2 to 4 feet

Description Purple coneflower is a branching perennial with coarse leaves. The stems are topped with numerous 4- to 6-inch daisylike flowers. These flowers have flat or drooping petals that are rose-pink to red-violet with orange centers. Purple coneflower blooms for a long time starting in midsummer and continuing into fall.

Landscape Use Purple coneflower is a very adaptable garden plant. It is a good addition to prairie gardens and perennial borders. The flowers are attractive to butterflies, and goldfinches enjoy the seeds, which remain on plants and are attractive into winter.

Site Average to rich soil in full sun or light shade.

Culture Plants grow from fibrous taproots. Divide only when you have to, since divisions usually don't produce as many flowers. Plants are drought tolerant once established. Self-sown seedlings will appear.

Good Companions In prairie gardens, plant it in clumps near other summer-blooming prairie flowers, such as black-eyed Susan, monarda, coreopsis, compass plant, blazing stars, butterfly weed, and tall bellflower, as well as native grasses. In perennial borders, combine it with phloxes, yarrows, and delphiniums.

Cultivars Many selections of purple coneflower have been made, some of which are quite removed from the original beauty of this plant. 'Bright Star' has mostly flat to slightly drooping flowers. 'Crimson Star' has deeper-colored flat flowers. 'White Lustre' has bright white flowers. Zone 3.

Eryngium yuccifolium
Rattlesnake master
Zone 4

Native Habitat Mesic to wet grass-lands in the far southwestern corner of Michigan.

Height 2 to 3 feet

Description Rattlesnake master has clusters of small, greenish white, fra-grant flowers in summer. They are tightly packed among pointed bracts to form globular flower heads about 3/4inch wide in branched clusters atop the stems. The blue-green leaves are large and narrow and have pointed teeth and clasping bases. Seed heads turn brown and remain on the plant for winter interest.

Landscape Use Rattlesnake master works well in sunny borders or in prairie gardens. The distinctive yucca-like leaves add interest when plants are not in flower. It can be used in a formal setting as an accent plant.

Site Prefers average to rich, moist but well-drained soil in full sun. Plants will grow in gravel and in sand in full sun.

Culture Add sand or gravel to improve soil drainage if necessary. Young leaves may need protection from rabbits and deer in spring. The deep taproot resents disturbance, so set out young plants in their permanent locations. Plants seldom need division. Rattlesnake master is on Michigan's threatened species list, so buy only nursery-propagated plants.

Good Companions Combine bold rattlesnake master with airy clusters of flowering spurge or sea lavender (*Limonium latifolium*). The flowers

Eryngium yuccifolium

look nice with blazing stars, Culver's root, Michigan lily, black-eyed Susan, coneflowers, goldenrods, autumn sneezeweed, asters, and grasses.

Erythronium americanum
Yellow trout lily
Zone 3

Native Habitat Moist, rich deciduous woods throughout most of Michigan.

Height 4 to 10 inches

Description Yellow trout lily has a pair of maroon-mottled green leaves 3 to 8 inches long, narrowly oval with smooth margins. The leaves clasp the base of a stem bearing a single yellow flower with three petals and three sepals, all reflexed. Plants grow from bulblike corms and bloom in April and early May. They form large mats of foliage on the forest floor but don't always produce a lot of flowers.

Landscape Use This ephemeral is one of the earliest wildflowers to bloom. Plant it in woodland gardens, where the interesting foliage makes an attrac-tive spring groundcover.

Site Likes lots of spring sunlight and a moist, rich soil. Once plants go dor-mant, they can be in shade.

Culture Add generous amounts of humus to the soil before planting. Plants may take five or six years before they flower. They self-sow and spread by stolons, eventually forming large drifts. Plants go dormant right after flowering; be careful not to dig into clumps in summer or fall.

Good Companions Interplant yellow trout lily with minor spring bulbs such as purple *Scilla siberica* (Siberian squill) and other spring ephemerals such as Dutchman's breeches, spring beauty, and bloodroot. Include ferns and foliage plants such as wild ginger, pul-monarias, and hostas to fill in after the plants go dormant.

Other Species *E. albidum* (white trout lily) is found in low, deciduous woods mainly in the southern half of the Lower Peninsula. The petals are white or dull pale-violet-tinged outside and yellow-tinged inside; the leaves are a slightly lighter greenish gray. Petals are strongly recurved. It flowers more pro-fusely in cultivation than yellow trout lily. Grow it in moist, rich, neutral soil in woodland or shade gardens. Zone 3.

Erythronium americanum

Erythronium albidum

Eupatorium purpureum
Sweet Joe-pye weed, purple Joe-pye weed
Zone 3

Native Habitat Wet slopes, low prairies, and woodland edges, mainly in the southern half of the Lower Peninsula.

Height 3 to 6 feet

Description Sweet Joe-pye weed has mounded or domed clusters of sweet-scented, pale rose or smoky lavender flowers. The leaves appear in whorls around the stems, which are often a deep purple color. Seed heads are attractive in winter.

Landscape Use Use sweet Joe-pye weed in prairie gardens, perennial beds, and mixed borders. It thrives at the edges of water gardens or in bog gardens. Butterflies are attracted to the flowers.

Site Prefers moist, average to rich soil in full sun or light shade, but tolerates drier conditions.

Culture Sweet Joe-pye weed is a good garden plant and easy to grow once established. New plants take at least two seasons to reach full size. It will perform well in dry situations, but best growth is in moist soil. Plants are late to emerge in spring but grow quickly after they are up. Several insects eat the leaves, which can leave plants looking a little rough in midsummer, but the damage is not life threatening. Divide oversized clumps in spring or fall. Sweet Joe-pye weed reseeds. Plants too close together may suffer from powdery mildew.

Good Companions Many plants look nice with a backdrop of Joe-pye weeds, including autumn sneezeweed, boltonia, coneflowers, black-eyed Susans, and daisies. In less formal situations, plant them with asters, wild bergamot, goldenrods, and grasses.

Other Species and Cultivars

E. maculatum (spotted Joe-pye weed) is native to wet prairies and other moist-soil areas throughout Michigan. It has flat-topped, 4- to 5-inch clusters of feathery rose-purple flower heads on top of purple or purple-spotted stems 24 to 72 inches tall. It blooms from late July to September in wet, average soil in full sun. Use it in wet prairies or naturalized plantings. 'Gateway' grows 6 feet tall or more and has pale mauve flowers in large clusters. It has sturdier, richly colored stems. 'Atropurpureum' is more compact, up to 5 or 6 feet tall, and has deep purple stems, dark leaves, and purple, sweet-scented flowers. Both cultivars are suitable for garden use. Zone 3.

E. perfoliatum (common boneset) is native to moist prairies and swamp margins throughout Michigan. It grows 2 to 4 feet tall and has short, hairy stems that support flat-topped clusters of off-white flower heads in mid- to late summer. Leaves have a wrinkled texture, and bases are fused so the stem appears to be pierced by a single long leaf. It requires consistently moist or wet soil in full sun. Use it in wet prairies or bog gardens, where it attracts bees and butterflies. Zone 3

E. rugosum (white snakeroot) is native to open woods scattered throughout most of Michigan. It grows 3 to 4 feet tall and has white flowers in small clusters in late summer. The seed heads are showy. It can tolerate drier soil in shaded woodland gardens but doesn't like full shade. Some references have started classifying it as *Ageratina altissima*. Zone 3. 'Chocolate' has dark chocolate-brown leaves and shiny purple stems, which are a great contrast with the clusters of domed white flowers in fall. It grows 2 to 4 feet tall. The silver seed heads offer fall and winter interest. Grow it with golden-leaved hostas for color contrast. Zone 4.

Eupatorium purpureum

Eupatorium perfoliatum

Eupatorium rugosum

Euphorbia corollata
Flowering spurge
Zone 3

Native Habitat Open woods, savannas, and prairies, mainly in the southern half of the Lower Peninsula.

Height 2 to 4 feet

Description Flowering spurge has clusters of small white flowers and pure white bracts that give it the look of a sturdy baby's breath. It blooms from June into September. The creeping slender stems have sparse pale green leaves, and plants bleed milky sap when picked or damaged. The foliage turns an attractive orange-gold color in fall.

Landscape Use The airy flower heads are easy to use in gardens, but its aggressive nature makes flowering spurge best suited to large sunny borders or naturalized plantings, where it weaves and helps tie plantings together. Because it grows well on dry, clay hillsides and roadsides where few other plants thrive, it's often used for erosion control and restoration projects.

Site Poor to average, well-drained soil in full sun or partial shade.

Culture This long-lived perennial tolerates drought and poor soil and needs little care once established. Plants grow from creeping rhizomes to form dense stands. Mature plants prefer to be left alone, but clumps can be divided as needed to control spread or for propagating. The white latex that oozes from cut stems can irritate skin.

Good Companions Good prairie companions include butterfly weed, blazing stars, coneflowers, wild bergamot, oxeye, Joe-pye weeds, goldenrods, and asters. In dry-soil gardens, plant it with sea hollies (*Eryngium*), sages, and ornamental grasses.

Euphorbia corollata

Filipendula rubra
Queen-of-the-prairie
Zone 3

Native Habitat Wet prairies and shorelines, widely scattered in the western half of the Lower Peninsula.

Height 3 to 7 feet

Description Queen-of-the-prairie is a stately plant with zigzag stems of large, deeply lobed leaves. The pink cotton-candy flowers, which resemble astilbes, appear at the top of plants in early to midsummer.

Landscape Use Although lovely, queen-of-the-prairie is difficult to use in perennial borders unless it is restricted in some way. It is great for massing in low areas, where it is a magnificent sight in flower, and for naturalizing in low areas along streams.

Site Fertile, evenly moist, neutral soil in full sun to partial shade.

Culture The rhizomes of this perennial spread far, and it will form a sizable stand in moist, fertile soils. Plants die back somewhat after flowering, so plan accordingly if it's used in a perennial border. It will not do well in hot, dry conditions. It is on Michigan's threatened species list because of its small natural range in the state.

Good Companions Site queen-of-the-prairie with other tall-growing moisture lovers such as Joe-pye weeds, autumn sneezeweed, boltonia, and possibly red-flowered cardinal flower.

Cultivars 'Venusta' is a popular selection with showy pink flowers that fade to light pink in fall.

Filipendula rubra

Fragaria virginiana

Fragaria virginiana
Wild strawberry
Zone 2

Native Habitat A wide variety of dry to moist open-woodland habitats throughout Michigan.

Height 3 to 6 inches

Description Wild strawberry is a delicate version of its cultivated relative. It has 1-inch-wide white flowers that peek out between deep green, three-part leaves in May, followed by small, bright red, juicy fruits that grow up to 3/4 inch in size.

Landscape Use The strawberries are edible and very tasty—if you can get to them before the wildlife. The 6-inch plants spread by runners, and a mass planting makes an interesting, easily cared for groundcover. It can also be grown in a rock wall or a rock garden.

Site Average to dry soil in part to full sun.

Culture Wild strawberry is very easy to grow and adaptable to a wide variety of conditions. If you want to harvest the edible fruits, you'll need to provide some type of protection from birds and other wildlife.

Good Companions Wild strawberry is usually grown alone as a groundcover.

Other Species *F. vesca* (woodland strawberry) is native in rich woods scattered throughout Michigan. It is very similar to wild strawberry, but is usually smaller, both in overall size and in flower size. 'Lipstick' has hot pink flowers. Zone 2.

Fragaria vesca 'Lipstick'

Gaultheria procumbens
Wintergreen
Zone 3

Gaultheria procumbens

Native Habitat Dry or moist woods, outcroppings, and forested bogs throughout Michigan.

Height 2 to 6 inches

Description Wintergreen has white, nodding, bell-shaped flowers that grow singly or in groups of two or three from the leaf axils of the creeping woody stem. The flowers turn to showy, bright red berries. Flowers bloom from April to May and the red fruits persist among leaves all winter and into spring. The leaves are dark green, shiny, and evergreen.

Landscape Use This low-growing plant has trailing woody stems that form broad, irregular colonies. It is a good groundcover under acid-loving shrubs such as azaleas. The bright red berries and evergreen foliage offer winter interest and can even brighten early spring gardens if birds do not eat the fruits.

Site Tolerates a wide range of conditions, but requires acidic soil with moderate humus content in partial shade.

Culture Acidify soil before planting, if necessary. Plants are slow to establish. Water well the first year. Divide rhizomes in spring to increase the population.

Good Companions Include wintergreen in northern coniferous garden habitats, where it looks nice with hepaticas, Canada mayflower, bunchberry, and wild ginger.

Other Species *G. hispidula* (creeping snowberry) grows in bogs, in damp coniferous woods, and on mossy logs mainly in the northern half of Michigan. It has intermittent, tiny white flowers along short, trailing stems that form a delicate mat. Stems grow 3 to 12 inches long. It blooms from May to June and has snow white berries later in the season. It needs a moist, rich, acidic soil in full shade and can be used as groundcover for moist, shady sites. Zone 3.

Gentiana andrewsii
Bottle gentian
Zone 3

Native Habitat Moist open woods, wet prairies, and marshes throughout most of Michigan.

Height 1 to 3 feet

Description Bottle gentian has deep blue, 1-inch, bottle-shaped flowers crowded into a terminal cluster, blooming from August to October. Other flowers may cluster in the axils of the opposite leaves below. Since the blossoms never open, pollinating insects must burrow through the petals. Plants are erect to sprawling and have glossy, oval, 4-inch leaves.

Landscape Use Bottle gentian's rich indigo-blue color is a welcome sight in autumn prairie gardens, when most plants are orange or yellow. It adapts well to the rich soil of perennial borders and can be grown in wet meadows and along ponds.

Site Prefers a sandy loam high in organic matter that stays moist throughout the growing season. Tolerates sun or partial shade; afternoon shade from summer sun is beneficial.

Culture Bottle gentian is easy to grow and long lived, requiring little care once established. Make sure the soil is high in organic matter, and mulch plants to conserve soil moisture. Plants seldom need dividing.

Good Companions Bottle gentian is a great companion for any of the fall prairie plants, including New England aster, obedient plant, and blazing stars. In a perennial border, use it with other moisture-loving plants such as turtlehead, ferns, and lobelias.

Other Species *G. flavida* [*G. alba*] (yellowish gentian) is native to dry-to-moist prairies and open woods in only a few locations in southern Michigan. It has creamy white flowers over semi-glossy, medium green to yellow-green leaves. Plants bloom in late summer. Plants are more upright than *G. andrewsii*, reaching a height of 2 feet or more. Use it in moist prairie plantings or mixed borders. It is a long-lived plant that grows into a good-sized clump over time. It is believed to be nearly extirpated in Michigan and is on the state's endangered species list. Zone 3.

Gentianopsis crinita (greater fringed gentian) is native to moist or wet open sites throughout most of the Lower Peninsula. This close relative (it is sometimes listed as *Gentiana crinita*)

Gentiana andrewsii

Gentiana flavida

has stunning, upward-facing, fringed flowers of satiny blue-violet. It grows 1 to 3 feet tall and is one of the few gentians to have open flowers. This biennial doesn't reliably reseed and must be sown each year. It is a challenge to grow, but is rewarding when successful. Zone 4.

Geranium maculatum
Wild geranium
Zone 3

Native Habitat Usually moist deciduous woods, mainly in the southern half of the Lower Peninsula.

Height 12 to 24 inches

Description Wild geranium has loose clusters of five-petaled, 1-inch-wide flowers rising above pairs of grayish green leaves, each with three to five distinct palmate lobes and coarse teeth. Flowers appear from early May into June and range from pale to deep magenta-pink to light purple. The fruits that appear after flowering resemble a crane's bill. Foliage turns a lovely red color in fall.

Landscape Use Wild geranium is easily adapted to culture. Plant it in drifts in woodland gardens. In perennial borders, it can grow in partial sun.

Site Prefers moist, rich soils in partial sun to light shade, but tolerates drier conditions.

Culture Wild geranium is easy to grow and transplant. Divide the slow-creeping rhizomes in early spring or early fall. Shelter plants from strong winds.

Good Companions Combine wild geraniums with other woodland denizens such as golden alexanders, blue phlox, Canada columbine, and ferns.

Cultivars 'Album' and 'Hazel Gallagher' are white-flowered cultivars.

Geranium maculatum

Native Habitat Dry-soil prairies and savannas in the east-central part of the Lower Peninsula.

Height 6 to 16 inches

Description Prairie smoke has pink- or rose-colored nodding flowers that look like they never completely open. They begin blooming in late April and continue well into summer, giving rise to showy, mauve seed heads that resemble plumes of smoke. The fern-like, light blue-green leaves are covered with soft hairs.

Landscape Use Prairie smoke is a good landscape plant, offering interest throughout the growing season. Use it in prairie gardens, perennial borders, and rock gardens. It eventually forms a dense groundcover. The seed heads attract goldfinches and can be dried for flower arrangements.

Site Dry, average, well-drained soil in full sun to light shade.

Culture Prairie smoke is a tough plant that withstands bitter cold, high heat, and drought. Rhizomes should be divided every third or fourth year to alleviate overcrowding. It is on Michigan's threatened species list, so purchase only nursery-propagated plants.

Geum triflorum
Prairie smoke
Zone 2

Geum triflorum

Good Companions In prairie gardens, combine it with butterfly weed, Canada columbine, prairie phlox, and bird's-foot violet. In perennial borders or rock gardens, it combines nicely with spring bulbs and low-growing perennials such as *Phlox stolonifera* (creeping phlox), perennial geraniums, and sedums.

Other Species *G. rivale* (purple avens) is native to bogs, swamps, and low woods throughout most of Michigan. It grows up to 2 feet tall and has purple, bell-like flowers that turn to plumes of seeds. It is not as showy as prairie smoke, but its interesting blooms are a nice addition to moist woodland gardens. Zone 2.

Helenium autumnale 'Butterpat'

Native Habitat Low woods, prairies, and marshes throughout most of Michigan.

Height 3 to 5 feet

Description Sneezeweed has abundant golden yellow, daisylike flowers 1 to 2 inches wide. They bloom from July through September. The bright

Helenium autumnale
Sneezeweed
Zone 3

green leaves are lance-shaped with toothed edges.

Landscape Use Sneezeweed provides nice late-summer color in perennial borders or prairie gardens. It does best in low, moist areas, such as in bogs or near streams, but it can be grown in many landscape situations.

Site Prefers a dampish spot in gardens, perhaps in a slight depression that can be given a good soaking during dry periods. Responds well to fertile soil. It grows in full sun to light shade.

Culture Although native to moist sites, sneezeweed adapts readily to most garden soils, especially if there is a low spot. Plants in moist, rich soil are quite robust, while those grown in drier soils are shorter and less vigorous.

Taller plants may need some sort of support to keep from flopping over. Mulch garden plants and give them extra water during dry times, especially in midsummer, to encourage good flowering. Prune plants in late May to keep them smaller and more compact. Plants will bloom better if they are divided every three or four years.

Good Companions Plant sneezeweed near ponds with irises, ferns, New England aster, and ironweed. In borders, use it with phloxes, asters, coreopsis, and goldenrods.

Cultivars Several cultivars are available, but they are not all easy to locate. 'Butterpat' grows to only 4 feet and has bright yellow flowers. 'Moerheim Beauty' has bronze-red blossoms. Zone 3.

Helianthus occidentalis
Western sunflower
Zone 4

Native Habitat Sandy savannas and barrens throughout the Lower Peninsula.

Height 2 to 4 feet

Description Large, long-stalked, ovate to oblong-lanceolate basal leaves, each up to 8 inches long, form a 4- to 8-inch-tall foliage clump. The flowers are up to 2 inches in diameter and have orange-yellow rays and yellow disks; they appear on stiff, almost naked flower stems that typically rise to a height of 2 to 3 feet (less frequently to 4 feet). Western sunflower blooms from midsummer to fall.

Landscape Use Western sunflower is one of the shortest native sunflowers. Use it in sunny borders or in prairie gardens. It attracts butterflies and goldfinches, and other birds eat the seeds. It is also a good choice for holding dry soils and preventing erosion.

Site Any well-drained soil in full sun; tolerates dry soil and drought.

Culture Western sunflower spreads over time by creeping rhizomes to form large colonies. Divide plants every three to four years to control invasiveness and to maintain plant vigor. Control it in smaller gardens by circling the clump in spring with a sharp spade, then pulling out any stems that travel too far afield.

Good Companions Plant western sunflower with other summer bloomers such as blazing stars, butterfly weed, prairie phlox, monarda, white wild indigo, garden lilies, daylilies, veronicas (*Veronica* species), asters, and grasses.

Other Species *H. divaricatus* (woodland sunflower) is native to dry open woods throughout the Lower Peninsula. It prefers moist to moderately dry soil in sun to light shade. It grows 2 to 4 feet tall and has yellow flowers in summer. It is an aggressive spreader for natural areas. Zone 3.

H. giganteus (tall sunflower) is native in moist soils in grasslands and open woodlands. It grows 6 to 10 feet tall, and its loose, branching panicles of deep yellow flowers bloom in fall. These terminal panicles of smaller blooms give the plants a fine texture despite their large size. Plants may need staking in garden situations. 'Sheila's Sunshine' has pastel yellow flowers. Zone 3.

H. mollis (downy sunflower) is rare in Michigan; native to dry prairies in the southern part of the state, it is on the state's threatened species list. It is a good choice for garden use, growing 3 to 6 feet tall; it has short rhizomes and a branching, bushy growth habit. It has yellow flowers in late summer and tolerates some drought and shade. Zone 4.

H. strumosus (pale-leaved sunflower) is native to a wide range of dry-soil habitats in the southern part of Michigan. It grows 3 to 5 feet tall and is somewhat shade tolerant, doing best when it receives a few hours of direct sunlight. Plant it in woodlands and woodland openings, where the large yellow flowers will add color from late summer into early autumn. Zone 4.

Helianthus occidentalis

Helianthus divaricatus

Helianthus strumosus

Heliopsis helianthoides 'Summer Sun'

Heliopsis helianthoides var. *scabra*

Heliopsis helianthoides
Oxeye
Zone 3

Native Habitat Woodland edges, open woods, and prairies throughout most of Michigan.

Height 3 to 5 feet

Description Oxeye is a rather coarse plant with large, rough, medium green foliage. It's redeemed by its abundance of sunny yellow, sunflower-like flowers that appear from June into September.

Landscape Use Oxeye is an excellent landscape plant, providing midsummer color in prairie gardens and perennial borders.

Site Moist or dry, average to rich soil in full sun or light shade.

Culture Oxeye adapts readily to garden culture. It is easy to grow from seed, often flowering the first summer if started indoors in winter. Plants require watering during dry periods to prevent wilting. Plants may get floppy; pinch them back in late May to reduce overall height. The named cultivars are less floppy. Oxeye will self-seed but seedlings are easily weeded out. It is occasionally attacked by aphids and powdery mildew.

Good Companions Plant oxeye with other summer bloomers such as blazing stars, butterfly weed, prairie phlox, monarda, white wild indigo, garden lilies, daylilies, veronicas (*Veronica* species), asters, and grasses.

Cultivars Several cultivars are available. 'Summer Sun' is the most popular and easiest to locate. It is more compact, growing to about 3 feet, and has large flowers. 'Prairie Sunset' is a newer introduction, having bright yellow flowers that have contrasting orange-red centers. Plants grow up to 6 feet tall and have attractive purplish stems and purple-veined leaves. Zone 4.

Hepatica americana
Round-lobed hepatica
Zone 3

Native Habitat Upland deciduous and coniferous woodlands throughout most of Michigan.

Height 4 to 6 inches

Description Round-lobed hepatica is one of the earliest flowers of spring, beginning its show in early April and continuing with scattered bloom into May. It has fuzzy, leafless stalks bearing pink, lavender, blue, or white flowers, each about 1 inch wide. Basal leaves are leathery and wine-colored on the underside and have three distinct rounded lobes. They keep plants interesting after flowers fade.

Landscape Use Plant hepaticas where you can enjoy their early bloom. A backdrop of rocks or a large tree trunk will help set off the early flowers. Plants will multiply to carpet the ground in woodland gardens. Hepaticas are an attractive addition to shaded rock gardens.

Site Moist, humus-rich soil in light to full shade.

Culture Plants self-sow and clumps get bigger every year, but never to the point of being invasive. Keep them away from larger, more-aggressive species that can overtake them. Round-lobed hepatica responds well to light fertilization in spring and an occasional application of limestone.

Good Companions Plant hepaticas with other woodland plants such as wild ginger, bloodroot, trillium, rue anemone, Dutchman's breeches, and spring beauties. They bloom at the same time as early species crocus, snowdrops, *Scilla siberica* (Siberian squill), and *Puschkinia* (striped squill) and are nice companions for these minor bulbs.

Other Species *H. acutiloba* (sharp-lobed hepatica) is native to rich deciduous maple-beech woods mainly in the Lower Peninsula. It grows 3 to 6 inches tall and produces dainty white or bluish flowers in early April. The almost evergreen leaves have three sharp-pointed lobes. It likes a more acidic soil than *H. americana*, preferring a soil acidifier to an application of limestone, but otherwise is similar in culture and use. Zone 3.

Heuchera americana
Alumroot, coral bells
Zone 4

Native Habitat Deciduous woods in southern Michigan.

Height 1 to 2 feet

Description Alumroot is an open, mounding plant. It has mottled silvery green, 3- to 4-inch, heart-shaped leaves with scalloped edges. Long slender stalks rise above the mounds and end in airy sprays of tiny cream-colored flowers. Leaves range from red to purple in fall.

Landscape Use Plant alumroot where you can enjoy the beautiful foliage, such as near the front of borders or along paths. It is well behaved and does well in a wide variety of landscape situations, including perennial borders, shade gardens, and rock gardens.

Site Does best in moist, rich, well-drained soil in partial sun. Can take full sun or partial shade, but leaves may bleach out in too much sun, and foliage color is paler in shade.

Culture Alumroot benefits from a spring application of compost or organic fertilizer. Plants may suffer from root rot if the soil is very heavy and wet. Crowns tend to rise above the soil as plants age. Winter mulch applied after the ground is frozen will help reduce heaving. Divide and replant older clumps every few years. Some people choose to highlight the foliage and clip off the tall, straggly flower stalks as they appear.

Good Companions Alumroot does well with other partial-sun plants such as columbines, wild geraniums, and bleeding hearts. In perennial borders, combine it with lady's mantle (*Alchemilla mollis*), gold-edged hostas, and perennial geraniums.

Cultivars and Other Species 'Green Spice' has green leaves frosted silver in the center with purple-brown along the veins. 'Silver Selection' ('Dale Strain') is a seed-grown strain with gray-green leaves and silver mottling. It has been crossed with other North American *Heuchera* species, resulting in many showy cultivars with red and silver leaves. These include 'Garnet', 'Montrose Ruby', 'Ruby Veil', and 'Pewter Veil'.

H. richardsonii (prairie alumroot) is native to dry soils in the southern parts of both peninsulas. It grows from a 12-inch-tall basal clump of heart-shaped, long-petioled leaves that show some white mottling or a purple blush when young, maturing to a more uniform green. Tiny, greenish, bell-shaped flowers in open, airy panicles are borne on slender, wiry stems extending well above the mound of leaves. The stems typically reach a height of 2 feet in

Heuchera americana 'Pewter Veil'

Heuchera richardsonii

spring to early summer, long enough to emerge above prairie grasses. Prairie alumroot's attractive foliage and airy flower panicles provide color and contrast to rock gardens, perennial borders, or open woodland gardens. It tolerates dry locations and is a good edging plant. It can be massed to form an attractive groundcover. Zone 2.

Hydrastis canadensis
Goldenseal
Zone 4

Native Habitat Rich deciduous forests, in scattered locations throughout the southern third of Michigan.

Height 6 to 8 inches

Description Goldenseal has attractive maple-like leaves that showcase the single white flowers with yellow stamens. Flowers appear in late April and May and are followed by raspberry-like red fruits.

Landscape Use Use goldenseal in shade gardens with other deciduous woodland plants. It will fill in when ephemerals go dormant. Plants are slow growing, but will eventually form a nice groundcover, spreading from rhizomes. Squirrels eat the fruits.

Culture Acidify soil before planting if necessary. Mulch garden plants to help ensure adequate soil moisture. Water during dry periods. Plants may go dormant during dry summers. Overharvesting has made goldenseal a threatened plant in Michigan; growing nursery-propagated specimens will help perpetuate the species.

Site Requires moist, slightly acidic to neutral soil in shade to partial sun.

Hydrastis canadensis

Good Companions Combine goldenseal with spring beauties, hepaticas, and other spring bloomers. The red fruits look nice with zigzag goldenrod.

Iris versicolor

Iris versicolor
Wild blue flag, northern blue flag
Zone 2

Native Habitat Wet prairies, ponds, shallow marshes, and bogs throughout the Upper Peninsula and in the northern half of the Lower Peninsula.

Height 2 to 3 feet

Description This emergent aquatic is a rhizomatous perennial. From May to July, it produces several bluish violet flowers on a stout stem, among a basal cluster of swordlike leaves.

Landscape Use Blue flag's flowers are attractive in early summer, and the erect, swordlike foliage provides textural contrast and a tropical feel throughout the growing season. Plant blue flag in a damp to wet spot, such as next to ponds or in bogs, where the leaves will lend a strong vertical accent. It can be grown in heavy soil in perennial borders where there is an ample water supply. Plants can be potted and sunk into wetland ponds.

Site Requires wet, rich soil in full sun to light shade. Grows best when the rhizome is just covered with water.

Culture If necessary, amend soil with organic matter to improve its water-holding capacity. Blue flag creeps slowly to form nice clumps, which are easily divided every third year for maximum bloom. To grow blue flag in water gardens, plant it in rich clay soil in a container. Cover the soil with 2 inches of pea gravel, and submerge the pot in up to 8 inches of water.

Good Companions Grow blue flag with other moisture lovers such as turtlehead, obedient plant, ferns, swamp milkweed, wild calla, pickerel-weed, arrowhead, and marsh marigold.

Cultivars and Other Species
'Kermesina' has flowers with bright red-purple petals and white centers. 'Version' is a pink selection. Zone 2.

I. lacustris (dwarf lake iris) is native to moist soils along the northern shores of Lake Michigan and Lake Huron. It grows 3 to 5 inches tall and has violet flowers in spring. It adapts well to cultivation when planted in slightly acidic to neutral soils in partial sun. It is on both state and federal threatened species lists and is difficult to find. Be sure any plants you purchase are nursery propagated. Zone 4.

I. virginica (southern blue flag) is native to pond shores and marshes in the Lower Peninsula. Cultural requirements and uses are the same as wild blue flag. It has narrower leaves and slightly darker flowers on shorter stems. The new growth has an attractive burgundy tinge that persists into summer. Zone 4.

Isopyrum biternatum

Isopyrum biternatum
False rue anemone
Zone 3

Native Habitat Rich deciduous woods and stream banks in the southern half of Michigan.

Height 8 to 12 inches

Description False rue anemone has delicate, blue-green basal and stem leaves and small, round-lobed leaflets. Snow white flowers appear in sparse clusters, covering plants for a month in early spring. It is one of the earliest wildflowers to bloom, starting in early to mid-April. Plants go dormant after blooming, and new leaves often appear in fall.

Landscape Use This early spring bloomer makes a nice groundcover in shade or woodland gardens. It weaves its way among other flowers without overpowering them.

Site Humus-rich, evenly moist soil in light to full shade.

Culture Amend soil with organic matter before planting, if needed, to create the necessary growing conditions. Plants grow from creeping roots to spread, but they rarely become a nuisance. Plants disappear after flowering, but new foliage may emerge in fall or late winter. This native flower is difficult to locate in the nursery trade.

Good Companions Plant false rue anemone with other shade-loving plants such as wild ginger, blue phlox, bloodroot, trilliums, primroses, epimediums, and pulmonarias.

Jeffersonia diphylla
Twinleaf
Zone 4

Native Habitat Rich deciduous forests, including floodplains and well-drained slopes, in the southern half of the Lower Peninsula.

Height 6 to 15 inches

Description A solitary, eight-petaled white flower, up to 2 inches wide, appears on this perennial's leafless stalk in early spring. The flower lasts only a day or two, but the plant redeems itself with its interesting foliage. The long-stemmed basal leaves are deeply divided into two lobes, resembling a perched butterfly, and they have an attractive reddish tinge. The flowers are followed by interesting pipe-like seed capsules in early summer.

Landscape Use Twinleaf can be used as groundcover in shade or woodland gardens, where the attractive leaves overlap and form layers.

Site Prefers an evenly moist, rich, neutral to alkaline soil in spring sun, but will tolerate fairly dry soils.

Culture Add limestone to the soil if the pH is too acidic. This plant is on Michigan's special concern list. Growing nursery-propagated specimens will help the species; do not use plants dug from the wild.

Jeffersonia diphylla

Good Companions Grow twinleaf with other deciduous woodland plants that have interesting foliage, such as bloodroot, ferns, meadow rue, trout lilies, and wild ginger.

Liatris spicata
Marsh blazing star
Zone 3

Native Habitat Moist, sandy plains and shores, and rarely in dry woodlands, mainly in the southern half of the Lower Peninsula.

Height 2 to 4 feet

Description This popular perennial has showy pink-purple, occasionally white, terminal flower spikes that crowd the upper portion of the stiff, leafy stems. The alternate, grass-like leaves increase in size from top to bottom. The midsummer bloom starts at the top of the flower spike and works its way down.

Landscape Use Marsh blazing star is a great plant for perennial borders and prairie gardens. Bees, hummingbirds, and monarchs and other butterflies gather on the flowers all summer, and birds eat the seeds. All blazing stars are good cut flowers, and they hold their color well when dried.

Site Moist, fertile, well-drained soil in full sun.

Culture Marsh blazing star is somewhat drought resistant once established. The tall stems usually need support, which can come from staking or from nearby grasses. Plants reseed but never become weedy, and they seldom need dividing. Cut back plants in spring rather than fall so birds can feast on the seed heads. Plants are sometimes sold as dormant tubers, which can be planted like bulbs. Pocket gophers, mice, and voles like to eat the tubers, and rabbits nibble on young foliage.

Good Companions Plant marsh blazing star with other summer prairie plants such as Culver's root, rattlesnake master, wood lily, mountain mint, coneflowers, monarda, and milkweeds.

Cultivars and Other Species Several compact cultivars are available, the most popular being 'Kobold', which grows about 2 feet tall. Zone 3.

L. aspera (rough blazing star) is native to dry, sandy soils, mainly in southern Michigan. In mid- to late summer, it has clusters of 1-inch, pale purple or pink, button-like flowers on short stalks atop 3- to 5-foot stems. The leaves are gray-green and grass-like. Grow it in sandy or loamy, moist but well-drained soil in full sun. It works well in prairie gardens or mixed borders. It will need staking or the support of nearby plants. Birds and butterflies enjoy the flowers. Zone 3.

L. cylindracea (cylindric blazing star) is native to dry, sandy soil in the Lower Peninsula. It is shorter, growing 8 to 24 inches, and has narrow clusters of pale purple flowers in open spikes in late summer. Culture and use are the same as marsh blazing star. Zone 3.

Liatris spicata 'Kobold'

Liatris aspera

Lilium michiganense

Lilium michiganense
Michigan lily
Zone 4

Native Habitat Moist to wet soils, mainly in the southern half of the Lower Peninsula but also in the Upper Peninsula.

Height 3 to 4 feet

Description From July to August, Michigan lily has nodding, deep orange flowers, the petals of which are strongly recurved and flecked with brown. The 2- to 3-inch flowers are held nicely above the stems, and the whorled leaves have smooth margins.

Landscape Use Michigan lily can be used in low areas in perennial borders or along ponds and streams. It is a good bog plant. Hummingbirds enjoy the flowers.

Site Wet, rich soil in full sun to light shade.

Culture Michigan lily likes a deep, rich soil, so add lots of organic matter before planting. Bulbs should be planted in fall. Rodents often eat the bulbs; deter them by surrounding planted bulbs with 1 to 2 inches of gravel or planting bulbs in wire cages.

Good Companions Plant Michigan lily with other moisture-loving natives such as turtlehead, ferns, and Joe-pye weeds.

Other Species *L. philadelphicum* (wood lily) is native to open, sandy or rocky dunes, woodlands, and bogs throughout most of Michigan. It has upright, 2-inch, cup-shaped, orange-red flowers that are spotted with purplish brown; erect, 1- to 3-foot stems; and whorled, widely spaced, lance-shaped leaves. It is one of the few lily species with upward-pointing flowers, and it blooms June to August. Grow it in dry, average, acidic, well-drained soil in full to partial sun. Plants are difficult to establish and tend to be short lived. Zone 3.

Lobelia cardinalis

Lobelia siphilitica

Native Habitat Moist to wet soils in open woods, swamps, and marshes throughout the Lower Peninsula and in some Upper Peninsula locations.

Lobelia cardinalis
Cardinal flower
Zone 3

Height 24 to 48 inches

Description Cardinal flower gets its name from the brilliant, rich red flowers that grow in an elongated cluster atop the stems from July to September. Leaves are alternate, dark green, canoe shaped, and 2 to 6 inches long.

Landscape Use Cardinal flower is one of the few native plants with true red flowers, and they are welcome additions to late-summer landscapes. Plant cardinal flower in groups of five to seven in a moist area of perennial borders or woodland gardens. A dark background will set off the flowers nicely. It thrives at the edges of water gardens and in bogs. It will naturalize when conditions are right. The showy tubular flowers attract hummingbirds.

Site Moist to wet, average soil in partial sun. It will tolerate full sun as long as the soil is always at least slightly damp.

Culture Cardinal flower adapts well to gardens, despite its native tendency to grow in moist areas at the edges of water. Amend soil with lots of organic matter and peat moss before planting. It transplants easily, but is short lived, so add seedlings every couple of years. Plants may not survive the winter if there is insufficient soil moisture; winter mulch is helpful.

Good Companions A backdrop of ferns will help set off the red flowers. Cardinal flower grows well with blue flags, sneezeweed, astilbes, turtleheads, and ligularias.

Other Species *L. siphilitica* (great blue lobelia) grows along bottomlands and riverbanks across the Lower Peninsula and into the Upper Peninsula. It has pretty, bright blue flowers in leaf axils that grow on the upper portion of leafy, 1- to 3-foot stems. It blooms for a long time, July to September. Give it a moist, rich soil in sun to light shade. It brings a welcome shade of blue to late-summer gardens. In the right conditions, it reseeds readily, but the seedlings are easy to pull. 'Alba' is a white-flowered form. Zone 3.

Lupinus perennis
Wild lupine
Zone 3

Native Habitat Dry, sandy soils of grasslands and barrens in the southern half of Michigan.

Height 15 to 30 inches

Description Wild lupine has pea-like, blue to purple flowers that grow in a 12-inch terminal cluster on erect, unbranched stems. Alternate leaves are palmately compounded, and each leaf has seven to eleven leaflets measuring 1 to 2 inches long. It blooms from mid-May into June.

Landscape Use A mass planting of wild lupine is a stunning sight. Plant groups in full sun in prairie gardens and woodland borders or clearings. It can be used in perennial borders, but plants often go into dormancy after flowering, so surround them with late-blooming plants. It is the only food plant eaten by the caterpillar of the endangered karner blue butterfly.

Site Prefers dry, slightly acidic, well-drained soil in full sun or light shade.

Thrives in poor soils and summer drought.

Culture Wild lupine can be a bit difficult to establish in landscape settings. Do not attempt to transplant mature plants. Start with young seedlings and include some of the soil from their mother plant to ensure the presence of specific nitrogen-fixing bacteria associated with the roots. Plants can also be started from seeds, which should be inoculated with the appropriate bacteria before planting. Once established, wild lupine enhances soil fertility by fixing nitrogen from the atmosphere. Space plants 8 to 12 inches apart in groups of five to seven. Plants will be short-lived on sites not suited to them.

Good Companions Although wild lupine looks best in large masses in naturalized settings, you can plant individual specimens with phloxes, spiderworts, blazing stars, and grasses in perennial borders.

Lupinus perennis

Native Habitat Moist woodlands, barrens, clearings, and dunes throughout Michigan.

Height 2 to 4 inches

Description Canada mayflower has zigzag stems topped by 1- to 2-inch racemes of minute white flowers resembling lily of the valley. It blooms from mid-May into June. Plants have 1- to 3-inch, alternate leaves with heart-shaped bases and smooth margins that clasp the stem. Flowers turn to reddish berries that are food for birds.

Landscape Use Canada mayflower makes a nice groundcover of glossy green in shade gardens. Under favorable conditions, it spreads to cover large areas, weaving itself among nearby plants.

Site Requires moist, acidic, humus-rich soil in partial to deep shade.

Culture Acidify soil before planting, if necessary. Mulch with pine needles or shredded leaves. Canada mayflower

Maianthemum canadense
Canada mayflower
Zone 2

Maianthemum canadense

spreads readily from rhizomes when conditions are right. It doesn't like to be crowded by other plants.

Good Companions Plant Canada mayflower in shade gardens with other acid-loving plants such as partridge-berry, starflower, dwarf lake iris, bunchberry, twinflower, and round-lobed hepatica.

Mertensia virginica
Virginia bluebells
Zone 3

Mertensia virginica

Native Habitat Moist deciduous woods in the southern part of Michigan.

Height 12 to 24 inches

Description Virginia bluebells has clusters of pinkish buds that open to showy, drooping clusters of sky-blue, trumpet-shaped flowers. The flowers begin opening in late April and last a long time, but plants go dormant soon after blooming. The lettuce-like leaves are oval shaped, thick veined, and deep green with smooth margins. They are a showy deep purple color in early spring when they first emerge.

Landscape Use Virginia bluebells is easily grown in woodland or shade gardens, where the flowers provide a soothing sea of blue for many weeks. It can also be used as a weaver in semi-shady perennial gardens, filling in spaces before other perennials are up and blooming. Gently pull mulch away from emerging plants so you can enjoy the striking deep purple color of the new foliage.

Site Prefers moist, rich sites in partial sun or shade.

Culture Plants die back after flowering in June, so interplant them with ferns or wild ginger. Be careful not to dig into dormant clumps. They will self-seed but not to the point of becoming a nuisance. Plants in the perennial border should be mulched and fertilized. Virginia bluebells is on Michigan's threatened species list, so purchase only nursery-propagated plants.

Good Companions Plant this early bloomer with yellow- or orange-flowered spring bulbs in perennial borders. In woodland gardens, combine it with celandine poppy, large-flowered bellwort, shooting star, columbines, and trilliums. Use wild ginger and ferns to fill in after Virginia bluebells goes dormant.

Mitella diphylla
Two-leaved miterwort, bishop's cap
Zone 3

Mitella diphylla

Native Habitat Rich deciduous woods throughout the Lower Peninsula and also in the Upper Peninsula.

Height 6 to 12 inches

Description Miterwort is a neat and compact rhizomatous perennial with evergreen, toothed, triangular leaves that stay low to the ground. Its small, dainty flowers grow in terminal racemes on top of 6- to 12-inch-tall stalks. The flowers are creamy white to green or purplish, and they bloom from early May into June.

Landscape Use Miterwort spreads slowly but eventually makes a nice groundcover in woodland gardens or under shrubs, such as viburnums, leatherwood, and dogwood. A generous planting of miterwort in flower has the same effect as baby's breath in a flower arrangement.

Site Prefers a humus-rich, moist but well-drained, neutral or slightly acidic soil in light to full shade.

Culture Amend soil with organic matter before planting. Space plants 8 to 10 inches apart. Miterwort is surprisingly tolerant of drought and will actually grow on top of limestone with only a few inches of rich soil.

Good Companions Grow miterwort in masses with columbines, woodland phlox, celandine poppy, bleeding heart, Jacob's ladder, and wild geranium.

Monarda fistulosa
Wild bergamot
Zone 3

Native Habitat Dry, open, sandy woodlands, barrens, prairies, and savannas throughout most of Michigan.

Height 2 to 4 feet

Description Wild bergamot has soft lavender to pale pink, 3-inch, tubular flowers in dense, round, terminal clusters. It blooms from June to August. The foliage is rather coarse, and the stems are square, a mint-family characteristic.

Landscape Use Wild bergamot is a beautiful summer-blooming perennial that adapts well to landscape use. It can be used in prairie plantings and in the middle to back of perennial borders. The flowers attract bees, butterflies, and hummingbirds.

Site Prefers average to rich, well-drained soil in full sun to light shade.

Culture Wild bergamot tolerates varying soil fertility as long as it is well drained. If the soil is too rich, stems can become weak. Plantings have a tendency to die out in the middle. Dividing plants every three to four years helps keep them vigorous and reduces their spread. Powdery mildew may be a problem in wet, humid conditions, but it is rarely serious. Avoid overhead watering.

Good Companions The soft color and uniquely shaped flower of wild bergamot is a nice complement to the brighter, deeper-colored flowers of other summer-blooming prairie plants such as black-eyed Susan, blazing stars, and butterfly weed. In perennial gardens, plant it with garden phlox (*Phlox paniculata*), yarrows (*Achillea* species), perennial geraniums (*Geranium* species), and ornamental grasses.

Other Species *M. didyma* (monarda, bee balm, Oswego tea) was native to rich woodland riverbanks in a small area of the far southeastern part of Michigan. There are no native stands left in the state. It adapts well to culti-

Monarda fistulosa

vation, and there are many cultivars of this popular garden perennial. Zone 3.

M. punctata (spotted bee balm, horsemint) is native to sandy soils in a wide variety of plant communities throughout the Lower Peninsula. It grows 2 to 3 feet tall and has unusually colored pink, green, and dark brown blooms in late summer. It is more tolerant of dry soils than other monardas. Zone 4.

Nymphaea odorata
American white water lily
Zone 2

Native Habitat Ponds, sloughs, marshes, and swamps throughout Michigan.

Height Floats on water surface

Description This rhizomatous aquatic has leaves and flowers that float on the water surface of lakes and ponds up to 5 feet deep. Its flowers are pure white or, rarely, pinkish and 3 to 5 inches wide; they have many petals and a multitude of yellow stamens. They bloom throughout most of the summer, opening in the morning and closing in the afternoon. Most flowers are fragrant. The round, flat, shiny green leaves are 4 to 12 inches across and usually purple on the back side.

Landscape Use American white water lily can be grown in large water gardens and ponds, where plants will spread to create a solid mat. Container-grown plants can be grown in small ponds and tub gardens.

Site Submerged, rich soil in full sun.

Culture American white water lily grows in deep ponds, the rhizomes barely covered with soil. In most landscape situations, it should be grown in pots to keep it from spreading too aggressively. Partially fill dark pots with clay topsoil low in humus, and plant rhizomes 3 to 4 inches deep. Cover the soil surface with 2 inches of fine gravel to hold in the topsoil. Keep the newly potted container within 6 to 8 inches of the water surface until several new leaves appear, then move it into water up to 4 feet deep. If planted in small, shallow garden ponds that may freeze solid, bring potted plants

Nymphaea odorata

indoors in late fall, wrap each one in wet newspaper, seal each package in a plastic bag, and store them in a cold basement where the temperatures remain a few degrees above freezing.

Good Companions Grow American white water lily with pickerelweed and arrowhead, two other native emergent aquatics.

Opuntia humifusa
Eastern prickly pear
Zone 4

Native Habitat Sandy prairies, mainly in the southwestern corner of Michigan.

Height 8 to 12 inches

Description Eastern prickly pear has large yellow flowers, 2 to 3 inches wide and with or without reddish centers. The flowers bloom from June to July. The stems have been modified into flattened, fleshy pads covered with clusters of short bristles. The barrel-shaped fruits turn reddish purple as they ripen.

Landscape Use Its alien look and cultural conditions limit how prickly pear can be used in landscapes, but it is great in rock gardens, stone walls, and xeriscapes.

Site Well-drained, sandy soil in full sun.

Culture Prickly pears are difficult to weed and cultivate around. The tiny spines can be irritating; wear heavy gloves when handling or working around plants. They survive winter temperatures by withdrawing most of the moisture from their pads, giving them a shriveled, unhealthy look in winter and early spring. They quickly plump up in spring, however. The clump-forming plants are easily cut back if they become too sprawling.

Good Companions Grow prickly pears with other plants that like the same hot, dry conditions, such as beardtongues, wild onions, harebell, purple prairie clover, rattlesnake master, and flowering spurge.

Opuntia humifusa

Penstemon digitalis
Foxglove beardtongue
Zone 3

Penstemon digitalis 'Husker Red'

Native Habitat Prairies and savannas, mainly in the Lower Peninsula.

Height 2 to 4 feet

Description This robust perennial has wide, lance-shaped leaves and tiers of many small, white, tubular flowers on long flower stalks.

Landscape Use Foxglove beardtongue can be grown in prairie gardens or perennial borders. Since plants have a short bloom time and the foliage isn't all that attractive, plant later-blooming species nearby to distract from non-blooming plants. Its tolerance of dry soil makes it well suited to rock gardens. The flowers are attractive to hummingbirds.

Site Average to rich, sandy or loamy, well-drained soil in full sun to light shade.

Culture Foxglove beardtongue is easy to grow in most garden situations. Plants spread by slow-creeping rhizomes to form dense clumps. Divide plants every four to six years to keep them vigorous. Plants will self-sow.

Good Companions Plant foxglove

Penstemon digitalis

beardtongue with other late-spring bloomers such as wild lupine, geraniums, yarrows, ornamental onions, prickly pears, garden phlox, and Siberian iris.

Cultivars and Other Species 'Husker Red' is a burgundy-leaved cultivar that does well in gardens. Zone 3.

P. gracilis (slender beardtongue) reaches the eastern edge of its range in Michigan, where it grows in oak woodlands in the far western part of the Upper Peninsula. It is a more delicate plant and has smaller, rose-pink to purple flowers on 2-foot stems. The narrow, toothed leaves are covered with soft hairs. Culture and use are the same. It is on Michigan's endangered species list because of its rarity. Zone 3.

P. hirsutus (hairy beardtongue) is native to sandy soils in prairies and savannas mainly in the southern half of the Lower Peninsula. It grows 12 to 18 inches tall and has violet to pale rose flowers tinged with yellow. It can be used in rock gardens. Zone 3.

Phlox divaricata
Blue phlox, woodland phlox
Zone 3

Native Habitat Rich mesic woods, moist deciduous woods, clearings, and floodplains, all in the southern two-thirds of Michigan.

Height 10 to 20 inches

Description Blue phlox has clusters of fragrant, pretty, pale blue to dark purple-violet flowers from late April into June. The glossy, semi-evergreen foliage spreads at a moderate rate by creeping rhizomes that form loose mats.

Landscape Use Blue phlox is one of the best groundcovers for woodland gardens. It is also ideal for planting beneath deciduous trees and large shrubs, where it will receive early spring sun and summer shade. Use blue phlox to hide dying spring bulb foliage. It forms natural drifts and is good for covering hillsides.

Site Thrives in partial to full shade in cool, well-drained soil that is rich in organic matter.

Culture Blue phlox has a shallow root system and benefits from a summer mulch to conserve soil moisture. Flowering will diminish and foliage will brown if conditions are too sunny or too dry. Cut back flower stalks after flowering to keep plants neat. Phloxes are favorite foods of deer and rabbits. To revive eaten plants, fertilize with a mixture of 1 tablespoon fish emulsion in 1 gallon of water. Plants seldom need dividing.

Good Companions Plant blue phlox with spring bulbs and wildflowers such as trillium, celandine poppy, columbines, Virginia bluebells, spring beauties, and wild ginger. In woodland gardens, plant it with foamflower, bleeding hearts, and ferns.

Cultivars and Other Species Var. *laphamii*, a naturally occurring selection that is native slightly farther west in Wisconsin, has deeper blue flowers. 'Fuller's White' is a good, white-flowered cultivar. 'Dirgo Ice' has pale blue to white flowers. 'Clouds of Perfume' has very fragrant ice blue flowers. 'Chattahoochee' is a hybrid of *P. divaricata* var. *laphamii* and *P. pilosa* that has lavender-blue flowers with dark purple centers.

P. bifida (sand phlox, cleft phlox) is rare and native to dry, sandy soils and outcrops in the southern part of Michigan. It grows 2 to 6 inches tall, and it has stiff, needle-like leaves and pale blue-violet flowers in spring. Its creeping habit makes it an excellent choice for rock gardens. It is on Michigan's threatened species list. Zone 4.

P. maculata (wild sweet William) barely reaches into Michigan, where it is native to moist soils in the far southwestern corner. It grows 2 to 3 feet tall and has large, conical clusters of pink or white flowers. The lance-shaped green leaves look nice all season. It prefers drier, sunnier conditions than its woodland cousin. Plant it in average to rich, moist but well-drained soil in full sun or light shade. It works well in perennial borders or prairie gardens with black-eyed Susan, prairie smoke, nodding wild onion, golden alexanders, wild bergamot, and mountain mint. Divide the multistemmed clumps every three to four years to keep plants vigorous. *P. maculata* is on Michigan's threatened species list. 'Alpha' has rose-pink flowers with darker eyes. 'Rosalinde' has deep pink flowers and grows 3 to 4 feet tall. Zone 3.

P. pilosa (prairie phlox) is native to prairies, dry open woodlands, and savannas in the southern half of the Lower Peninsula. It grows 10 to 30 inches tall. It has clusters of lavender, pink, or sometimes whitish, fragrant flowers atop downy stems and leaves. It blooms in late spring and early summer. Grow it in sandy, well-drained, slightly to moderately acidic soil, in full sun or light shade. It works well in prairie gardens or perennial borders. Zone 3. Var. *fulgida* is another naturally occurring variety native in Wisconsin; its leaves have a more lustrous appearance. Zone 3.

Phlox pilosa

Phlox maculata

Phlox divaricata

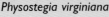

Physostegia virginiana

Physostegia virginiana 'Vivid'

Physostegia virginiana
Obedient plant
Zone 3

Native Habitat Moist soils throughout most of Michigan.

Height 2 to 3 feet

Description Obedient plant has tall vertical stems lined with narrow, jaggedly toothed leaves. The showy tubular flowers bloom from midsummer to early fall. They appear successively up the stalk in somewhat elongated clusters of pinkish, two-lipped, 1-inch-long, snapdragon-like flowers arranged in two rows.

Landscape Use Obedient plant's aggressive nature limits its landscape use. Use it in wet prairie gardens and naturalized plantings. The flowers have an old-fashioned look and are good for Victorian gardens and cut bouquets. There are several good cultivars that are less aggressive than the species and better for garden use.

Site Prefers a moist, rich, well-drained soil in full sun, but tolerates drier conditions and partial sun.

Culture Plants spread by underground rhizomes and can become invasive. In perennial borders, plants can be grown in buried 3-gallon nursery containers to keep them in bounds. Garden plants may need staking, especially if grown in fertile soils.

Good Companions Obedient plant's pink-to-white flowers are a welcome addition to late-summer borders. Plant it with New England aster, bottle gentian, blazing stars, Culver's root, ironweed, Joe-pye weeds, goldenrods, and grasses.

Cultivars 'Miss Manners' is much less aggressive than the species and well behaved enough to be used in perennial borders. It has bright white flowers from late summer through fall. 'Pink Bouquet' has bright pink flowers on 3- to 4-foot stems. 'Variegata' has pale pink flowers and leaves edged in creamy white. 'Vivid' has vibrant rose-pink flowers on 2- to 2 1/2-foot stems.

Podophyllum peltatum
May apple
Zone 3

Podophyllum peltatum

Native Habitat Moist deciduous woods and clearings in the southern half of the Lower Peninsula.

Height 12 to 18 inches

Description May apple is a rhizomatous, spreading perennial with nodding, creamy white, 2-inch flowers from mid- to late May. The single flower is hard to see, because it grows beneath the large, umbrella-like, deeply lobed, paired leaves that spread up to a foot in diameter.

Landscape Use May apple is good for covering large shady areas of bare ground; its large, tropical-looking leaves emerge in mid-April and remain fresh-looking all season and in cooler temperatures. Its aggressive nature can overtake more delicate species, so it is usually planted in large masses. If you want to see the spring flowers, plant it on slopes, so you can look up under the leaves.

Site Grows in evenly moist to damp, humus-rich soil in light to full shade, but tolerates drier sites once it is established.

Culture Once established, May apple spreads rapidly by long rhizomes and may crowd out nearby plants. It can be kept under control with annual removal of some rhizomes, which are easily dug out. If you want to grow it with less-aggressive plants, plant it in a large, sunken, nursery pot. The green, apple-like fruits are poisonous until they are fully ripe, as are all other parts of the plant.

Good Companions Few plants can compete with May apple, and it is usually grown as a large groundcover. In large shaded areas, it can be grown with other large plants such as Solomon's seal, baneberries, bugbane (*Cimicifuga racemosa*), and large ferns. It can also be grown with early ephemerals that go dormant before it shades them.

Polemonium reptans
Spreading Jacob's ladder
Zone 3

Native Habitat Barely reaches into southern Michigan, where it grows in moist soils in deciduous woodlands.

Height 8 to 16 inches

Description Spreading Jacob's ladder is a low-branching, clumping plant with attractive, dark green, pinnately divided leaves. The plants are covered with small sky-blue flowers in terminal clusters held slightly above leaves, starting in late April and lasting well into June.

Landscape Use This long-blooming plant works well in woodland or shade gardens and under shrubs or flowering trees.

Site Prefers a fertile, damp soil with a pH of 6 to 7, in partial shade, but can be grown in almost full sun.

Culture Cut bloom stalks to the ground after flowering; foliage will remain attractive all season. Plants do not creep, and they seldom need division. The brittle flower stems are easily broken, so any staking should be done before plants flower. *P. reptans* is on Michigan's threatened species list, so purchase only nursery-propagated plants.

Good Companions Combine Jacob's ladder with Virginia bluebells to provide blue color after the latter goes dormant. It looks nice under flowering trees such as serviceberry, redbud, or

Polemonium reptans

flowering dogwood. In shade gardens, combine it with bloodroot, wild geranium, foamflower, wild ginger, hostas, and ferns.

Cultivars 'Blue Pearl' is 10 inches tall and has abundant, rich blue flowers.

Polygonatum biflorum
Giant Solomon's seal
Zone 3

Polygonatum biflorum

Native Habitat Rich, moist deciduous woods and floodplains in the southern half of the Lower Peninsula.

Height 1 to 3 feet

Description Giant Solomon's seal has greenish yellow flowers that dangle from leaf axils in May and June, but the deep purple fruits that appear later in summer are much more ornamental. They hang from the arching stems and offer great contrast to the foliage, which turns a striking gold color in fall. The alternate, oval, 2- to 6-inch, parallel-veined leaves clasp the stem.

Landscape Use The graceful, arching stems of giant Solomon's seal bring a strong architectural element to gardens. Use it as groundcover at the base of large trees, where it tolerates the dry shade. Tuck clumps here and there for accent, setting off the bright green leaves with a tree trunk or fallen log. Birds eat the berries.

Site Prefers moist, high-humus soil in partial sun to deep shade, but tolerates drier sites.

Culture Giant Solomon's seal grows slowly from creeping rhizomes to form natural patches, but seldom becomes invasive. For faster growth, mulch with pine needles or oak leaves to increase soil acidity and moisture. Plants grown in sun may need watering during dry periods.

Good Companions Plant giant Solomon's seal with other tall foliage plants for an interesting textural display. Good choices are ostrich fern, wild ginger, May apple, and false Solomon's seal.

Varieties and Other Species Var. *commutatum* (great Solomon's seal) is a rare, naturally occurring tetraploid form (having more than the regular number of chromosomes). It can grow 6 feet tall or more and is truly spectacular, but it is difficult to find in the nursery trade. Zone 3.

P. pubescens (hairy Solomon's seal) is native to rich deciduous woodlands throughout Michigan. It is a little smaller than giant Solomon's seal, growing to only about 28 inches, and has hairy veins on the lower leaf surfaces. Culture and use are the same as giant Solomon's seal. Zone 3.

Pontederia cordata

Pontederia cordata
Pickerelweed
Zone 4

Native Habitat In and along marshes, streams, shallow lakes, and shallow ponds throughout most of Michigan.
Height 1 to 2 feet above water surface
Description This emergent aquatic grows in shallow water (3 feet or less) or saturated soil near water features, often forming large colonies. It has attractive clublike clusters of violet-blue (or rarely white) flowers from June to August. The flowers emerge from a sheathing basal spathe. Plants have heart-shaped, glossy leaves 2 to 10 inches long.
Landscape Use Pickerelweed is an ornamental plant that forms spreading patches by means of a thick, creeping rhizome. It can be grown in bog gardens or in shallow, large ponds. In smaller ponds, grow it as a container plant. It makes a nice cut flower. Ducks and geese eat the seeds, and muskrats may eat the leaves. This plant is the sole nectar source for one bee species (*Dufourea novae-angliae*).

Site Requires a fertile, heavy loam soil at water edges, or a submerged soil in full sun, but tolerates low fertility and partial shade.
Culture Once established, it is important to maintain year-round water depths greater than saturation but shallower than the leaves. Pickerelweed responds well to organic fertilizers. Plants slowly spread to cover the sediment with a tough vegetative mat, but they are easily weeded out if needed.
Good Companions Grow pickerelweed with American white water lily and arrowhead, two other native emergent aquatics.

Potentilla anserina
Silverweed
Zone 4

Native Habitat Moist, sandy and gravelly soil along shores of lakes and ponds throughout most of Michigan.
Height 2 to 8 inches
Description An interesting groundcover, silverweed spreads via runners that root at leaf nodes. The sharply toothed leaflets are silvery green underneath and sometimes on top. The cherry yellow flowers first appear in May, and plants bloom intermittently into September.
Landscape Use Silverweed is a tough plant that thrives in damp areas and can be used on heavy soils as a groundcover. It is also effective for dune restoration.

Site Moisture-retentive soil in full sun to light shade.
Culture Silverweed needs little care once established, but young plants will need supplemental water if the soil is on the dry side.
Good Companions Silverweed is usually planted alone as a groundcover or with other tough dune plants along shorelines.
Other Species *P. tridentata* (three-toothed cinquefoil) is native to acidic, well-drained soils mainly in northern Michigan. It forms a 3- to 8-inch mat of dark green, strawberry-like leaves that turn a nice wine-red color in fall. The small, white flowers are numerous, starting late May and continuing into summer. It needs a cool, acidic, well-drained, sandy or even gravelly soil in sun to partial shade. Use it in rock gardens or for edging, where it will spread but not become too weedy. Zone 2.

P. arguta (tall cinquefoil) is native to dry soils throughout most of the state. It grows 1 to 3 feet tall, has pale yellow flowers all summer, and tolerates dry conditions and full sun in rock gardens and perennial beds. Zone 2.

Potentilla anserina

Pycnanthemum virginianum
Virginia mountain mint
Zone 3

Native Habitat Wet to mesic open woods and prairies, mainly across the southern half of Michigan.

Height 2 to 3 feet

Description Virginia mountain mint is a stiff, erect, clump-forming plant with leaves that smell like mint or oregano. The whitish to lavender flowers have purple spots and are borne in 1-inch terminal clusters in summer. The attractive 2-inch leaves have a bright yellow fall color, and the gray seed heads cling to plants through winter.

Landscape Use Virginia mountain mint is a little coarse for perennial borders, but it can be used in informal wild gardens and prairies. It is often grown for its aromatic foliage rather than for its flowers. It offers winter interest and attracts butterflies and bees. It makes a good cut or dried flower.

Site Prefers moist, humus-rich soil in full sun.

Culture This stoloniferous plant can become invasive. If you want to grow it in butterfly or herb gardens, plant it in large sunken nursery containers. Plants need division every few years to keep them from overwhelming nearby plants.

Good Companions Grow Virginia mountain mint with other summer bloomers such as purple prairie clover, blazing stars, black-eyed Susans, butterfly weed, prairie phlox, coneflowers, and beardtongues.

Other Species *P. muticum* (broad-leaved mountain mint) is thought to possibly be native in the far southwestern corner of Michigan. Its rarity in the state puts it on Michigan's threatened species list. It is an attractive plant with broad clusters of dense heads of white flowers accented by sil-

Pycnanthemum virginianum

very white bracts. The peppermint-scented leaves appear on 3-foot-tall plants that spread by creeping underground stems to form large clumps. It requires an even moisture supply. Zone 4.

P. tenuifolium [*P. flexuosum*] (slender mountain mint) is native to sandy soils widely scattered in the Lower Peninsula. It grows 12 to 18 inches tall. The leaves are narrower than *P. virginianum*, giving it a finer texture. It has an abundance of flowers that are attractive to butterflies. Zone 3.

Ratibida pinnata
Gray-headed coneflower
Zone 3

Native Habitat Dry prairies and savannas, mainly in the southern part of Michigan but also found in Menominee County.

Height 3 to 5 feet

Description Gray-headed coneflower is a stiff, erect plant with rough-feeling, coarse leaves. It is redeemed by its showy 2½-inch flowers that appear throughout summer. They have drooping, soft yellow rays and elevated, globose, cone-like green centers that change to dark purple or brown.

Landscape Use The soft yellow color of gray-headed coneflower is a welcome and relaxing contrast to other hot-colored summer flowers. It adapts well to perennial borders and weaves nicely through prairie gardens. The flowers bloom a long time, attracting

butterflies and bees, and they are good for cutting. Once established, it is drought tolerant and can be used in xeriscapes.

Site Requires average to rich, well-drained soil in full sun or light shade; cannot tolerate heavy, wet soils.

Culture Gray-headed coneflower is easy to grow. It transplants readily and seldom needs division. Plants reseed in the garden and prairie. Seedlings can be replanted to refresh the supply of plants. Garden plants may need staking in fertile soils.

Good Companions Plant gray-headed coneflower with other summer-blooming plants such as blazing stars, butterfly weed, purple prairie clover, wild bergamot, blue giant hyssop, and prairie grasses.

Ratibida pinnata

Rudbeckia fulgida 'Goldsturm'

Rudbeckia triloba

Rudbeckia hirta 'Indian Summer'

Rudbeckia fulgida [R. sullivantii]

Black-eyed Susan, orange coneflower
Zone 3

Native Habitat Moist soils of grasslands in southern Michigan.

Height 1½ to 3 feet

Description Black-eyed Susan may well be the most recognizable native flower. It is a short-lived perennial. Its 3-inch, flat flowers have golden yellow rays surrounding a conical cluster of rich brown disc florets. It blooms for a month or more in late summer. The dark green, lance-shaped leaves appear on stiff, branched stems.

Landscape Use Black-eyed Susan brings long-lasting color to prairie gardens and mixed borders. Plants bloom there the first year from seed. The flowers attract bees and butterflies and provide winter interest if left standing.

Site Prefers moist, average, well-drained soil in full sun, but tolerates light shade and a wide range of soil conditions.

Culture Black-eyed Susan is a slow-spreading plant. Plants should be divided every 3 to 4 years. Overly rich soils tend to produce weak-stemmed plants. Plants are easy to propagate from seeds or by transplanting seedlings.

Good Companions Good native companions include blazing stars, obedient plant, asters, butterfly weed, wild bergamot, little bluestem, and prairie dropseed. The list of suitable nonnative companions includes Russian sage (*Perovskia*), garden phlox (*Phlox paniculata*), sedums, and ornamental grasses such as *Calamagrostis* and *Pennisetum*.

Cultivars and Other Species 'Goldsturm', a very popular selection, is supposed to have darker green foliage, more flowers, and a longer bloom time. Var. *speciosa* has smaller leaves and flowers but in greater numbers. Zone 3.

R. hirta (black-eyed Susan) is native to sandy soils in a wide variety of plant communities throughout Michigan. It grows 2 to 3 feet tall, and it is a biennial or short-lived perennial with similar flowers. It can be used in the perennial border, where it will perpetuate itself by reseeding. Zone 2. 'Indian Summer' is a popular tetraploid form with larger flowers. 'Prairie Sun' has 5-inch flowers; the golden petals are tipped in primrose yellow and surround a light green cone. 'Cherokee Sunset' is a mix of fully double flowers in shades of yellow, orange, bronze, and russet. All three cultivars are short lived and usually grown as annuals. They make good containers plants. Showy tetraploid hybrids called gloriosa daisies are derived from *R. hirta*. They are annuals or short-lived perennials and have 5- to 6-inch, yellow, orange, red, or multi-colored flowers on 2- to 3-foot plants. They bloom all summer and are good for cutting.

R. laciniata (cut-leaved coneflower) is native to moist open areas throughout most of Michigan. It grows 3 to 6 feet tall and has leaves with cut, irregular lobes. The abundant clusters of yellow flowers have light green central disks. It requires moister soil conditions than other coneflowers and is great for soggy stream banks. Use it in informal gardens and wet prairies. Plants can take light shade, but will have fewer flowers. 'Gold Drop' is a 2- to 3-foot-tall selection with double flowers; it is good for perennial borders and containers. Zone 3.

R. triloba (three-lobed coneflower) is native to moist prairies and open woodlands in the southern part of the state. It grows 2 to 5 feet tall, blooming from July into October. It has brilliant yellow, smaller sized flowers with jet black centers and three-lobed leaves. It is a short-lived perennial that blooms its second year from seeding and self-sows readily in open soil. Use it in prairie gardens, perennial borders, and for naturalizing. Zone 3.

Ruellia humilis
Wild petunia
Zone 4

Native Habitat Found rarely in dry prairies in the southwestern corner of Michigan.

Height 1 to 2 feet

Description Wild petunia has hairy stems and 3-inch, stalkless leaves. The tubular, violet-blue flowers resemble annual petunias and bloom from June to August.

Landscape Use Wild petunia is a great plant for dry, rocky, shallow soils such as in rock gardens, but it can also be grown in well-drained garden loam. Keep it at the front of perennial borders so larger plants don't overwhelm it. The lovely flowers bring the rare blue color to prairie gardens.

Site Needs well-drained soil in full sun.

Culture Wild petunia is easily grown in gardens if the soil is well drained. Add sand and organic matter to heavier soils. Plants grow from fibrous-rooted crowns to form clumps, but never become invasive. It is on Michigan's threatened species list, so purchase only nursery-propagated plants.

Good Companions Plant wild petunia with other small plants that won't hide its showy flowers. Good choices include prairie smoke, wild onions, pussytoes, little bluestem, and butterfly weed.

Ruellia humilis

Sagittaria latifolia
Broad-leaved arrowhead
Zone 3

Native Habitat Along stream margins and in still ponds throughout Michigan

Height 12 to 36 inches

Description Broad-leaved arrowhead is an emergent aquatic with 4- to 16-inch leaves shaped like exaggerated arrowheads, with two long, pointed lobes projecting down. The delicate, white-petaled flowers have yellow centers and grow in widely spaced whorls of three on a leafless stem from July to August. Fruits are round and green.

Landscape Use The leaves of broad-leaved arrowhead vary widely in width and shape, and a mass planting offers an interesting study in texture. It is not well suited to small pools because it spreads rapidly. Waterfowl, snapping turtles, and muskrats eat arrowhead fruits and tubers.

Site Requires a fertile, heavy, loamy soil at water edges, or a submerged soil, in full sun or light shade.

Culture Arrowhead grows from a potato-like tuber in water 2 to 3 inches deep or in the moist soil at edges of ponds or lakes. Plants will eventually multiply and form a large colony. Restrict growth by planting in nursery containers.

Good Companions Grow arrowhead with pickerelweed and American white water lily, two other native emergent aquatics.

Sagittaria latifolia

Sanguinaria canadensis

Native Habitat Rich, moist woods and floodplains throughout most of Michigan.

Height 4 to 10 inches

Description Bloodroot has simply elegant, pure white flowers in early spring. The flowers are 1¹/₂ inches wide; they have eight to ten petals and

Sanguinaria canadensis
Bloodroot
Zone 3

golden stamens on smooth, leafless stalks. The beautiful rounded basal leaves are deeply lobed and wrap around the stalks of young plants, unfurling with age. The first blooms will appear in early April on sunny south-facing slopes, but the main bloom begins in mid- to late April.

Landscape Use The short-lived but showy pure white flowers of bloodroot really say spring has arrived. It makes a great groundcover in shade or woodland gardens, because the leaves remain through most of summer and are ornamental in and of themselves. Tuck small groups here and there in shady borders.

Site Prefers moist, humus-rich soil with direct sunlight in early spring and summer shade, but will tolerate drier soils if well mulched.

Culture Improve poor or sandy soil by adding generous amounts of peat moss and compost. Mulch plants with a thin layer of pine needles or shredded leaves. Heavy mulch can lead to stem rot at the soil surface. Plants may go dormant during dry spells. The thickened, elongated rhizome exudes red sap when broken. Self-sown seedlings will appear when conditions are favorable and are usually a welcome sight.

Good Companions Plant bloodroot with other early spring bloomers such as false rue anemone, bellworts, spreading Jacob's ladder, and Virginia bluebells. It also combines nicely with lady fern, spring bulbs, and pulmonarias.

Cultivars 'Flore Pleno', also sold as 'Multiplex', is an exquisite double-flowered cultivar. Zone 3.

Senecio plattensis

Native Habitat Moist woods and swamps throughout most of Michigan.

Height 1 to 2 feet

Description Golden ragwort is an early blooming perennial with handsome clusters of golden-yellow, daisy-like flowers. These are borne atop 1- to

Senecio aureus [Packera aurea]
Golden ragwort
Zone 3

2-foot scapes in May and June. The heart-shaped, toothed, basal leaves resemble violet leaves; they are dark green above and purplish beneath, turning yellow in fall.

Landscape Use The showy blooms of golden ragwort persist for several weeks in spring, and the leaves look nice when the plant isn't flowering. Its golden yellow color is a nice contrast with other spring blooms, which are usually pink or purple shades. It thrives in moist soils and will even do well in wet sites such as bog gardens. It can be grown in groups of three to five in perennial borders, or used as a small-scale groundcover in wet areas.

Site Prefers a moist, slightly acidic soil in full sun to partial shade.

Culture Amend soil with organic matter before planting to ensure adequate

soil moisture. Plants in drier sites should be mulched to help keep the soil moist. This rhizomatous plant will spread slowly when conditions are right.

Good Companions Combine golden ragwort with other late-spring bloomers such as blue phlox, columbine, blue flag, goatsbeard (*Aruncus*), and creeping phlox (*Phlox stolonifera*).

Other Species *S. obovatus* (round-leaved ragwort) is native to rich woods and moist grasslands in the far southern part of the state. Zone 4.

S. plattensis (prairie ragwort) is native to open woods, savannas, and prairies throughout the Lower Peninsula. It is a self-sowing biennial with similar flowers and heart-shaped basal leaves. It is not quite as ornamental but tolerates drier sites. Zone 3.

Silene virginica
Fire pink
Zone 4

Native Habitat Found rarely in open woods in the southeastern part of Michigan.

Height 8 to 14 inches

Description This short-lived perennial has dark green, narrow leaves that form dense low clumps. Its plants send out wiry stems laden with starry crimson red flowers in summer.

Landscape Use Fire pink can be used in rock gardens and on sandy banks. It is attractive to hummingbirds and bees.

Site Moist to dry, well-drained soil in sun to partial shade.

Culture Drought tolerant and adaptable. Fire pink can be short lived, but its plants self-sow. Remove spent flowers to encourage plants to live longer. Fire pink is on Michigan's threatened species list because of its rarity in the state.

Good Companions Consider growing fire pink with coreopsis, coneflowers, rattlesnake master, wild petunia, blue-eyed grass, and beardtongues.

Other Species *S. stellata* (starry campion) is native to dry oak woodlands in the southwestern corner of Michigan.

Silene stellata

It grows 1 to 2 feet tall and has nodding white flowers. It is rugged, is shade and drought tolerant, and can be naturalized along woodland paths. It is also on the state's threatened list. Zone 4.

Silphium laciniatum
Compass plant
Zone 3

Native Habitat Dry to moist prairies and savannas along the far southern edge of Michigan.

Height 3 to 12 feet

Description There is nothing small about compass plant. It has lemon yellow, sunflower-like flowers that can be up to 5 inches across. The flowers grow at the ends of branched, hairy, sticky stems from July to September. The 12- to 18-inch cut-leaf blades orient themselves horizontally in a north-south direction to avoid the intense rays of midday sun.

Landscape Use Compass plant can be used in large perennial borders, but it is best suited to prairie gardens. Try to find a spot where you can enjoy the beautifully cut and lobed basal leaves as well as the flowers. Goldfinches, chickadees, and sparrows like the large seeds.

Site Prefers moist, average soil in full sun, but tolerates a wide range of soil moisture and pH. Mature plants are drought tolerant.

Culture Compass plant needs plenty of room, so space new plants 3 to 4 feet apart. New plants take a year or two to become established. The large taproot of mature plants can go down 15 feet, making established clumps difficult to divide or move, so choose a site carefully. Young plants may need protection from deer. Plants will self-sow. If you don't want the seedlings, weed them out while they are still young and easy to pull. Because of their rarity in the state, this species and *S. perfoliatum* are on Michigan's threatened species list. Be sure to purchase only nursery-propagated plants.

Good Companions Plant compass plant with other tall prairie flowers such as rattlesnake master, purple prairie clover, Culver's root, New England aster, Joe-pye weeds, big bluestem, and Indian grass.

Other Species *S. perfoliatum* (cup plant) is native to low, open woods and wet prairies in the far southern part of Michigan. It grows 3 to 8 feet tall and has leaves that encircle tall stems, forming cups that collect dew and become drinking fountains for birds. The 3-inch yellow flowers bloom in branched clusters just above the leaves in mid- to late summer. It can take light shade. It has a commanding presence in perennial borders, and it can be used at the edge of woodland gardens or in prairie gardens. Goldfinches love the seeds. Plants may self-sow. Aphids can

Silphium laciniatum

Silphium perfoliatum

be a problem during hot, dry periods. Zone 3.

    S. terebinthinaceum (prairie dock) is native to the grasslands of southern Michigan. It grows 4 to 8 feet tall and is recognized by its huge paddle-like leaves. Zone 3.

Sisyrinchium angustifolium

Sisyrinchium angustifolium
Blue-eyed grass
Zone 3

Native Habitat Grasslands and shorelines mainly in the Lower Peninsula but also farther north.

Height 10 to 20 inches

Description This iris relative has small, blue to violet-blue flowers with yellow centers. The flowers form loose clusters on top of flattened stems from mid-May to June, and bloom sporadically throughout the growing season. The basal leaves are narrow and grasslike.

Landscape Use Blue-eyed grass should be planted in groups and in places where it can be seen in the morning when the flowers are open. Use it in rock gardens or at the edges of perennial borders or prairie gardens. The fine, grass-like foliage has great garden value when plants are not in flower.

Site Prefers a moist, average, well-drained soil in full sun, but tolerates light shade.

Culture Blue-eyed grass is easy to grow, quickly forming large clumps by spreading and by self-sown seedlings. Divide plants every other year for the best bloom. Moderate fertility and summer moisture will encourage repeat blooms. Plants can be cut back lightly after flowering to prevent seed formation and self-sown seedlings.

Good Companions Plant delicate blue-eyed grass with late-blooming spring bulbs, prairie smoke, bird's-foot violet, and pussytoes.

Cultivars 'Lucerne' has larger blue-purple flowers and is less aggressive in the garden. Zone 4.

Smilacina racemosa

Smilacina stellata

Smilacina racemosa
[Maianthemum racemosa]
False Solomon's seal, false spikenard
Zone 2

Native Habitat Rich deciduous woods throughout most of Michigan.

Height 1 to 3 feet

Description False Solomon's seal grows from creeping rhizomes. It has attractive, 5- to 7-inch, egg-shaped, pleated leaves with smooth margins that clasp the stem. Conical plumes of small white flowers develop at the end of an arching stem and rise above the foliage in late spring into summer. The showy fruits start out green and take on a red marbling in summer, eventually turning translucent red.

Landscape Use Use this shade lover in woodland or shade gardens, in clumps of one to three plants. It can also be used as groundcover under trees. Be sure to place it where you can enjoy the interesting berries that appear in mid- to late summer and persist into winter.

Site Requires a moist, rich, acidic soil in light shade to full shade; best bloom comes with some sunlight.

Culture False Solomon's seal is easily grown when the soil conditions are right. If necessary, amend soil with organic matter and acidify before planting. Mulch plants with a thin layer of pine needles or shredded leaves. Groundcover plants should be spaced 12 inches on centers. Plants spread, but rarely become invasive. Slugs can be a problem.

Good Companions Grow false Solomon's seal with other shade plants such as baneberries, foamflower, bloodroot, Virginia bluebells, ferns, hostas, pulmonarias, and epimediums.

Other Species *S. stellata* (starry false Solomon's seal) is native to open woods, barrens, savannas, and dunes mainly in the Lower Peninsula but also farther north. It is a more delicate plant. It has smoother, narrower leaves; arching zigzag stems to 24 inches tall; and terminal, plume-like clusters of white, star-shaped flowers from May to June. The alternate, pointed, gray-green leaves that fold along the midrib are a distinctive feature. Use it in woodland gardens with native wildflowers. Zone 2.

Solidago rigida
Stiff goldenrod
Zone 3

Native Habitat Dry to moist grasslands and open woodlands in the southern halves of both the Upper and the Lower Peninsulas.

Height 3 to 5 feet

Description Stiff goldenrod has wide, flat, or somewhat rounded clusters of gold flowers in early fall. The light green leaves have short, stiff hairs and turn an attractive dusty rose in fall.

Landscape Use Goldenrods are a staple of prairie gardens, but they also adapt well to sunny perennial borders. The flowers attract bees and butterflies, including monarchs, and work well in fresh and dried arrangements.

Site Prefers average to infertile, well-drained soil in full sun.

Culture Keep the soil on the lean side; plants in rich soil often become floppy. Plants grow from clumps or rhizomes that will spread but can easily be kept under control if needed. Goldenrods are wrongly accused of causing hay fever; they are insect-pollinated plants, so their pollen is heavy and sticky rather than wind-borne. Self-sown seedlings can become weedy in small gardens.

Good Companions Plant goldenrods with other late-summer plants such as asters, Joe-pye weeds, blazing stars, purple coneflowers, and grasses.

Other Species *S. caesia* (blue-stemmed goldenrod) is native to rich deciduous woods as well as drier woods and dunes throughout most of the Lower Peninsula. It ranges from 1¹/2 to 4 feet in height. It is shade tolerant and can be used in woodland gardens, where fall color is hard to come by. Zone 3.

S. flexicaulis (zigzag goldenrod) is native to woods and woodland edges throughout most of Michigan. It grows 2 to 4 feet tall with erect, somewhat zigzagged stems, and flowers in small clusters. It prefers richer soil and light shade and is another good candidate for woodland gardens. Zone 3.

S. houghtonii (Houghton's goldenrod) is nearly endemic in Michigan, native to dunes along the northern shores of Lakes Michigan and Huron. It is on both Michigan and federal threatened species lists. It is not practical for garden use, but is included here because of its endemic nature.

S. juncea (early goldenrod) is native to dry grasslands and barrens throughout Michigan. It is the first native goldenrod to bloom, usually starting in late July. Yellow flower clusters resemble fireworks. Zone 3.

S. nemoralis (gray goldenrod) is native to dry grasslands, barrens, and open woodland throughout Michigan. It has tight, 1- to 2-foot clumps of gray-green basal leaves and one-sided, plumed clusters of lemon yellow flowers on 2-foot stems. Its smaller stature opens it up for use in rock gardens. Zone 2.

S. ohioensis (Ohio goldenrod) is native on shorelines and dunes as well as wet grasslands throughout most of Michigan. It has flat-topped clusters of large lemon yellow flowers on 2- to 3-foot stems. It is suitable for borders as well as prairie gardens. Zone 3.

S. rugosa (rough-stemmed goldenrod) is native to a wide variety of habitats throughout the Lower Peninsula and into the Upper Peninsula. It is too weedy for most landscape situations, but the cultivar 'Fireworks' is an excellent clump-forming selection well suited to garden use. Zone 4.

S. speciosa (showy goldenrod) is native to grasslands, dunes, and open woods throughout most of Michigan. It is one of the most beautiful goldenrods, growing 2 to 5 feet tall with small yellow flower heads crowded into dense, pyramidal, terminal clusters. Plants form tight clumps of leafy, red-tinged stems. Divide clumps every third year to promote vigorous growth and better flowering. It is an excellent choice for perennial borders. Zone 3.

Solidago rigida

Solidago flexicaulis

Solidago rugosa 'Fireworks'

Stylophorum diphyllum

Stylophorum diphyllum
Celandine poppy
Zone 4

Native Habitat Deciduous woods in the southwestern corner of Michigan.

Height 12 to 20 inches

Description This woodland beauty has exquisite, four-petaled, bright yellow, 2-inch flowers that have a sort of crepe-paper look. It blooms in spring. The sea green oaklike leaves have undulating margins and are decorative in their own right.

Landscape Use The best place to use celandine poppy is the woodland garden, where it offers much-needed yellow color for up to four weeks. It can also be used in shade gardens, but the seed heads should be removed after flowering to prevent too much of a good thing.

Site Prefers rich, moist soil in shade to partial shade.

Culture Celandine poppy often goes dormant after flowering if soil conditions are dry, so plan accordingly. Plants will self-sow, sometimes to the point of becoming weedy, but they are easy to remove.

Good Companions An awesome spring combination includes celandine poppy planted with woodland phlox, Virginia bluebells, showy trillium, and ostrich fern.

Thalictrum dioicum

Thalictrum dasycarpum

Thalictrum dioicum
Early meadow rue
Zone 3

Native Habitat Moist deciduous woods, mainly in the southern half of the Lower Peninsula, but also farther north and west in the Upper Peninsula.

Height 1 to 3 feet

Description Early meadow rue is grown mainly for its fine-textured foliage and bushy shape. The much-divided, thinly spreading compound leaves are bluish green. Plants are either male or female. The female flowers are insignificant. The greenish male flowers appear in mid- to late April in candelabra-like clusters of fuzzy-petaled flowers with pendant golden stamens that tremble in the slightest breeze.

Landscape Use Treat early meadow rue like a fern in the landscape, using its foliage to blend and soften other plants. It can be used in shade or rock gardens, along stone walls, or in masses in woodland gardens. The delicate flowers will be much more effective if you can get them up to eye level.

Site Prefers a fertile, moist, slightly acidic soil in light shade, but tolerates drier soil and deep shade.

Culture Early meadow rue is easily grown in gardens, seldom needing division or weeding out. Leaf miners can ruin the foliage; get rid of plant debris to remove overwintering sites.

Good Companions Grow early meadow rue with showier woodland wildflowers such as bloodroot, violets, and Virginia bluebells, using the foliage to tie the plantings together.

Other Species *T. dasycarpum* (tall meadow rue) is native to wet soils, wetland margins, and floodplains throughout Michigan. It grows 4 to 6 feet in height. The stems are often purple, and its inflorescence is made up of numerous drooping white flowers. It needs a larger spot with moist soil and can tolerate more sun. Zone 3.

Tiarella cordifolia
Foamflower
Zone 3

Native Habitat Moist woods, mainly in the northern half of the Lower Peninsula, but also farther southeast and north.

Height 3 to 10 inches

Description Foamflower gets its name from the frothy conical clusters of white flowers that are sometimes flushed with pink. They appear in spring. The handsome maple-leaf foliage is attractive all summer long, turning a beautiful red in autumn. Plants spread by trailing stolons.

Landscape Use Foamflower is an attractive, shady groundcover that will eventually form a weed-smothering mat of foliage. Use it under trees or shrubs or in combination with other woodland groundcovers.

Site Evenly moist, rich, slightly acidic soil in partial to full shade.

Culture Remove unwanted rooted

Tiarella cordifolia

runners at any time to keep plants from spreading too far. Foamflower is not drought tolerant and may need supplemental water during dry periods.

Good Companions Foamflower and wild ginger make an attractive and very tough groundcover in shady areas. In woodland gardens, combine foamflower with tougher species such as columbines, wild geraniums, and hostas, which won't be overtaken by this aggressive spreader.

Cultivars 'Running Tapestry' has light green leaves that have a distinct red speckling along the veins. 'Winterglow' has pointed, dissected foliage that appears gold with red flecking in winter.

Tradescantia ohioensis
Ohio spiderwort
Zone 3

Native Habitat Dry, sandy savannas and open woods in the southern part of Michigan.

Height 2 to 4 feet

Description Ohio spiderwort is a slender, branching plant; it has narrow blue-green leaves and deep medium-blue flowers with rounded petals. The foliage has long, leafy stems that resemble daylily foliage, especially when first emerging. Leaves are blue-green. The three-petaled flowers are flat faced and deep rose-pink to purple. They last only a day and usually close by midafternoon, but the plants produce blooms for most of June and July.

Landscape Use Plant spiderwort in prairie gardens or along the edge of woodland gardens. Its drought and heat tolerance make it a good choice for xeriscaping. It can also be grown in perennial borders, but the foliage often looks old and tired by midsummer. Plants may go dormant after flowering, so try to place them where they will be masked by other plants.

Site Grows best in lean, well-drained soil in full sun or light shade, but will grow in heavier, richer soils. Plants grown in shade will have fewer flowers.

Culture In fertile soils, plants may become aggressive. They also reseed. Foliage can be cut back to the ground after flowering to keep plants neat and to halt seed production.

Good Companions Plant spiderwort with other tough plants that offer late-season interest, such as mountain mints, asters, goldenrods, and ferns.

Cultivars and Other Species 'Alba' is a white-flowered form. Zone 3.

T. virginiana (Virginia spiderwort) is native to sandy soils in only a

Tradescantia ohiensis

few locations in the southern part of Michigan. It is a little shorter, with blue-purple flowers and similar foliage. It is on Michigan's special concern list. Zone 3.

Trillium grandiflorum

Trillium erectum

Trillium nivale

Trillium grandiflorum
Large-flowered trillium
Zone 3

Native Habitat Fertile, moist woodlands (primarily deciduous) and floodplains throughout most of Michigan.

Height 10 to 18 inches

Description Large-flowered trillium has a single white flower with three waxy petals and six yellow stamens; the flower is borne on a stalk above a whorl of three roundish leaves, on an erect stem. The funnel-shaped flower is 2 to 4 inches wide and turns pink with age. Flower time is from mid- to late April through May.

Landscape Use Large-flowered trillium really says "Michigan woodland" and is a great addition to any shade or woodland garden, either as specimen groupings or massed. It makes a nice underplanting beneath spring-blooming shrubs and trees.

Site Requires rich, well-drained soil in light to dense shade.

Culture Large-flowered trillium adapts surprisingly well to cultivation, but is slow to establish. The ideal site is one with a humus-rich sandy loam soil that remains consistently moist and where plants receive spring sun and summer shade. If massing, space plants 10 inches on center. It can take as many as seven years to flower when grown from seed. Be sure to purchase only container-grown, nursery-propagated specimens.

Good Companions Set off the pure-white flowers with blue phlox, Virginia bluebells, wild geraniums, and woodland ferns.

Cultivars and Other Species 'Flore Pleno' is a rare, fully double-flowered form.

T. cernuum (nodding trillium) is native to rich, damp woods throughout Michigan. It has short, curved flower stalks, so the flowers hang beneath the leaves. The nodding white flowers have reflexed petals that reveal rose or maroon anthers. It blooms anytime from late April to June. Zone 2.

T. erectum (purple trillium, stinking Benjamin) is native to rich, moist, deciduous woods in the Lower Peninsula. It grows 6 to 20 inches tall and has deep red flowers. Its vigorous clumping growth habit makes it a good choice for gardens. Flowers may have a fetid odor. Zone 3.

T. flexipes (white wake robin, drooping trillium) is native to rich deciduous woods in the southern part of Michigan. The white flower is on a rather long stalk and usually below the leaves. Zone 4.

T. nivale (snow trillium) is rare, found in moist forests and bottomlands in southern Michigan. It is the earliest trillium, starting its bloom in early April, sometimes poking up through snow. Plants are smaller than large-flowered trillium and have narrower leaves and flowers. Grow this 6-inch plant where it will be seen up close or it will get lost. It adapts well to cultivation, but is difficult to locate. It is on Michigan's threatened species list, so buy only nursery-propagated plants. Grow it in moist, humus-rich, limey soil in light to partial shade. Plants usually go dormant after flowering. Zone 4.

T. recurvatum (red trillium, prairie trillium) is rare, found in rich deciduous woods in the far southern part of Michigan. It grows 4 to 12 inches tall, and it has narrow-petaled, maroon flowers and mottled leaves. It adapts readily to garden use. It is on Michigan's threatened species list. Zone 4.

Uvularia grandiflora
Large-flowered bellwort
Zone 3

Native Habitat Deciduous woods and bottomlands, and occasionally under conifers, throughout most of Michigan.

Height 12 to 16 inches

Description Large-flowered bellwort has 1- to 2-inch, lemon yellow flowers that dangle bell-like from downturned stems. It blooms from late April to mid-May. The alternate, long, sea green leaves have smooth margins and downy white undersides, and they clasp the stem at their bases. The foliage expands after flowering to create a soothing, soft green groundcover.

Landscape Use The bright yellow color is a real attention getter in early spring woodland gardens. Place clumps here and there for interest. It is a good choice next to foundations on the north sides of buildings, as it can take the higher pH soil conditions often found next to concrete blocks. Plants compete well with the roots of trees, and the long-lasting, attractive foliage is an added bonus.

Site Prefers a moist, average, neutral to limey soil in spring sun and summer shade.

Culture An annual dusting of limestone may be needed in some sites to keep the soil pH in line.

Good Companions Large-flowered bellwort grows well with almost any early flowering woodland plant, but it is especially attractive with blue flowers such as Virginia bluebells and woodland phlox. In shade gardens, grow it with epimediums, foamflower, and pulmonarias.

Other Species *U. sessilifolia* (pale bellwort, wild oats) is native to woods and thickets mainly in the southeastern corner of Michigan, but also in the Porcupine Mountains. It is smaller, growing 4 to 12 inches tall, and more delicate and lighter yellow in flower. Culture and use are the same, but it prefers a more acidic soil. 'Variegata' is a rare variegated form for collectors. Zone 3.

Uvularia grandiflora

Uvularia sessilifolia

Verbena hastata
Blue vervain
Zone 3

Native Habitat Wet to moist soils of swamps and shorelines throughout Michigan.

Height 3 to 5 feet

Description Erect branches hold strongly vertical, candelabra-like spikes of small, dark blue flowers in summer and early fall. The leaves are long and narrow-toothed.

Landscape Use Plants are a little too coarse for specimen use, but the dark blue flowers are easily combined with gold and yellow late-summer bloomers and grasses in perennial borders and prairie gardens, where they add a strong vertical accent. Blue vervain can also be grown in bog gardens and alongside streams and ponds. All vervains make good cut flowers.

Site Prefers rich, evenly moist to wet soil in full sun or light shade.

Culture Hoary vervain adapts well to garden use. Self-sown seedlings occur but are rarely a nuisance.

Good Companions Grow blue vervain with wild bergamot, phloxes, coneflowers, and grasses.

Cultivars and Other Species 'Alba' is a hard-to-locate cultivar with pure white flowers.

V. stricta (hoary vervain) is thought to be native to dry soils of Michigan grasslands, but the exact range is unclear. It grows 1 to 3 feet tall and has erect branches holding strongly vertical spikes of very attractive blue-violet flowers in summer and early fall. Bloom starts at the bottom of the flower spike and works its way up, resulting in a long bloom time. The leaves are wedge shaped and hairy. It tolerates a wide variety of soil types in full sun. Zone 3.

Verbena stricta

Verbena hastata

Native Habitat Prairies, floodplains, and woodland edges, mainly in the southern half of the Lower Peninsula.

Height 3 to 6 feet

Description Culver's root is a strong architectural plant. The dark green, whorled leaves give the plant a horizontal effect that contrasts with the strong vertical spires of the white or pale lavender candelabra-like flowers. The flowers start blooming in midsummer and continue into early September.

Landscape Use This durable plant can be used in the middle or back of a perennial bed, where it offers a strong upright accent. It tolerates wet soil well. The flowers are good for cutting.

Site Prefers a moist to wet, rich soil and full sun to light shade, but grows well in ordinary garden soil that has been enriched with ample organic matter.

Culture Work generous amounts of organic matter into the soil before planting. Mulch plants and give them

Veronicastrum virginicum
Culver's root
Zone 3

Veronicastrum virginicum

an annual application of compost to keep soil rich and moist. Culver's root forms clumps as it ages but is not overly aggressive. Water plants during dry spells.

Good Companions The long bloom time and tall stature of Culver's root make it a good backdrop for many border plants, including blazing stars, lilies, oxeye, monardas, milkweeds, rattlesnake master, goldenrods, and asters.

Cultivars 'Apollo' has lavender flowers. 'Roseum' has pale rose-pink flowers. Zone 3.

Viola pedata

Native Habitat Sandy soils of grasslands and barrens, mainly in the eastern half of the Lower Peninsula.

Height 4 to 8 inches

Description Bird's-foot violet has bluish purple flowers that are up to 1 1/2 inches wide, bilaterally symmetrical, and have five petals and orange centers. They start blooming in late April. The leaves, which are shaped like bird's feet, rise directly from the roots.

Landscape Use Use this charming plant as a groundcover on sandy banks

Viola pedata
Bird's-foot violet
Zone 3

or in large rock gardens. It adapts well to container culture and is pretty in trough gardens. Plants may rebloom sporadically in summer and fall.

Site Prefers sandy, acidic, well-drained soil in full to partial sun.

Culture Bird's-foot violet is a bit more finicky than other violets, but is worth the trouble. It will rot if the soil is not well drained. It is not a strong competitor, so keep it free of weeds and other aggressive plants. Maintain soil acidity with a mulch of pine needles or shredded oak leaves. Plants may be short lived, but seedlings are plentiful. Rabbits can be a problem.

Good Companions Plant bird's-foot violet with other delicate early bloomers such as prairie smoke, blue-eyed grass, and spring bulbs. It really stands out against the brown grasses when it blooms in prairie gardens in spring.

Other Species *V. canadensis* (Canada violet) is native to deciduous wood-

lands throughout Michigan. It grows to 1 foot tall. It has heart-shaped leaves and white flowers with a purplish blush and yellow centers. It spreads by runners to form patches. Zone 3.

V. pubescens (yellow violet) is native to moist woodlands throughout Michigan. It is a robust plant, growing 6 to 16 inches tall and having lemon yellow flowers. Plants have hairy, heart-shaped leaves and form dense clumps in rich, evenly moist soil and in light to full shade. Use it in woodland or shade gardens. Zone 3.

V. sororia (common blue violet) is native to woodlands and clearings throughout Michigan. It grows about 10 inches tall and has deep purple-blue flowers. It makes a lush green groundcover where few plants will grow. It likes moist soil in sun or shade, but tolerates a wide variety of conditions. It is a prolific self-sower and can become weedy. Zone 3.

Waldsteinia fragarioides
Barren strawberry
Zone 4

Native Habitat Open woods and savannas scattered throughout Michigan.

Height 3 to 6 inches

Description Barren strawberry is a rhizomatous perennial somewhat resembling cultivated strawberry plants. The basal leaves have three leaflets, and the flowering stems bear several small yellow flowers from April to May, followed by tiny inedible fruits.

Landscape Use This unique-looking groundcover forms a dense mat where conditions are favorable. It leafs out early and can tolerate the dry shade under large trees or on slopes. It can be used in large rock gardens, in stone walls, or between pavers in walkways.

Site Prefers a moist, acidic soil in full sun to light shade, but tolerates drier sites.

Waldsteinia fragarioides

Culture If necessary, before planting, acidify the soil and/or use organic matter and sand to improve drainage. Plant crowns even with the soil surface, as you would plant strawberries. Plants are fairly drought tolerant once established but require regular watering their first year.

Good Companions Barren strawberry makes a good groundcover under azaleas and other shrubs and under large trees.

Zizia aurea
Golden alexanders
Zone 3

Native Habitat Open woods, floodplains, and moist grasslands in the southern half of the Lower Peninsula.

Height 1 to 3 feet

Description From May to June, this erect, bushy perennial has umbels of small yellow flowers that resemble Queen Anne's lace. The compound leaves have elongated leaflets and a bluish cast.

Landscape Use The flattened heads of yellow flowers are a bright accent in a spring garden, and the foliage looks nice all summer. Use golden alexanders in prairie gardens, open woodland gardens, or perennial borders, where it will weave its way through other plants. It spreads rapidly and should not be planted where space is limited. Plants are food sources for several butterfly larvae.

Site Prefers moist, well-drained soil and light shade or full sun.

Culture Once established, golden

Zizia aurea

alexanders are carefree plants that tolerate summer dryness. Individual plants may be short lived, but they will self-sow to maintain the population.

Good Companions The cheery yellow flowers combine nicely with prairie smoke, blue phlox, butterfly weed, wild lupine, columbines, and wild geraniums.

Other Species *Z. aptera* (heart-leaved alexanders) is only found in one location, on a dry shaded bluff in the east-central part of the Lower Peninsula. Flowers are similar but smaller, and the 1- to 2-foot flower stalks arise from rosettes of attractive, leathery, basal leaves. It is not as invasive as golden alexanders and can be used in more formal landscape situations. Unfortunately, it is difficult to locate in nurseries. It is on Michigan's threatened species list. Zone 3.

Additional Native Flowers and Groundcovers

Acorus americanus (sweet flag) is native to wet, open places throughout most of Michigan. It is an upright plant growing 3 feet tall and wide. The flowers are yellowish green and not particularly ornamental. The crushed leaves and rhizomes give off a cinnamon-like aroma. Sweet flag requires a moist soil in sun or partial shade. It spreads by means of rhizomes and is a good choice for wetland restoration. 'Variegatus' has leaves marked with white. Zone 5; trial in zone 4.

Agastache nepetoides (yellow giant hyssop) is native to open deciduous woods in the southern half of the Lower Peninsula. It grows 4 to 6 feet tall. Its greenish yellow flower spikes appear from mid- to late summer and can last well into fall. Grow it in full sun to partial shade in perennial borders, in prairie gardens, and along woodland edges, where it will attract bees and butterflies. Zone 2.

A. scrophulariifolia (purple giant hyssop) is native to woodland borders and floodplains in the southern part of Michigan. It is similar to yellow giant hyssop but has purplish red flowers and prefers a moister soil. Zone 2.

Angelica atropurpurea (angelica) is a native of wet to moist soils in grasslands and open woodlands, mainly in the southern half of the Lower Peninsula, but also in scattered locations in northern Michigan. It grows 4 to 6 feet tall and has a smooth, dark purple stem 1 to 2 inches in diameter. The leaves are divided into three parts, each of which is again divided into many broad leaflets. The 8- to 10-inch, greenish white flowers are produced in roundish heads from June to July. Angelica's size and need for moist soil limits its use, but it makes an interesting specimen plant in perennial borders and along water features. Zone 4.

Astragalus canadensis (Canada milk vetch) is native to grasslands and shorelines, mainly in the southern part of Michigan. This robust clump perennial grows 1 to 4 feet tall and has pinnately compound leaves with many leaflets. The elongated, loose clusters of interesting flowers are cream colored and appear in July and August. They are attractive to hummingbirds and can be used in cut bouquets. Grow Canada milk vetch in full sun to partial shade in perennial borders and prairie gardens. It does not transplant well, so choose a site carefully. Its limited occurrence in Michigan has put it on the state's threatened species list. Zone 2.

Astragalus canadensis

Cacalia atriplicifolia (pale Indian plantain) is native to dry soils of grasslands and dunes in the southern part of Michigan. It is a striking plant, growing 5 to 10 feet tall. It has fan-shaped, waxy, blue-green foliage and white flower clusters in summer. It makes an interesting accent plant in prairie gardens, where it grows in medium to moist soils in full sun to light shade. Zone 4.

Cacalia atriplicifolia

Calla palustris (wild calla) is native to bogs, swamps, and ponds throughout Michigan. It grows 12 inches tall. It has a broad, white, 2-inch spathe that partially surrounds a 1-inch spadix bearing tiny yellow flowers from May to August. The long-stalked basal leaves are dark green, glossy, heart-shaped, and 2 to 6 inches long. Plant wild calla in submerged soil in full sun at the edge of streams or ponds where it can form colonies. It will extend the season of color after marsh marigolds go dormant midsummer. Zone 2.

Camassia scilloides [C. esculenta] (wild hyacinth) is native to wet to moist soils along rivers in the far southwestern corner of Michigan. It is a neat, clump-forming plant growing 12 to 16 inches tall with whorls of strap-like green leaves and stalks of pale blue-violet or white flowers in loose racemes in spring. It requires moist to wet soil in spring, but somewhat drier summer conditions are okay, in sun or part shade. Wild hyacinth is an excellent choice for an accent near water features. It can also be used for naturalizing in moist areas. Keep in mind that plants go dormant in summer and leaves must be allowed to remain until plants go dormant so plants can store food for the next year. Wild hyacinth is on Michigan's threatened species list because of its rarity in the state. Zone 5; trial Zone 4.

Corydalis sempervirens (pink corydalis) is native to rock ledges and sandy woodlands in all but the far southeastern quarter of Michigan. It grows 18 to 30 inches tall and has elegant, drooping, tubular, pink-and-yellow flowers from May through September and deeply cut and divided blue-green leaves. It is a reseeding biennial that grows in dry soil in sun to partial shade. It is good for rock gardens. Zone 4.

Epilobium angustifolium

Epilobium angustifolium (fire-weed) is native to dry, open woodlands throughout Michigan. It grows 3 to 6 feet tall and has spiked clusters of flamboyant magenta flowers that bloom from the bottom up, starting in July and continuing into late August. It is especially abundant in an area two to three years after a fire, where it can grow into dense groundcover. Fireweed is a little too aggressive for most landscape situations, but it can be used in naturalized plantings and for erosion control. The flowers are attractive to hummingbirds and bees. It requires a moist, well-drained soil in full sun. Zone 2.

Equisetum hyemale (tall scouring rush) is native to damp places near streams and in dunes throughout Michigan, except in the far southeastern corner. It is an interesting plant, growing 20 to 36 inches tall and having evergreen, unbranched, jointed stems. It is an instant focal point in Japanese-style gardens or near garden pools. Grow it in moist, slightly acidic soil in partial shade to almost full sunlight. It can become invasive; plant it in a buried nursery container to keep rhizomes contained. Zone 2.

Erigeron pulchellus (Robin's plantain) is native to rich, moist-to-wet woodlands mainly in the southern half of the Lower Peninsula. It grows about 18 inches tall and has 1- to 1½-inch, aster-like flower heads with violet

or pink petals surrounding a flat, yellow, central disc. It blooms spring to early summer. It spreads readily by runners and is best used for naturalizing at the edge of woodlands. Zone 3.

Galium boreale (northern bed-straw) is native to prairies and open woodlands throughout Michigan. It grows about 12 inches tall from creeping roots, and it forms large patches, weaving its way among other plants. It is easy to grow in any soil in sun or partial shade, and it is drought tolerant once established. Use it to create a lacy backdrop for darker-colored prairie plants such as butterfly weed and bird's-foot coreopsis. Zone 2.

Galium boreale

Goodyera pubescens (downy rattlesnake plantain) is native mainly to dry, upland oak or pine woods, usually in sandy, acidic soil, throughout Michigan. A ground-hugging, mat-forming orchid, it has small white flowers in dense clusters, which appear on stalks reaching 6 to 18 inches tall. It starts flowering in late July and continues into September. The foliage is very showy; dark green leaves cover a network of whitish veins. It spreads slowly by rhizomes and is a good groundcover for the acidic conditions found under conifers and oaks. Zone 3.

Hibiscus moscheutos (swamp rose mallow) is native to moist soils in the southeastern and southwestern corners of Michigan. It is a

shrub-like perennial that grows 4 feet tall or more. Broad, shallowly lobed leaves grow on erect stalks from a woody crown. Open clusters of 6- to 8-inch, white or pinkish flowers with deep red centers appear at the tops of the stems in summer. Flowers only last one day but are produced in abundance for a long time. Tropical-looking and showy, swamp rose mallow is a great accent plant, livening up borders in summer. It does well in bog and rainwater gardens and alongside ponds. The dried seed capsules add winter interest. It needs evenly moist soil in full sun to light shade. Established plants tolerate drier conditions. Swamp rose mallow's range just barely extends into Michigan, and it is on Michigan's special concern list. Be sure to purchase only nursery-propagated plants. Var. *palustris* [*H. palustris*] has deep pink flowers. Zone 4.

Hydrophyllum virginianum (Virginia waterleaf) is a native of moist to wet woods and openings in most of Michigan. It has showy, silvery gray, "watermarked" leaves that provide early interest in woodland gardens. The pale to deep violet flowers appear in airy, rounded clusters in mid-May. Plants are easy to grow but can become weedy. It is a good plant to use in woodland areas where buckthorn has recently been eradicated. Plants fill bare areas quickly and help reduce soil erosion. Zone 3.

Hydrophyllum virginianum

Hypericum ascyron [*H. pyramidatum*] **(giant St. John's wort)** is a native of wet to moist soils throughout most of Michigan. It is an upright plant that grows 2 to 6 feet tall. In summer it has yellow-orange, five-petaled flowers that can grow up to 2 inches across. For an awesome color display, use it in lightly shaded, moist places near streams and ponds with great blue lobelia. Zone 3.

Hypoxis hirsuta **(yellow star grass)** is native to sandy grasslands and open woods in the southern half of the Lower Peninsula. It grows only 3 to 6 inches tall and has bright yellow flowers late spring into summer. It grows in moist to dry soil in sun to partial sun. A clump of star grass has the look of miniature daffodils, and it will form a tidy groundcover after a few years. It can also be grown along pathways and in rock gardens. Zone 3.

Lespedeza capitata **(round-headed bush clover)** is native to dry prairies and savannas mainly in southern Michigan. It grows 30 to 48 inches tall on sturdy stalks. Inconspicuous whitish flowers emerge in summer, but the main attraction is the bronze seed heads, which provide fall and winter color and are an important food supply for birds. It prefers a dry, well-drained, sandy soil in full sun or very light shade. Plant it in prairie gardens. Zone 4.

Linnaea borealis **(twinflower)** is native to moist, cool, northern woodlands and bogs in the northeastern quarter of Michigan. It is a creeping evergreen growing 3 to 6 inches tall and has stems that root as they spread. Each upright branch bears a pair of nodding, white or pinkish, bell-shaped flowers from June to August. The rounded, light green leaves are finely toothed at their tips and occur in pairs along the trailing stems. Plant twinflower near the edges of paths where you can see it up close. This dainty little groundcover looks very nice in mossy habitats and growing over rotting stumps and logs. It

requires a moist, high-humus, acidic, peaty soil in partial shade. Plants will form dense colonies over time but do not become invasive. Zone 2.

Lysimachia ciliata **(fringed loosestrife)** is native along streams throughout Michigan, usually in moist, shaded places but sometimes in full sun. It grows 2 to 3 feet tall and forms a sprawling mass. The pretty yellow flowers are arranged in whorls and borne on slender stalks arising from leaf axils from June to September. Use fringed loosestrife for naturalizing in low, moist areas in light shade; it is aggressive and may overcrowd nearby plants. 'Atropurpurea' and 'Purpurea' have purple-bronze foliage and are supposedly less invasive. Zone 3.

Lysimachia ciliata

Mimulus ringens **(monkey flower)** is native to wet soils throughout Michigan. It grows 2 to 4 feet tall and has light violet flowers in summer. It grows best in moist to wet soils in full sun and is good for naturalizing in wet areas. It is a short-lived perennial that will reseed. Zone 4.

Mitchella repens **(partridge-berry)** is native to rich, moist woodlands, pinelands, and clearings mainly in east-central Michigan, but also farther north and south. It is a low (1 to 3 inches tall), creeping evergreen that

forms large mats. Paired, white, tubular flowers with four spreading lobes appear in May. Each pair of flowers forms one bright red berry in fall. Leaves are opposite, round, and shiny green, and they have a distinct white vein down the center. Use this dainty groundcover in shade gardens, where it will weave among other shade plants. It makes a nice underplanting for acid-loving shrubs such as azaleas. The wintergreen-scented berries are showy all winter if not eaten by birds. Mulch with a thin layer of pine needles, and water during dry periods. Do not allow this low-growing plant to be smothered by fallen leaves. Zone 3.

Oenothera biennis **(common evening primrose)** is native to dry, sandy soils in grasslands and sometimes on dunes throughout most of Michigan. It is a biennial, growing up to 6 feet tall and has cheery yellow flowers from mid- to late summer. It can become weedy and is best used in large naturalized plantings, where it will perpetuate itself by reseeding. Zone 4.

Oenothera fruticosa **(sundrops)** is native to dry soils in the southern third of the state. It grows 16 to 30 inches tall and has yellow blooms in summer. It is a somewhat aggressive spreader, but can be used in large perennial borders, grassland gardens, and for xeriscaping. Zone 4.

Mimulus ringens

Porteranthus trifoliatus [Gillenia trifoliatus] **(Bowman's root)** is found in oak clearings in the southern part of Michigan. This shrubby, 2- to 3-foot perennial has zigzag stems of three-part leaves. In early summer, five-petaled, star-shaped, white to pinkish flowers "float" above the foliage. The showy red sepals below the flowers persist after the petals drop. The leaves turn orange-yellow in fall. Bowman's root is most effective in masses, where the flowers lend a light airy texture to the back of large borders and edges of woodland gardens. Give it moist to dry soil in sun to partial shade; plants are drought tolerant once established. Bowman's root is on Michigan's threatened species list because of its rarity in the state. Zone 4.

Sanguisorba canadensis **(Canadian burnet)** is native to a few wet prairies in the southern part of Michigan. It grows 6 feet tall and has small white flowers borne in spikes from late summer into fall. It prefers moist soil in full sun to partial shade. Grow it near water or in a well-mulched site at the back of a perennial border, where it provides late-season interest. It is on Michigan's threatened species list. Zone 3.

Sarracenia purpurea **(common pitcher plant)** is native to the wet soils of bogs and swamps throughout Michigan. It is a very interesting plant, growing 6 to 12 inches tall and having evergreen leaves arranged in a rosette that catches water and attracts insects, which the plant then "eats." Dark red flowers rise about the rosettes in spring. Grow this attention-getting, unique specimen in acidic bog gardens in full to partial sun. Zone 2.

Scutellaria lateriflora **(mad-dog scullcap)** is a native of moist to wet soils, usually in shaded locations, throughout Michigan. It grows 1 to 2 feet tall and has violet to lavender tubular flowers, each with a flared lower lip and protruding upper lip. It blooms in late summer. The quilted, toothed foliage resembles spearmint but lacks a strong fragrance. It is best suited for naturalizing in a woodland garden or along a stream or pond. It needs moist to wet soil in sun to partial shade. Zone 3.

Streptopus roseus **(rose twisted stalk)** is native to rich woods and stream banks in northeastern Michigan. It has 12- to 30-inch succulent stems clothed in clasping, deeply veined, succulent leaves. Small rose-pink bells hang from the leaf axils in spring and are followed by showy red fruits in summer. Plant small groups or large colonies in cool shade, in moist but not wet sites, and in rich, acidic soil. Zone 3.

Trientalis borealis **(starflower)** is native to rich, moist, acidic woods and bogs, mainly in the northeastern quarter of Michigan. This delicate ephemeral grows 4 to 8 inches tall and spreads by thin rhizomes with fibrous roots. It can have one to three flowers, but usually has two. The white flowers have golden anthers and arise on slender stalks from a whorl of five to nine canoe-shaped leaves. Starflower blooms from mid-May into June. It is a good groundcover in moist, rich, acidic soils, spreading rapidly but not too aggressively. Plants go dormant in mid-summer, so plant them with ferns and other summer-foliage plants. Mulch with sphagnum moss or pine needles to maintain soil acidity, and grow in full or partial shade. Zone 2.

Vernonia missurica **(Missouri ironweed)** is native to low, wet places in the southern half of the Lower Peninsula. It grows 3 to 5 feet tall and has magenta-purple flowers in late summer. It can be used toward the back of large perennial borders, where it offers a strong vertical presence. It is also good for prairie gardens and screening. The flowers are good for cutting. Although native to moist soils, Missouri ironweed adapts well to garden settings as long as it is not drought stressed. Mulch plants to keep soil moist. Pinch back stems in late May to keep plants compact. Unpinched plants may need staking or support of some kind. Zone 4.

Trientalis borealis

Grasses and Sedges

Grasses are an important part of native landscapes. They are easy to grow and care for, and they wave in the slightest breeze, bringing a sense of movement to a landscape. They have four-season interest, but are especially valuable in fall and winter, when they combine beautifully with evergreens and fruiting shrubs. Taller types can be used similarly to shrubs—as background plants, as specimens, or even as a hedge. Smaller types work well with annuals and perennials in herbaceous borders.

Grasses have a pure, abstract quality that blends well with modern architectures, and their shapes, colors, and textures contrast nicely with wood, stone, and other hard structural surfaces. Some people choose to create entire gardens of grasses. Beyond their landscape value, many are valuable sources of food and cover for birds, and the mature seed heads are prized for dried arrangements.

Being wind pollinated, grasses don't need brightly colored flowers to attract insects. They release their pollen into the air to float from flower head to flower head on gentle breezes. That doesn't mean their flowers aren't attractive, however. Flowers can be lacy panicles, stiff brushes, or waving plumes, often with beautiful fall color. Most grasses flower from August into fall, but some flower earlier. To make it easier to see the flowers, plant grasses against dark fences or backgrounds of evergreens.

Leaves of grasses are lance-shaped with parallel veins, and they come in many shades of green. Plants have round, hollow stems and branching roots—never a taproot. Grasses are classified as mounded,

upright, arching, open, irregular, and combinations of these forms. Most grow from clumps and are easy to use in the landscape, but some spread by creeping rhizomes (underground stems) or stolons (horizontal stems that creep just above or just below ground and root at nodes).

These spreading types are best used in prairie gardens, for erosion control, or groundcover.

Sedges are grass-like plants, but are not true grasses. They can be distinguished from grasses by their solid, three-angled flower stems (grasses have round, hollow flower stems). Most sedges form dense, compact clumps of bright green foliage.

Planting

Some native grasses are available only as seeds and are often found in mixtures used for seeding prairies or other restoration projects. Many of the types better suited to landscape use are available in containers, which is the easiest way to plant them. Plant grasses after all danger of frost has passed in spring, spacing plants according to their final size. Smaller grasses can be planted as close as 1 foot apart, but taller types require 3 to 5 feet between plants. Water well after planting and as needed the first year until plants are established. A summer mulch will help conserve water and keep weeds down. Place 2 inches of compost, shredded leaves, dried grass clippings, or pine needles around plants in late spring.

Most grasses grow best in well-drained soil that is not overly fertile. In all cases, the addition of organic matter to the soil increases plant health. If possible before planting, mix in compost, rotted manure, or peat moss. Most grasses flower and grow best in full sun, but some tolerate light shade, and a few prefer full shade. Most are tolerant of wind and can be used in open, exposed areas where other plants would be damaged. It is important to remove all grassy weeds from the site before planting, since it is difficult to remove grass weeds from grass plants. If not eliminated, weedy perennial grasses such as quack grass and canary reed grass will overwhelm desirable plants.

Care

Grasses require little maintenance once established. To help ensure survival the first winter after planting, cover the soil with weed-free straw or leaves after the ground has frozen. Remove mulch before growth begins in spring. On established plants, leave the foliage so you and the birds can enjoy the flowers in winter. Cut back plants in late winter before new growth begins. If you only have a few plants, use a hand pruner or hedge shears. A string trimmer can be used if you have a large number of grasses to cut back. If practical, burning is also effective.

To look their best, grass plants need dividing at some point, some more frequently than others. Early spring is best. If the clump is crowding its neighbors or looks dead in the middle, remove the center and replant the smaller outside clumps.

Possible Problems

Grasses are generally disease and insect free. Poorly drained soils may lead to crown rot on some plants. To reduce problems, choose the right grass for the site or improve the soil before planting.

Special-Use Native Grasses and Sedges

There are many other native species suitable for grasslands, restorations, and other specialized uses. These are usually available as seeds, often as part of mixtures, from specialty nurseries.

Agropyron trachycaulum (slender wheat grass)
Beckmannia syzigachne (slough grass)
Brachyelytrum erectum (long-awned wood grass)
Bromus species (bromes)
Calamovilfa longifolia (sand reed grass)
Carex species (sedges)
Cinna arundinacea (wood reed grass)

Cladium mariscoides (twig rush)
Danthonia spicata (poverty oat grass)
Diarrhena americana (beak grass)
Eleocharis acicularis (spike rush)
Elymus species (rye grasses)
Glyceria species (manna grasses)
Juncus species (common rushes)
Leersia oryzoides (rice cut grass)
Melica smithii (Smith's melic grass)

Muhlenbergia species (satin grasses)
Paspalum ciliatifolium (hairy lens grass)
Poa palustris (fowl bluegrass)
Rhynchospora macrostachya (tall beak rush)
Scirpus species (bulrushes)
Scleria verticillata (nut rush)
Sparganium eurycarpum (giant bur-reed)
Stipa spartea (porcupine grass)

Left: Native grasses are essential to prairie gardens, but many can also be used to add interest to other areas of the landscape in autumn and winter. Here *Panicum virgatum* 'Rostrahlbusch' grows with *Picea pungens* 'Globosa' (Colorado spruce) and *Hylotelephium* 'Autumn Joy' (sedum).

Andropogon gerardii
Big bluestem
Zone 3

Andropogon gerardii

Native Habitat Grasslands and woodland openings throughout the Lower Peninsula and in select spots on the Upper Peninsula.

Height 4 to 8 feet

Description Big bluestem is a clump-forming grass. It has blue-green stems topped with fingerlike racemes of fruiting clusters. The flower clusters, which resemble upside-down turkey feet, really stand out in late summer. The fall foliage color is an attractive bronzy reddish brown.

Landscape Use Although attractive, big bluestem gets too large for many landscape situations. Use single plants in prairie gardens or large mixed borders. It is great for massing in naturalistic plantings, where birds can enjoy the seeds.

Site Prefers full sun to partial shade and a moist, fertile, well-drained soil, but is adaptable to soil type.

Culture This warm-season grass is easy to grow. Space plants 1 to 2 feet apart. Mow or cut back in spring. Big bluestem is long lived, so choose a site carefully.

Good Companions Combine this large grass with other tall prairie plants such as asters, goldenrods, Joe-pye weeds, and Indian grass, or grow it as a backdrop for butterfly weed, milkweeds, coneflowers, and blazing stars.

Other Species *A. virginicus* (broom sedge) is native in sandy soil, mainly in the southwestern corner of Michigan but also in the southeast. It is shorter, growing to about 4 feet; it has a stiff, upright growth habit and bright orange fall color. It is very drought tolerant. Broom sedge can become weedy, so it is best reserved for large grassland gardens. Zone 3.

Bouteloua curtipendula
Side-oats grama
Zone 3

Bouteloua curtipendula

Native Habitat Grasslands and open woodlands in the southern part of Michigan.

Height 2 to 3 feet

Description Side-oats grama gets its name from the way the flowers are arranged on one side of the stem. The purplish spikes of oatlike flowers appear in midsummer, hanging downward from the stalks, and the seed heads remain attractive into fall. It produces short rhizomes and tends to a bunch-type growth. This warm-season grass has gray-green summer foliage, changing to straw color in fall.

Landscape Use This grass is often overlooked for a specimen, but the unique flowers serve as a striking focal point in prairie gardens or in sunny rock gardens. Birds eat the seeds in winter. This sod-forming grass can take occasional mowing and is sometimes part of native lawn mixtures.

Site Prefers an average to dry, well-drained garden soil in full sun.

Culture Space plants 1 foot apart. Mow or cut back in spring. Side-oats grama spreads relatively slowly, but plant it in a buried nursery container if you need to restrict root growth. It is on Michigan's threatened species list.

Good Companions Plant side-oats grama with other dry-soil prairie plants or massed as a groundcover.

Carex pensylvanica
Pennsylvania sedge
Zone 3

Native Habitat Moist and dry woods throughout most of Michigan.

Height 8 to 10 inches

Description This grass-like plant grows in cute but persistent tufts on the forest floor. Its long rhizomes allow it to spread out and colonize nearby open areas, and it often appears in pure stands in woodlands. This cool-season plant provides some of the earliest green color in spring.

Landscape Use Use individual clumps or small groupings to soften stones in woodland gardens. In shady rock gardens, Pennsylvania sedge's uncommon grass-like form will add interest. It is sometimes planted as a no-mow groundcover under maples, basswoods, or pines.

Site Grows on well-drained sites, in soils ranging from loam to sand. Some soil types are slightly acidic and relatively infertile. Does well in shade or sun.

Culture Pennsylvania sedge is adaptable to a wide variety of conditions. It spreads but is not overly aggressive. It does not appear to be bothered by deer.

Good Companions Pennsylvania sedge looks nice with almost any woodland plant and is especially attractive planted with spring ephemerals.

Other species *C. grayi* (Gray's sedge) is native to moist soils mainly in the southern half of the Lower Peninsula. This semi-evergreen sedge grows 24 inches tall and has starlike seed heads that are interesting in dried arrangements. It is tolerant of wet soil and partial shade. Zone 4.

C. muskingumensis (palm sedge) is native along rivers and in low woods mainly in southeastern Michigan. It grows 2 to 3 feet tall and has wide, straplike, light green leaves that resemble palm fronds. Grow it in moist, fertile soil in partial to full shade. The creeping rhizomes spread slowly to form an effective groundcover. 'Wachtposten' is more upright and tolerates drier sites. Zone 4.

C. plantaginea (plantain-leaved sedge) is native in moist woods throughout Michigan. It has broad

Carex pensylvanica

evergreen leaves that are reddish at the base. Use it to soften stones along shady water gardens. Zone 3.

C. stricta (tussock sedge) is native to wetlands throughout most of Michigan. It forms a dense, 2-foot clump of long, slender leaves that arch outward, creating a symmetrical fountain-like effect. As the plants develop, they form vertical-sided columns on which they grow, raising them above their surroundings and further adding to their distinctive appearance. Zone 3.

Deschampsia caespitosa
Tufted hair grass
Zone 4

Native Habitat Widely scattered fertile wetlands or sandy lakeshores throughout most of Michigan.

Height 3 to 4 feet in flower

Description Tufted hair grass is a well-mannered bunch grass with dark green stems and rolled leaves that give the plants a stiff, wiry appearance. During summer it produces large, open panicles of glistening, silver-tinted flower heads that have a cloudlike quality. The tight basal tufts grow about 1 foot tall and spread 2 feet wide.

Landscape Use A tolerance for wet soils makes this plant useful for planting near water; it can even be used in bog gardens. It is good for naturalizing, as the billowy masses of fine-textured

flower stalks become cloudlike. A dark background will set off the delicate flowers.

Site Grows best in moist soils in full sun, but does tolerate partial shade. Avoid sunny, droughty conditions.

Culture This cool-season grass needs regular water; it will turn brown if allowed to dry out. Garden plants grown in drier soil should be mulched and given supplemental water as needed. It tolerates a fair amount of shade, but flowering will be reduced. Plants often self-sow. Plants can be sheared off in late summer if they start to look tired.

Good Companions Plant tufted hair grass with other moisture lovers such

Deschampsia caespitosa

as cardinal flower, Joe-pye weeds, blue flags, and obedient plant.

Cultivars 'Bronze Veil' ['Bronzeschleier'] flower heads have distinct bronze-yellow tones when they open, fading to amber as they mature. 'Northern Lights' has cream-and-green variegated leaves and a pinkish blush on new growth. 'Scotland' ['Schottland'] has dark green leaves and airy, yellow-green flower panicles that fade to light buff. Zone 4.

Elymus canadensis
Nodding wild rye
Zone 3

Elymus canadensis

Native Habitat Mesic grasslands, open woodlands, and dunes throughout most of Michigan.

Height 3 to 6 feet

Description From July to August, this cool-season bunching grass has dense, silvery leaves and large, nodding, golden seed plumes that resemble cultivated rye seeds.

Landscape Use This fast-growing prairie grass is not only attractive in prairie gardens, but it is also a good grass to plant on bare ground, as it looks nice, keeps out weeds, and reduces erosion. Birds eat the seeds.

Site Prefers a well-drained soil with plenty of moisture and full sun, but tolerates dry soils and full shade.

Culture Nodding wild rye grows in an incredible range of soils, including bare sand, gravel, clay, and even damp soils. It also serves as an excellent native nurse crop for prairie seedlings. Plant it at a rate of 2 to 3 pounds per acre, as part of a prairie seed mix. It will mature in the first or second year, ahead of the longer-lived prairie grasses and flowers.

Good Companions Nodding wild rye combines nicely with other prairie plants.

Other Species *E. hystrix* [*Hystrix patula*] (bottlebrush grass) is native to moist soil in oak savannas and woodlands throughout much of Michigan. It is a tall, graceful grass with large, showy, bottlebrush seed heads that catch the sunlight, even in light shade. Use it in prairie gardens and restorations. Zone 3.

E. virginicus (Virginia wild rye) is native to moist soils in grasslands and open woodlands throughout most of Michigan. It has green leaves; the seed heads are upright rather than nodding, and they appear earlier. It is also shorter (reaching 5 feet), less drought tolerant, and more shade tolerant. It does particularly well in slightly moist soils along woodland streams and floodplains, where it will readily reseed. It is excellent for wooded openings and forest edges, especially along cooler north- and east-facing forest edges. Zone 3.

Koeleria macrantha
June grass
Zone 3

Native Habitat Grasslands, dunes, and savannas throughout most of the Lower Peninsula.

Height 1 to 2 feet

Description This cool-season bunch grass blooms earlier than most prairie grasses—as early as May but usually in June—with yellowish or greenish white flowers that are quite showy.

Landscape Use June grass is one of the first native grasses to green up, offering a nice green color in prairie gardens while most other grasses are still brown. It usually remains as clumps rather than forming dense stands. It can be used for dune restoration or as a groundcover on hot, dry sites.

Site Well-drained soil in full sun.

Culture Make sure soil is well drained before planting. Amend heavy soils with sand and organic matter. Plants may go dormant in summer. It withstands occasional mowing.

Good Companions June grass is a nice backdrop for spring bulbs and early blooming grassland plants such as prairie smoke and bird's-foot violet.

Koeleria macrantha

Panicum virgatum
Switch grass
Zone 4

Native Habitat Mesic to wet prairies, dunes, and oak woodlands throughout much of the Lower Peninsula.

Height 3 to 6 feet

Description This warm-season grass forms handsome upright clumps of medium-textured foliage. Airy conical flower heads appear in late summer and are green with a pinkish cast, turning yellow to golden brown in fall.

Landscape Use Switch grass is one of the best native grasses for landscape use. It can be used in mixed borders, as a screen, or in natural gardens. The open flower panicles look best when viewed against a dark background. The dense foliage stands up well in winter and provides excellent cover for wildlife.

Site Any average garden soil in full sun.

Culture Allow 2 to 3 feet between plants, as clumps become large. Switch grass tolerates poor conditions, including poor drainage and occasional flooding. Plants are fairly slow to spread, but division will be needed to keep plants under control in gardens. Self-sown seedlings will appear.

Good Companions Plant switch grass with other late-summer prairie plants such as asters, goldenrods, coneflowers, and boltonia. It looks nice with an evergreen background in winter.

Cultivars 'Heavy Metal' has metallic blue foliage that turns yellow in fall. Zone 4. 'Rotstrahlbusch' has good red fall color. Zone 4. 'Shenandoah' has reddish purple foliage by midsummer and a distinct reddish cast to the 3-inch flower heads. Zone 4.

Panicum virgatum

Schizachyrium scoparium
Little bluestem
Zone 3

Native Habitat Well-drained soils of dunes, barrens, and savannas throughout most of the Lower Peninsula and in scattered locations on the Upper Peninsula.

Height 2 to 3 feet

Description This attractive clump former has light green to blue foliage in summer, turning golden to reddish brown in fall. The slender stems hold attractive silvery white seed heads. The fluffy seed heads and crimson-colored foliage are extremely showy in the fall landscape.

Landscape Use Little bluestem is among the best native grasses for fall color, and its small size makes it easy to use in most landscapes. Plant it in mixed borders, in prairie gardens, along walkways, and in foundation plantings.

Site Prefers well-drained sand or loam in full sun, but will grow in rocky soils and partial shade. Not recommended for heavy clay or damp soils.

Culture Little bluestem is a warm-season grass and is slow to emerge in spring. Burn or mow clumps in late winter. It will not do well on heavy soils that hold moisture. It is sometimes sold under the outdated name of *Andropogon scoparius*.

Good Companions The blue-green foliage provides a great backdrop for summer prairie flowers, as well as perennials, in a mixed border. Plant it with chrysanthemums, coneflowers, monardas, blazing stars, asters, boltonia, and Indian grass.

Cultivars 'The Blues' was selected for its good blue-green foliage color. Zone 3.

Schizachyrium scoparium

Sorghastrum nutans
Indian grass
Zone 4

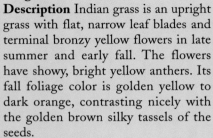

Native Habitat Moist to dry savannas and open woodlands throughout most of the Lower Peninsula.

Height 5 to 7 feet

Description Indian grass is an upright grass with flat, narrow leaf blades and terminal bronzy yellow flowers in late summer and early fall. The flowers have showy, bright yellow anthers. Its fall foliage color is golden yellow to dark orange, contrasting nicely with the golden brown silky tassels of the seeds.

Landscape Use The silky soft, golden seed heads of Indian grass impart a special beauty and drama to prairie gardens in autumn, and this grass makes a powerful late-season statement in mixed borders. Finches and sparrows feast on seeds all winter.

Site Prefers a slightly moist to well-drained soil in full sun, but will tolerate very light shade. Plants may open up or flop in moist, rich soils.

Culture Space plants 1 to 2 feet apart. Mow or burn this warm-season grass in late winter. Plants tolerate drought once mature. It is not overly aggressive.

Good Companions Indian grass should be planted with little bluestem and other late-summer and fall prairie plants such as asters, boltonia, oxeye, black-eyed Susans, wild bergamot, and Joe-pye weeds.

Cultivars 'Sioux Blue' is an upright form with metallic blue summer foliage. Zone 4.

Sorghastrum nutans

Spartina pectinata
Prairie cordgrass
Zone 4

Spartina pectinata 'Aureomarginata'

Native Habitat Wet prairies, sandy shores, and marshes throughout most of the Lower Peninsula and the southern part of the Upper Peninsula.

Height 6 to 9 feet

Description This warm-season grass has a graceful, arching form. The seed heads start out purple in summer and turn yellow-gold in fall. Its fall foliage color is yellow.

Landscape Use Prairie cordgrass is good in naturalistic plantings and for stabilizing stream banks and pond edges, where it thrives in the wet soil.

Site Requires a moist, fertile soil in full sun. Even moisture is necessary, and it can even be submerged for short periods.

Culture For stream-bank erosion control, space plants 2 feet apart and apply mulch or erosion fabric to hold soil during establishment. In about two years the entire area will be a solid mat of rhizomes that defy erosion. Prairie cordgrass is too invasive for most landscape situations, but it will spread slower in a heavy soil.

Good Companions Plant prairie cordgrass in moist soils along with other tall moisture lovers such as Joe-pye weeds and autumn sneezeweed.

Cultivars 'Aureomarginata' ['Variegata'] has long, graceful, ribbon-like foliage striped with yellow bands; it has good fall color. Zone 4.

Sporobolus heterolepis
Prairie dropseed

Native Habitat A few widely scattered grasslands in the southern part of the Lower Peninsula.

Height 2 to 4 feet

Description Prairie dropseed is a clump-forming grass, which slowly expands to form a fountain-like mound about 18 inches in diameter. It has narrow individual blades that are bright green in summer, turning yellow and orange in fall. It blooms in late summer, producing many upright flower stalks topped with pale pink panicles. These flowers have a luscious scent reminiscent of fresh popcorn and later turn gold.

Landscape Use This graceful, well-behaved grass will add a touch of elegance to any planting. Use it in perennial gardens, mixed borders, or foundation plantings. Space plants 18 to 24 inches apart for distinctive borders. A mass planting is a beautiful site in late summer. The seeds are an important food source for birds in fall and winter.

Site Prefers a well-drained soil with moderate moisture levels and full sun, but will tolerate drier conditions. Avoid constantly wet soils.

Culture Prairie dropseed is slow to grow from seeds; start with plants if possible. Dig and divide clumps in spring as needed. It is on Michigan's special concern list, so purchase only nursery-propagated plants.

Good Companions Plant fine-textured prairie dropseed with butterfly weed, coreopsis, asters, coneflowers, and blazing stars in perennial borders or in prairie gardens.

Sporobolus heterolepis

Other Species *S. cryptandrus* (sand dropseed) is much more prevalent in Michigan—native on sandy shores, barrens, and dunes. It grows 1 to 2 feet tall and in small tufts. It can be used on hot, dry sites and for dune restoration. Zone 4.

Additional Native Grasses

Ammophila breviligulata **(beach grass)** is the main stabilizing grass on dunes and beaches along the Great Lakes. It grows 2 to 3 feet tall in dry to average sandy soil and full sun. It has tall, stiff, pale yellow or purplish flowers that rise above the narrow leaves. The long, spreading rhizomes can spread up to 8 feet in one year. Use it for dune and beach restoration or to control erosion on a sandy slope. Zone 3.

Calamagrostis canadensis **(blue joint)** is native to marshes, bogs, and lakeshores throughout Michigan. This cool-season, rhizomatous grass grows 2 to 5 feet tall and often makes a solid stand that excludes other plants. It blooms from June to July with highly variable flowers. Use it over septic tanks, in bog gardens, and along streams and large ponds. It requires moist or wet soil in full sun and can even be partially submerged for part of the year. Zone 3.

Chasmanthium latifolium **[***Uniola latifolia***] (wild oats)** is native in only the far southwestern corner of Michigan. It grows 2 to 3 feet tall and has a spread of 2 feet. The showy dangling seed heads start out green and turn a coppery brown. It prefers moist, well-drained, humus-rich soil and partial shade, but will tolerate full sun if given adequate moisture. Wild oats is a good grass for woodland gardens or along streams or ponds. The seed heads are interesting additions to cut- and dried-flower arrangements. Plants will self-sow. Wild oats is on Michigan's threatened species list. Zone 5.

Eragrostis spectabilis **(purple love grass)** is native to well-drained soils of open areas, mainly in the southeastern section of Michigan. It grows 12 to 24 inches tall and in a clump. The light green summer foliage turns bronzy red in fall. The showy amethyst seed heads emerge in July. Drifts of the reddish purple flowers are especially attractive from a distance, but purple love grass could be tried as a specimen plant or even in a container planting. It prefers a well-drained soil in full sun, but tolerates sandy soils and light shade. Individual plants may be short lived, but they will self-seed to maintain a colony. Zone 4.

Hierochloe odorata **(sweet grass)** is native to wet meadows, woodland edges, bogs, stream banks, and lakeshores throughout most of Michigan. The glossy leaves have a pleasant vanilla fragrance. The golden flowers turn to seed by July, but leaves remain green until winter. Growing 1 to 2 feet tall, it prefers a moist soil and full sun near a pond or stream bank. It slowly creeps by rhizomes to form a patch; encircle plants with a root barrier to restrict growth. Zone 4.

Luzula acuminata **(hairy wood rush)** is native to various soils in woodlands throughout most of Michigan. It grows only 6 to 10 inches tall, forming an evergreen spreading clump. Use it as a groundcover in the partial shade of a woodland garden. It will adapt to the dry shade found under deciduous trees. Zone 4.

Milium effusum **var.** *cisatlanticum* **(American millet grass)** is native to rich deciduous-forest openings throughout most of Michigan. It is a nice green grass that grows only 8 to 18 inches tall and tolerates quite a bit of shade. Use it near ponds or in woodland gardens. Keep it well watered until it is established. Zone 4.

Ferns

Ferns evoke the essence of Michigan's woodlands, where most native ferns grow in moist, rich, acidic soil in part to full shade. They are actually a conspicuous part of the state's vegetation in all but the driest prairie ecosystems. Many adapt well to shady landscape situations, where their foliage provides interesting textural contrasts to other plants. They add visual buoyancy, lightening the garden with their wide assortment of foliage shapes and varying shades of green. With adequate soil and moisture, fern foliage will be attractive until fall frost kills them back or winter snow covers them.

Ferns are typically used in shade gardens, where they are excellent background plantings, fillers, blenders, groundcovers, or focal points. Although the small fiddleheads appear fairly early in spring, the leaves do not fully mature for quite awhile. This growth pattern makes ferns good companions for many of the early flowering ephemerals and spring bulbs, which die back in early summer, leaving room for the ferns to fill in. Some ferns can be used in foundation plantings, and some of the sun-tolerant types can be used in mixed borders. Ferns are fun for collectors, and some gardeners choose to devote gardens solely to these plants. They look good around water gardens, and some of the smaller types can be used in shady rock gardens. They can be used to create a soft boundary between one section of a garden and another. They can even be used to form a small hedge in the right spot.

The most recognizable feature of a fern is its frond, or leaflike structure. Fronds range from 1/16 of an inch up to several feet long and may be feathery to coarse in texture. They have two main parts: the stipe, or leaf stalk, and the blade, which is the leafy portion. Fronds are often divided and subdivided, and sometimes divided again. Most ferns have two different shapes of fronds—sterile and fertile—and these can be quite different on some species.

Most ferns grow from underground perennial rhizomes, which can lead to large stands of a single species. They push up new, tightly curled fronds called fiddleheads. This method of growth protects fern tips during emergence. Instead of growing from seed like most flowering plants, ferns come from a single spore that develops into the sporophyte. Spores are borne in a spore case. The case contains many individual spores and is usually found on the underside of a frond or on separate stalks. Inexperienced gardeners often become concerned over these fruiting bodies and assume their plants are infested with a rust disease or unusual insect.

Planting

Native ferns are easy to grow if a few simple cultural requirements are met. Most prefer filtered shade as opposed to deep, heavy shade. Dappled shade, where patterns of sunlight move across the plants as the day progresses, is best. In some cases you may need to limb-up some trees to allow more light to reach ferns. Some ferns will grow in full sun if sufficient moisture is provided. In general, the larger and more robust the fern, the more it will tolerate sunlight. Most need protection from midday sun.

Most ferns grow best in slightly acidic, humus-rich soil. Dig or till at least 6 to 8 inches deep and add 3 to 4 inches of organic matter in the form of peat moss, ground pine bark, or shredded leaves. Well-rotted manure and compost also work.

When planting, do not allow roots to become dry. Bare-root ferns should be unpacked immediately upon arrival; their roots should be wrapped in wet newspaper and placed in the shade out of any wind until they can be planted, which should be as soon as possible. Plant bare-root ferns in fall or early spring only. Plant them as you would any perennial: dig a hole, spread out rhizomes, and plant the crown no deeper than 1 inch below the soil surface. Remove any broken fronds, as they will not be repaired. Container-grown ferns can be planted at any time during the growing season if you can provide the young plants with adequate water and protection from sun. Plant at the same depth as in the container. Space small ferns about 1 foot apart, medium-sized ferns about 2 feet apart, and large ferns 3 feet apart.

Ferns are the backbone of shade garden. Not only do they offer color and texture throughout the summer months when most shade plants are less showy, they also serve to fill in the bare spots when spring ephemerals fade away.

Care

Ferns should never be allowed to become bone dry. Plant them in an area where you will be able to supply supplemental water during droughts. Water deeply several times a week during dry spells, right up until they go dormant for winter. An organic mulch applied at planting time will help conserve water as well as retard weed growth. Good mulches are shredded bark, pine needles, and dry oak leaves. Dig and divide ferns every few years in spring to keep plants vigorous. Replant divisions with the crowns at soil level.

In spring, gently brush away any leaves that have matted over the ferns, and crumble any erect dead fronds by hand. Add mulch if needed, and the ferns are ready to go for the season. They shouldn't need additional fertilizer if you allow leaves to remain on the bed each fall. Pull weeds by hand; don't use a hoe or tiller. Rhizomes are close to the soil surface and can be easily injured.

Possible Problems

Most ferns are not bothered by diseases, but slugs can be a problem. Unfortunately, there is no foolproof method for eradicating these slimy pests. All you can really hope to do is reduce their numbers and protect young, vulnerable plants. You can install physical barriers, such as plastic-bottle cloches, or sprinkle lime, eggshells, or sawdust around plants. Slugs are attracted to saucers or plastic pots of milk or beer. Lay rolled-up newspaper or boards on the soil. Slugs will seek out these protected areas and can be easily removed. Drop them in a bucket of a 5 percent alcohol-water solution or soapy water, or spray the slugs with an ammonia-water solution. Remember that toads, frogs, and beetles eat slugs and are worth encouraging in your garden.

Several fern species are in jeopardy in Michigan and must not be dug from the wild. As with all native plants, purchase native ferns only from nurseries selling nursery-propagated plants. Growing nursery-propagated plants in your garden will help to maintain biodiversity and help to ensure the survival of endangered species.

Adiantum pedatum
Maidenhair fern
Zone 3

Adiantum pedatum

Native Habitat Moist, well-drained woodlands throughout Michigan.
Height 12 to 24 inches
Description Maidenhair fern has horizontal, lacy, fan-shaped, arching branches and wiry, black stems. The individual fronds are green and fan-shaped with black petioles, and they turn golden yellow in fall.
Landscape Use This delicate fern is attractive from spring through fall. Its fine texture adds softness to the landscape. It can be grown in the dry shade under large trees or in shady rock gardens.

Site Prefers partial shade and moist, slightly acidic, rich soil, but tolerates all but very dry soils.
Culture Maidenhair fern is easy to grow in the garden. Transplant it carefully to avoid damaging the thin stems. Plant it in groups spaced about 18 inches apart or tucked here and there. With time, 2-foot-wide clumps will cover the ground.
Good Companions Fine-textured maidenhair fern combines well with almost all woodland plants, but it is especially effective with coarse-textured plants such as hostas.

Asplenium platyneuron
Ebony spleenwort
Zone 4

Asplenium scolopendrium

Native Habitat Moist woods, often on rocks, mainly in the southern part of Michigan but also farther north.
Height 8 to 18 inches
Description Ebony spleenwort has spreading sterile fronds that lie close to the ground and showy, erect fertile fronds that are dark green with small leaflets. Fronds are sword-shaped and evergreen.
Landscape Use Ebony spleenwort is an excellent smaller fern for the shaded rock garden or for planting among rocks bordering a woodland path.
Site A loose, woodsy, near-neutral pH soil in partial shade.
Culture Once established, ebony spleenwort generally maintains itself with little additional care. It will tolerate dry periods.
Good Companions Plant ebony spleenwort with showy spring woodland natives such as Jacob's ladder and trilliums, which will detract attention from the tired-looking fronds in early spring.
Other Species *A. rhizophyllum* [*Camptosorus rhizophyllus*] (walking fern) is native to a few damp, shady places widely scattered throughout Michigan. It is so named because the tips of the long-tapering, 4- to 12-inch fronds arch over and root, producing new plantlets as it "walks" along the ground. It is on Michigan's threatened species list, so purchase only nursery-propagated plants. Zone 4.

A. scolopendrium (Hart's-tongue fern) is native to only a few moist shady sites in the far eastern part of the Upper Peninsula. It grows 8 to 18 inches tall and has bright to dark green, straplike, leathery fronds. It is challenging to grow, but rewarding when successful. It is on Michigan's endangered species list. Zone 5.

A. trichomanes-ramosum (green spleenwort) is found on ledges and in crevices on moist cliffs, widely scattered in the northern part of the state. It is a small, delicate fern, growing 3 to 6 inches tall and having spreading leaves. It is a good choice for cool, moist rock gardens. It is on Michigan's threatened species list, and it may be difficult to find sources. Zone 3.

Athyrium filix-femina
Lady fern
Zone 2

Native Habitat Wide range of habitats throughout most of Michigan.
Height 2 to 3 feet
Description Lady fern forms a cool green carpet of lacy, deeply cut fronds that arch from the crown. The bright green to light yellow, 5- to 12-inch fronds are produced continually during growing season, keeping plants fresh looking.
Landscape Use Lady fern is an excellent groundcover and makes a nice backdrop for smaller plants in moist woodland gardens. It can be naturalized along stream banks or shady water gardens. It is large enough to be used with shrubs in foundation plantings.
Site Prefers partial to full shade and a slightly acidic, moist to wet soil, but tolerates a wide variety of soils. Can take some sun if the soil is kept moist.

Culture Lady fern is easy to grow, provided plants receive consistent moisture. Mulch plants and water during dry periods. The fronds are somewhat brittle, and older fronds may become tattered by late summer if they are grown in high-traffic areas or on windy sites. It is slow spreading.
Good Companions Use lady fern to brighten a shady spot. Its light color sets it off nicely from other ferns, and it is a good backdrop for bloodroot, trilliums, and other native flowers.
Cultivars 'Frizelliae' has narrow fronds (less than 1 inch wide) with fuzzy, green, earlike projections along the sides. It is an interesting specimen plant for a special spot in woodland gardens. Zone 3. 'Vernoniae Cristatum' and 'Victoriae' were selected for the attractive crests at the ends of their leaves. Zone 4.

Athyrium filix-femina

Cystopteris bulbifera
Bulblet fern
Zone 3

Native Habitat Moist, rocky woods and streams banks scattered throughout most of Michigan.
Height 12 to 30 inches
Description Bulblet fern has narrow, lacy, twice- or thrice-cut triangular fronds that are widest at the base. Bulblets form along its main stem and fall off to form new plants. The young stems are dark red when they emerge in spring, offering an interesting color contrast to other spring plants.
Landscape Use Grow bulblet fern in a shady nook of a rock garden or in a moist spot in a shade garden. In its native habitat it is often found clinging to rocks wet with water spray, so it would look at home near a pool or waterfall. It grows in humus-packed limestone crevices.
Site Requires shade and a moist, rich soil with a pH of 7.0 to 7.5.

Culture Bulblet fern is easy to establish, and it eventually forms large colonies. Young plants are easy to cull out, however.
Good Companions Place bulblet fern near a water feature with other moisture-loving plants such as cardinal flower, obedient plant, and blue flag; good fern companions include *Dryopteris* species and *Polypodium virginianum*.
Other Species *C. fragilis* (fragile fern) is native to moist spots on the Upper Peninsula and some Lower Peninsula locations. It is a delicate, slow spreader that often grows in shady, rocky crevices. It prefers soils that are slightly alkaline. Zone 2.
C. protrusa (protruding fragile fern) is native to the moist, shady slopes of woodlands in the southern part of Michigan. It grows 10 to 12

Cystopteris bulbifera

inches tall and in clumps 2 feet or more across. The fronds are 10 inches long and 3 inches wide. It continually forms new fronds, and the fresh, light green clumps attract attention in a shade garden, especially in spring. It grows best in a slightly acidic to neutral soil in moist shade. Extra water during the growing season will keep plants green and encourage production of new fronds. Zone 4.

FERNS

Dryopteris marginalis
Marginal wood fern
Zone 4

Dryopteris marginalis

Dryopteris filix-femina

Native Habitat Rich, rocky woods throughout most of Michigan.

Height 18 to 24 inches

Description Marginal wood fern is a large, leathery woodland fern with fronds borne in a crownlike cluster 18 to 24 inches long and 6 to 10 inches wide. The fiddleheads are densely covered with golden brown hairs.

Landscape Use Use marginal wood fern in shady rock gardens or in woodland gardens. The evergreen foliage provides year-round interest.

Site Prefers a cool, shady site protected from sun and drying winds.

Culture Incorporate lots of organic matter into the soil before planting. Provide water during dry periods.

Good Companions The dark green fronds of marginal wood fern set off white and red flowers nicely. Grow it with cardinal flower and trilliums. Other good companions include wild sarsaparilla, large-leaved aster, blue-bead lily, and Canada mayflower.

Other Species *D. carthusiana* [*D. spinulosa*] (spinulose wood fern) is native to damp wooded areas throughout most of Michigan. It is an erect fern with outward-curving evergreen fronds that are often used in floral arrangements. Give it partial shade and moist, acidic soil, and it will perform nicely as an accent plant or a mass planting in a woodland garden. Zone 3.

D. cristata (crested shield fern) grows in moist woodlands throughout most of Michigan. The erect, 18- to 30-inch fertile fronds have horizontally arranged, widely spaced pinnae and a slight twist to them. Grow crested shield fern in light shade in moist soil. Zone 3.

D. filix-mas (male fern) is native to moist, calcareous soils in scattered locations in the northern part of the state. It grows 24 to 28 inches tall and does best on evenly moist soils, but will tolerate drier soils. The dark green stiff fronds are 8 inches wide. Many cultivars are available. 'Barnesii' has longer, narrower fronds. 'Crisspatissima' has upright fronds with crinkled margins. Male fern is on Michigan's special concern list, so purchase only nursery-propagated plants. Zone 4.

D. goldiana (Goldie's fern) is rare in Michigan, found in cool, moist woods and shady ravines widely scattered in the state. It is a large, impressive fern, growing 3 to 5 feet tall in clumps up to 2 feet across. It makes a spectacular clump in woodland gardens. Its fiddleheads are covered with showy, shaggy, brownish scales. It requires a cool, moist, shady location in slightly acidic, humus-rich soil. Zone 4.

D. intermedia (evergreen wood fern) is native to moist to dry, shaded soils throughout Michigan. It grows 18 to 36 inches tall and is a good fern for heavy shade. Zone 3.

132

Gymnocarpium dryopteris
Oak fern
Zone 2

Gymnocarpium dryopteris

Native Habitat Rich, moist to wet, acidic soils, mainly in the northern half of Michigan but also farther south.

Height 6 to 12 inches

Description This deciduous fern has three-parted delicate fronds held horizontally under stalks. It spreads by rhizomes to form small patches of bright green on the forest floor.

Landscape Use Oak fern is good for colder areas of Michigan. It is a diminutive fern that requires careful siting so it doesn't get lost. Use it along pathways, in bog gardens, and next to ponds. It is great as groundcover in full-shade areas of woodland gardens.

Site Rich, moist to wet, acidic soil in full to partial shade.

Culture Amend soil before planting, if necessary, to make sure soil is acidic and will hold moisture.

Good Companions Place oak fern near a water feature with other moisture-loving plants such as cardinal flower, obedient plant, and blue flag; good fern companions include *Cystopteris* species and *Polypodium virginianum*.

Other Species *G. robertianum* (limestone oak fern) is native to shaded limestone rocks widely scattered across the state. It has triangular, pale apple green fronds and forms a spreading clump. It does well on limey (higher pH) soils. It is on Michigan's threatened species list, so purchase only nursery-propagated plants, which will probably be difficult to locate. Zone 3.

Matteuccia struthiopteris
Ostrich fern
Zone 3

Matteuccia struthiopteris

Native Habitat Swamps and wet woods throughout Michigan.

Height 2 to 5 feet

Description Ostrich fern is vase shaped. It has large, plume-like, leathery sterile fronds and smaller fertile fronds that appear in late summer. The fertile fronds become brown and woody in fall and persist through winter, offering interest even into early spring.

Landscape Use Ostrich fern has a regal look to it and can be used in more formal landscape situations, such as north-facing foundation plantings, shade gardens, and mixed borders. The young fiddleheads are up early in spring. They are edible, having a taste similar to asparagus.

Site Prefers a cool, wet, slightly acidic soil in partial to full sun, but is adaptable to drier conditions.

Culture Ostrich fern is easy to grow if given suitable conditions. It spreads readily by rhizomes, but it is fairly easy to keep in check. Leaves will scorch if soil becomes dry.

Good Companions Ostrich fern can be planted with shade-tolerant shrubs, and it is a good choice for filling in after spring bulbs and ephemerals are gone.

FERNS

Onoclea sensibilis

Onoclea sensibilis
Sensitive fern
Zone 2

Native Habitat Swamps; wet, open woods; and other moist areas throughout Michigan.
Height 12 to 30 inches
Description Sensitive fern has interesting, deeply pinnate fronds that grow to 18 inches in length. They are light green, large, and lobed, somewhat resembling a green glove. The sterile fronds die with the first frost, but fertile fronds persist through winter. Fiddleheads emerging from rhizomes form a distinctive pale red mass in spring.

Landscape Use Sensitive fern is best for large gardens as a mass planting. It will grow in still water along ponds and stream banks, even in full sun.
Site Prefers wet to slightly moist, acidic soil in light shade; sun is okay if the soil is quite wet.
Culture Sensitive fern produces long, robust rhizomes and may become invasive in the right conditions.
Good Companions Sensitive fern is best planted in masses or with other large ferns as groundcover.

Osmunda cinnamomea
Cinnamon fern
Zone 3

Native Habitat Wet soils of wooded swamps, marshy places, and wet savannas throughout Michigan.
Height 30 to 36 inches
Description This upright fern has waxy, deep green foliage. The fertile fronds occur in spring, just above the foliage. They are cinnamon-colored spikes in the center of the clump of hairy fiddleheads, which can reach up to 8 inches before unfolding. The fertile fronds are soon replaced by sterile

fronds, which are yellow-green, deeply pinnate, and have a dense tuft of rusty hairs beneath the base of each pinna.
Landscape Use This large fern makes a bold statement in the landscape. Use it as a background planting or along water's edge. It can also be used in foundation plantings or as a background for flowers. It is difficult to see individual plants in established plantings.
Site Does best in acidic, moist soil and partial shade, but adapts fairly well to a

wide range of conditions, including full sun if the soil is continually wet.
Culture Cinnamon fern is very easy to grow and requires little care once established.
Good Companions Plant cinnamon fern in masses or with other large ferns in a fern garden. It can be used as a backdrop for cardinal flower and turtleheads in moist-soil areas.
Other Species *O. claytoniana* (interrupted fern) is native to rich, shaded woods throughout Michigan. The upright-growing, vase-shaped deciduous clump looks a bit like cinnamon fern, except that the normal fronds along the stem are suddenly "interrupted" by a few brown, fertile fronds. Culture and use are the same. Zone 2

O. regalis (royal fern) is native to swamps and moist, acidic soils throughout the state. It grows 24 to 36 inches tall or more and is coarser than the other two species. The fronds unfurl with a wine-red color before turning green. The light green, leathery leaves give it a tropical appearance, and it looks especially nice planted near water, where it will thrive in the damp soil. Zone 3.

Osmunda cinnamomea

Osmunda claytoniana

134

Polystichum acrostichoides
Christmas fern
Zone 3

Native Habitat Moist to well-drained upland soils, mainly in the southern half of the Lower Peninsula.
Height 18 to 24 inches
Description Christmas fern has dark green evergreen fronds. The fertile fiddleheads are covered in silvery scales. Smaller sterile fronds are produced later in the season.
Landscape Use Christmas fern can be massed as groundcover, or a clump looks nice tucked into the base of a stump. The evergreen foliage adds year-round interest but looks rather tired by spring. It is often used for cut greenery during the holidays.

Site Prefers fertile, well-drained woodland soil in partial to almost full shade.
Culture Plants are easy to establish if grown in partial shade and constantly wet soil. This clump former stays nicely in place.
Good Companions Christmas fern's dark green color is a good backdrop for smaller woodland plants and spring bulbs.
Other Species *P. braunii* (Braun's holly fern) is native to cool, shaded gorges on the Upper Peninsula. It requires cool woodland soil that has good moisture retention. Zone 3.

Polystichum acrostichoides

Additional Native Ferns

Dennstaedtia punctilobula (hay-scented fern) was once native in a small area in southern Michigan, but is no longer found naturally. The pale green, lacy fronds grow 15 to 30 inches long. It is easy to grow in moist to dry, acidic soil and in sun to partial shade. It may form dense stands and become invasive where conditions are favorable. Zone 3.

Phegopteris connectilis [Thelypteris phegopteris] (northern beech fern) is native mainly to the northern half of Michigan, where it grows in moist, acidic soils and in shade to partial sun. It grows 8 to 18 inches tall and has triangular-shaped fronds. It spreads by rhizomes to make a nice groundcover. Zone 2.

Polypodium virginianum (rock-cap fern, common polypody) is native to rocks and cliffs throughout most of Michigan. The rhizomes grow in a mat. The leaves form a dense, yellow-green mass. The deeply pinnate, 4- to 12-inch fronds are leathery and evergreen. Use rock-cap fern to soften ledges and crevices of rock walls or to cover large boulders in woodland gardens. It can be grown in a rock garden in partial shade. It can take several years for rock-cap fern to permanently establish itself. Mats can be placed on suitable rock surfaces with a bit of humus and weighted down. Supply additional moisture in periods of drought. Zone 3.

Pteridium aquilinum (bracken) is native to the well-drained soils of thin woods and barrens in all but the far western part of the Upper Peninsula. It grows 12 to 48 inches tall and has coarsely textured, broadly triangular fronds. It tolerates well-drained soil in partial sun and can be used as groundcover along roadsides or at the edge of a woodland. It may become invasive under favorable conditions, but it is easily controlled by mowing or cultivation. Zone 3.

Thelypteris palustris (marsh fern) is native to marshes and bogs throughout Michigan. It grows 18 inches tall and has light green, lacy fronds, each arising individually from a creeping rhizome without forming clumps. Marsh fern spreads rapidly, especially when given supplemental water or grown in damp soil. Use it to edge streams and ponds. Zone 3.
T. noveboracensis (New York fern) is native to moist soils and in sun to partial shade, mainly in the southern part of the state but also farther north. It grows 12 to 24 inches tall and has yellow-green fronds that are tapered at both ends. It can be aggressive, especially when given some sun. Zone 4.

Woodsia obtusa (blunt-lobed woodsia, cliff fern) is native to rock crevices in a few locations in the south-central part of the Upper Peninsula. It has deep green fronds and grows 6 to 18 inches tall. Use this slow spreader in rock gardens or wall gardens. Plants prefer a neutral soil rich in organic matter. Once established, they will survive prolonged dry periods. It is on Michigan's threatened species list. Zone 4.

Evergreen Conifers

When you have the potential for five or more months of snow cover each year, it is important to include landscape plants with winter interest. Evergreens excel in this area, but they are also valuable for the many other benefits they bring to a landscape. Their evergreen foliage provides a dark backdrop for flowering and fruiting herbaceous plants. They provide year-round screening, and many make good hedges. Many can also be used in foundation plantings, where they offer a certain stability, and the shrub types offer interest and texture in shrub borders. Most provide shelter for birds and other forms of wildlife, and some provide food as well. The aromatic cut foliage is often used for indoor holiday arrangements.

Most people would agree that mature evergreens are a real asset when it comes to property value. However, their value quickly goes down if they are diseased or improperly pruned, which is often the case. It is so easy to fall in love with cute little "button" or pyramidal evergreens, but keep in mind than many landscape plants tend to outgrow their sites. They grow into large trees or spreading shrubs that aren't easy to keep small with pruning, and they are more susceptible to insect and disease problems when they are growing in a contained space. Most evergreens look best when they are allowed to grow naturally, without a lot of shaping. If you want an evergreen to stay within a certain size range, look for a dwarf or compact cultivar, rather than trying to restrict the growth of full-sized species.

When choosing an evergreen, consider hardiness, light requirements, rate of growth, attractiveness to wildlife, and winter appearance. Select a tree or shrub based on your soil conditions if you don't want to drastically change them. Keep in mind also that some evergreens are favorite foods of deer.

Planting

You will have the best success planting northern-grown nursery plants that have been properly root pruned. They will survive transplanting best and start growing quickly. Bare-root trees must be planted in spring as soon as the soil can be worked. Balled-and-burlapped plants, container plants, and tree-spade trees can be planted any time except the hottest days of summer, from mid-June to mid-August. Spring is still the best time to plant, however. If you have the opportunity to move a native evergreen, stick with one that has a trunk less than 2 inches in diameter and move it in early spring.

Before planting, amend the soil with a good amount of organic matter such as compost, peat moss, or well-rotted manure. Mix this organic matter thoroughly with the planting-hole soil. Place the evergreen at the same depth it was growing in the container or burlap wrap. Bare-root plants should be planted so that the crown is level with the ground. Newly planted evergreens should not need additional fertilizer, but it is a good idea to surround them with a 2- to 4-inch layer of organic mulch, such as wood chips, shredded bark, or pine needles. Replenish the mulch as needed throughout the growing season.

Care

The first two or three years after planting, make sure the soil is evenly moist from spring until the ground freezes in fall. Once established, many evergreens can tolerate some dry periods, but don't hesitate to water as needed, especially in sandy soils. Always saturate the soil thoroughly with each watering to encourage deep rooting. To avoid brown needles in winter, make sure the plants have plenty of moisture right up until the ground freezes.

Most young evergreens will benefit from a spring application of an acidic fertilizer. Spread a layer of rotted manure or compost around each plant or use a fertilizer such as cottonseed meal, Milorganite, or fish emulsion. If possible, allow needles to fall and decay under plants to return nutrients and acidity to the soil. Keep weeds pulled or smother them with organic mulch. Never cover the roots of these forest trees with plastic or rock.

Maintenance needs of evergreens differ depending on the species. Most shrubs will benefit from regular trimming to help maintain their natural shape. Light trimming is okay from spring into early summer, but do not cut branches too far back—stay in young green growth. Most evergreens do not generate new growth in older sections. Remove any dead, damaged, or diseased parts of evergreens at any time of year.

This planting of *Pinus resinosa* (red pine) provides winter interest as well and a windbreak.

Possible Problems

Native evergreens are susceptible to insects and diseases, some of which can become serious. The best defense against insect and disease problems is a vigorously growing plant. By choosing a tree or shrub appropriate for your site conditions and by providing it with the necessary nutrients and ample water, most pest problems will not become serious in landscape situations. Many insect and disease problems are purely cosmetic and don't really threaten the life of the tree. On large trees, control measures are rarely practical. On young plants, keep an eye out for aphid feeding (spray foliage daily with a strong blast of the hose), iron chlorosis (acidify soil to lower pH), and scale (spray with a dormant oil in early spring).

Winter burn, or browning of needles, is common on evergreens and caused by insufficient water during winter. Water insufficiency can be due to a sudden drop in temperature, direct sun, desiccating winds, or drought conditions in fall. The sun, reflected from a white snow surface on a still day in February, may cause the temperatures in the plants to rise as much as 50 to 60 degrees above air temperatures. If the sun goes behind a cloud or a building, the temperatures drop suddenly and tissue within the leaves is killed. Plant sensitive evergreens such as arborvitaes, Canada yew, and some junipers on sites where they will receive some winter shade, and make sure plants receive ample water going into winter.

Abies balsamea
Balsam fir
Zone 2

Native Habitat Moist soils, shaded forests, and along bogs, throughout the Upper Peninsula and in the northern half of the Lower Peninsula.

Size 30 to 50 feet tall, 25 feet wide

Description Balsam fir is an aromatic and handsome tree with a straight-tapering trunk from bottom to top. The spreading branches form a symmetrical, slender pyramid. Its bark is smooth, grayish, and prominently marked by blisters filled with resin. The needles are flat with rounded points, dark green and lustrous above and silvery white beneath. Showy female cones are upright, bluish purple, 2 to 3 inches tall, and clustered near the tops of trees. Balsam fir is often found growing with white spruce in native stands.

Landscape Use Balsam fir is especially attractive as a young tree, which is good because it is one of the slower growing evergreens (6 inches or less a year). It tends to be a little sparse looking as it ages, especially when you compare it to a spruce. It is a good choice for naturalizing on a north slope or in moist conditions. Plant a group of three in a large shade garden. Trees provide winter cover for wildlife. It is one of the most popular Christmas trees, since it holds its needles well and smells wonderful.

Site Does best in cool, damp places; moisture-retentive, acidic soils; and partial shade to sun. Keep it away from hot, drying winds.

Culture Amend soil with organic matter before planting balsam fir. Acidify the soil if necessary. Landscape trees should be mulched and watered as needed. Older trees will shade and mulch their own root systems. Balsam fir does not have any serious insect or disease problems and rarely needs pruning. Winter browning is rarely a problem if plants are sited right.

Cultivars 'Nana' is a mounded, low-spreading form, growing only 18 to 24 inches tall. It is available from some specialty nurseries. Zone 3.

Abies balsamea

Abies balsamea 'Nana'

Juniperus communis
Bush juniper
Zone 2

Native Habitat Sandy or rocky soils on steep bluffs, river bottoms, and swamps throughout the state. Also on or near sandy shores and dunes along the Great Lakes.

Size 1 to 3 feet tall, 3 to 10 feet wide

Description This spreading shrub has a sharp, angular form and a rather coarse texture. The dense, awl-shaped needles are green in summer and take on a purplish color in fall. Bark is reddish brown, peeling off in strips. Plants are dioecious—only females have the potential to produce showy berries. Most native plants are var. *depressa*, a low-growing form with erect branch tips.

Landscape Use Junipers are among the best evergreen shrubs available for northern landscapes. Use the coarser species for naturalizing or as groundcover. The cultivars are better choices for use in shrub borders, foundation plantings, and rock gardens. All types provide winter cover for wildlife. Avoid planting junipers under drip lines, where crashing snow can damage them. Native junipers tolerate road salt better than most evergreens.

Site Prefers neutral to slightly acidic, well-drained soil in full sun; tolerates drought and wind well. Foliage will be sparser in shade.

Culture Make sure plants are well watered going into winter to reduce chances of winter burn. Plants can easily outgrow their space. Regular pruning of the branch tips in June will keep them from becoming overgrown and needleless in the middle. Pruning back overgrown plants does not work well. Browned needles may need to be combed out from plants to keep them looking neat. Trimming upright forms so that the upper part is slightly narrower than the base will allow light to get to the lower foliage. Bagworms can be a problem; remove and destroy any bags as soon as you see them. Deer are usually not interested in junipers.

Cultivars and Other Species 'AmiDak' (Blueberry Delight™) was selected for its ability to produce prolific blue fruits when pollinated. Zone 3. 'Depressa Aurea' has new growth with a golden yellow color. Zone 4. 'Repanda' is a compact, rounded form, growing to 1 foot tall and spreading 6 feet wide. Zone 4.

J. horizontalis (creeping juniper) is native to rocky or sandy soils and dunes mainly in the Upper Peninsula and the far northern part of the Lower Peninsula. This low, creeping shrub is usually less than 1 foot tall, spreading 3 to 6 feet to form dense groundcover. Leaf color is bluish green to steel blue, taking on purplish tints in fall. Juniper blight is a disease that can show up during wet springs, turning portions of the plant brownish. Snip off diseased parts and dispose of them. Some cultivars are more resistant to blight. Creeping juniper is on the state's special concern list, so do not dig plants from the wild. Zone 2. Many cultivars have been selected for wonderful textures, foliage color, and a variety of shapes and forms. They are good landscape plants that can be used in foundation plantings, in rock gardens, and as groundcover in sandy soil. 'Bar Harbor' spreads up to 10 feet wide and has trailing bluish green branches that turn purple in fall. 'Blue Chip' is very low growing and has good blue color throughout the year. 'Hughes' is somewhat resistant to juniper blight. It has distinct radial branching and silvery blue leaves, and it spreads up to 10 feet. 'Wiltonii' is a low form (3 inches tall by 4 feet wide) with intense silvery blue color. All cultivars are hardy into zone 3.

J. virginiana (eastern red cedar) is native to stabilized sand dunes, lake shores, low deciduous woods, oak-hickory woods, and swamps in the southern half of the Lower Peninsula; it is often found on river bluffs where few other trees are found. Growing 25 to 40 feet tall, it has a straight trunk and a broad, conical head. The thin, reddish brown bark peels off in long strips. Leaves are dark green and scale-like; newer growth may be sharp-pointed and whitened underneath. Dark blue, berry-like cones on female trees are a favorite winter food of wildlife, and trees provide winter shelter for birds. Eastern red cedar is the alternate host of cedar apple rust, a disease that causes strange-looking orange galls on trees. Snip off any plant parts infected with the galls and destroy them. Use this durable tree for screening, windbreaks, or in natural settings on tough sites. Zone 3. 'Canaertii' stays at 20 feet in height and spreads 8 feet. It has a dense, pyramidal form and dark green leaves. 'Gray Owl' is a spreading form with silvery gray foliage. It grows 4 feet tall and 5 feet wide. Both cultivars are hardy into zone 4.

Juniperus communis var. *depressa* 'Amidak'

Juniperus horizontalis 'Blue Chip'

Juniperus virginiana

Picea glauca
White spruce
Zone 2

Native Habitat Coniferous swamps, mixed woods, bogs, and stream borders, throughout the Upper Peninsula and in the northern part of the Lower Peninsula.

Size 40 to 60 feet tall, 40 feet wide

Description This large tree is pyramidal when young, becoming narrower as it matures. Bark is scaly and dark gray or grayish brown. The stiff, bluish green needles are crowded along branchlets. Slender, 2-inch cones hang from branches.

Landscape Use Spruces are vital to northern landscapes and long lived if properly cared for. Their large size restricts their use, but they can be used for screening, windbreak and shelterbelt plantings, and background plantings. Don't plant a spruce tree if you want to mow right up to the trunk. Their natural shape is pyramidal, with branches all the way to the ground—not palm-tree-like. They provide food and cover for wildlife and make good Christmas trees. Dwarf and compact forms can be used as specimens or accents in the landscape and in rock gardens.

Site Does best in well-drained, slightly acidic soils in full sun. Foliage is thinner in shade. Keep away from winter winds and road salt.

Culture Give white spruce plenty of space. Crowded trees will drop needles. Keep soil evenly moist. Trees do poorly in overly wet soils and in drought conditions. Spruces require little or no pruning. If you want to shape a spruce tree, do a little trimming in June just as the new growth is hardening, rather than a lot all in one year. If possible, keep snow off branches in winter, to reduce branch breakage. Sawflies can leave bare spots on trees. Remove them by hand as soon as you see them. Cankers show up as wounds on trees and branches and they lead to defoliation. Prevent cankers by growing healthy trees. Once a tree is infected, there is little you can do.

Cultivated Varieties and Other Species 'Conica' is a compact, slow-growing form that grows about 5 feet tall and 3 feet wide. Protect it from winter sun and winds or shade it with burlap to reduce winter burn. Zone 4.

P. glauca var. *densata* (Black Hills spruce) seldom grows taller than 40 feet and is denser and more drought tolerant than the species. Foliage is also a little bluer. It is a good choice for landscape use. It is often sold as 'Densata'. Zone 3.

P. mariana (black spruce) is native to the wet soils of swamps and bogs in all but the far southern part of Michigan. It usually stays at 20 to 30 feet, but it can grow to over 50 feet in favorable conditions. It has a narrow, pyramidal shape, widely spaced branches that are somewhat drooping, and bluish green needles. It is fairly drought tolerant in landscape situations if well mulched, but it does best in wetter soils. Zone 2. 'Nana' is a slow-growing, mounded cultivar growing 2 feet tall and 3 feet wide. It needs partial shade. Zone 3. 'Ericoides' is a slow-growing dwarf that eventually becomes rounded and flat-topped. Zone 3.

Picea mariana 'Ericoides'

Picea glauca var. *densata*

Pinus strobus
White pine
Zone 3

Native Habitat Wide variety of soils, from dry and sandy to moist upland sites, throughout most of Michigan.

Size 60 to 100 feet tall, 50 feet wide

Description White pine, the state tree, is the largest conifer in Michigan. It has a pyramidal shape and whorls of horizontal branches evenly spaced along the trunk. The bark is thin, smooth, and greenish gray on young trees, but thick, deeply furrowed, and grayish brown on older trees. The soft, flexible, gray-green needles are 2½ to 5 inches long and occur in clusters of five. Cones are 4 to 8 inches long, thick, and usually gummy.

Landscape Use There's nothing like the scent of pine trees or the sound of wind whistling through their branches. They can be used as specimens on large landscapes, but are usually used for screening and windbreaks. They don't adapt well to urban conditions.

Site Grows best in fertile, acidic, well-drained soils in full sun. Pines do not need protection from wind, but keep them away from road salt.

Culture Pruning is not recommended for white pine, but it does help form more compact growth on cultivars. Prune in spring when the candles are beginning to lengthen, pinching or cutting back no more than one-third to one-half of the candles. Although native trees are susceptible to several insect and disease problems, landscape trees are usually not bothered. White pine blister rust shows up as powdery red rust on the bark. The alternate host is *Ribes* species (gooseberries and currants). Don't plant these where white pines are a priority. Pick off sawflies as soon as you see them. Scale insect damage shows up as whitish flecks on needles. For serious infestations, you may need to spray plants with dormant oil or lime sulfur in late fall or early spring. Deer browsing can be a problem, and young trees can get winter burn on exposed sites. Needles in the center of trees brown before falling, and this change often confuses uneducated homeowners, who think their tree is dying.

Cultivars and Other Species 'Blue Shag', 'Compacta', and 'Nana' are rounded, dense shrubs growing 6 to 8 feet tall and 6 feet wide; 'Compacta' has softer foliage than the species. 'Fastigiata' is a columnar form growing about 25 feet tall and 8 feet wide. 'Pendula' is a 10-foot weeping form that must be staked when young. It takes several years to really look nice. All cultivars are hardy in zone 4.

P. resinosa (red pine) is native to dry, sandy soils, often in pure stands, throughout the Upper Peninsula and the northern half of the Lower Peninsula. Mature trees are 40 to 80 feet tall or more and have an open, rounded, picturesque head. Bark develops reddish brown plates as it matures, giving this tree its common name. The stiff, 4- to 6-inch needles appear in clusters of two. Cones are about 2 inches long, light brown fading to gray, and free of resin. Red pine is impressive when seen in windbreaks and shelterbelts. It thrives in sandy loam and dry soils in full sun, and it is disease and insect resistant. Winter burn can be a problem on younger trees. Zone 3. 'Wissota' is a dwarf form that grows about 6 feet tall and wide. Use it as a specimen or in rock gardens. Zone 3.

P. banksiana (jack pine) is native to acidic, sandy soils of low fertility throughout the Upper Peninsula, in the northern half of the Lower Peninsula, and in the south along Lake Michigan.

It grows up to 60 feet tall, but usually stays closer to 20 to 40 feet in landscape situations. It is an open tree with many small, dead branches that often remain on trees for many years. Bark is a dull red-brown to black color and has loose scales or plates. Needles are flat, grayish green, and twisted two in a bundle. Cones are strongly curved, and brown when ripe, then turning gray. It is tolerant of poor, sandy soil and shade, thriving in sites unsuitable for white or red pine. It is fast growing when young, making it good for windbreaks and screening. Its stark, open growth habit can be adapted to landscape use, especially with modern architecture. Zone 2. 'Uncle Fogy' is an interesting selection with an irregular, often weeping form. It grows about 6 feet tall and 10 feet wide. Use it as a specimen or accent plant. Zone 3.

Pinus strobus

Pinus banksiana 'Uncle Fogy'

Taxus canadensis
Canada yew
Zone 2

Taxus canadensis

Native Habitat Cool, rich, damp woods and bog margins throughout most of Michigan.

Size 3 to 6 feet tall, 6 to 8 feet wide

Description This low-spreading, open, irregular shrub has attractive, dark green needles that usually take on a purplish cast in fall. Plants are dioecious, and female plants produce red, berry-like fruits.

Landscape Use Canada yew is good for naturalizing under large trees, especially pines. It can be planted along the north or east side of buildings in informal foundation plantings, in shrub borders, or in woodland gardens. Plants are slow growing and easy to keep under control with pruning.

Site Prefers a slightly acidic soil in full to partial shade, but keep out of winter winds.

Culture Although Canada yew is hardy, it is subject to winter burn if planted in the wrong conditions. Make sure plants have winter shade or reliable snow cover. If you can't provide these conditions, protect plants with a burlap screen during winter. Landscape plants should be well mulched. Unlike other evergreens, yews have the ability to sprout new growth from fairly old wood, so they can be cut back severely and still develop good foliage. It is still better to prune plants regularly rather than resort to drastic cutting back. The foliage and seeds of yews are poisonous and should be kept from small children. Unfortunately, the poison does not deter deer. This plant is difficult to find in the nursery trade.

Thuja occidentalis
White cedar, arborvitae
Zone 2

Native Habitat Moist or wet soils, often in pure stands, in all but the far southern sections of Michigan.

Size 30 to 50 feet tall, 30 feet wide

Description This upright, pyramidal evergreen has dense, scale-like, green to yellowish green foliage arranged in flat, fanlike branches. On mature trees the bark is gray to reddish brown, separated in long shreds, and the trunk is often twisted. Foliage and bark are aromatic. Foliage often looks slightly yellow, purple, or brown in winter, but returns to green in summer.

Landscape Use The large size of this species limits its use to screening and windbreaks. The cultivars are good choices for hedging, specimen plants, and foundation plantings. All provide excellent shelter for birds.

Site Does best in a moisture-retentive soil in full sun or partial shade. In deep shade, plants are open and have sparse foliage. Keep plants away from dry, windswept locations.

Culture Arborvitaes are easy to grow in any moisture-retentive soil. They are slow growing and long lived. They are subject to winter burn, especially when planted on the south side of buildings;

This planting includes, pictured left to right, *Thuja occidentalis* 'Holmstrup', 'Techny', 'Hetz Midget', and 'Woodwardii'.

however, the winter burn is easy to prune out in spring, since it occurs on the outside of the leaves. Do not confuse winter burn with the normal browning of inside leaves as plants age or with the normal color change arborvitaes go through in winter. Prune just after new growth has emerged. Formal hedges can be pruned again once later in the season, but do not prune in late fall. Plants are susceptible to damage from heavy snow or ice. Try to plant them away from the roofline. Deer are a serious problem, often completely defoliating the lower parts of trees.

Cultivars Many cultivars have been selected for foliage color and growth habit. Here are some good choices for northern use. 'Hetz Midget' is a dense, globe-shaped selection that grows 2 feet tall and 3 feet wide. 'Holmstrup' is a tough, upright grower that stays under 8 feet tall. 'Techny' is a broad, pyramidal tree that is 25 feet tall and has good dark green color; it is a good choice for a tall hedge. 'Wintergreen' and 'Wareana' grow to 15 feet tall and are good for midheight hedging. 'Woodwardii' is a true globe, growing 5 to 6 feet tall and wide. All cultivars are hardy in zone 3.

Tsuga canadensis
Eastern hemlock
Zone 3

Native Habitat Cool, acidic, moist soils containing considerable organic matter; found in all but the far southern and southeastern counties of Michigan.

Size 40 to 60 feet tall, 30 to 50 feet wide

Description Eastern hemlock is a willowy, flexible evergreen with horizontal branches that droop gracefully. The flattened, deep green sprays of soft, short needles hold their color well all year. The cinnamon red bark is deeply divided into narrow ridges. The flat, blunt needles are borne in many rows; they are dark yellow-green above and lighter colored below. The 1/2- to 3/4-inch-long cones hang down from the ends of twigs.

Landscape Use Eastern hemlock is a long-lived, fine-textured evergreen that has much to offer if it has the proper growing conditions. Use it as a specimen or in odd-numbered groupings. It can be used as a hedge or as a background or screening plant.

Site Does best in partial shade and cool, moist, well-drained, acidic soil. Eastern hemlock can be grown in full sun as long as it has a highly organic soil and receives no strong, drying winds. Avoid windswept sites and polluted conditions.

Culture Eastern hemlock is one of the few evergreens that can tolerate shade, but it is sensitive to environmental extremes. Avoid heat, drought, wind, road salt, air pollution, and poor drainage. It tolerates winter cold but can be damaged by unseasonable frosts. Sun scorch can occur when temperatures reach 95 degrees, killing ends of branches. Pruning is not usually necessary, but trees are amenable to late-spring pruning. Purchase plants propagated from a local seed source for best results.

Tsuga canadensis

Tsuga canadensis

Deciduous Shrubs and Small Trees

Shrubs and small trees fulfill many important roles in the landscape. They are the basis for most foundation plantings and hedges. They fill out mixed borders, providing interest all season long, especially in winter when flowers and groundcovers have little to offer. Many shrubs and small trees have fruits that provide winter interest as well as attract birds and other wildlife. In shade gardens, they provide that middle tier that is often forgotten in the home landscape. Shrubs are valuable for hedges and massing. Small trees are important for adding height to entry and patio gardens, and many make nice lawn trees in small yards. Most large shrubs can be pruned into small trees, adding another dimension to their landscape use.

To use shrubs and small trees intelligently you must know their mature size and under what conditions they grow best. Consider hardiness, light requirements, growth rate, and seasonal aspects such as flowers, fruits, fall color, and winter appearance. It is best to select a plant based on your existing soil, but it is fairly easy to change soil conditions if necessary.

Planting

Deciduous shrubs and small trees are best planted in spring, but early fall is also a good time. If you have the opportunity to move a native tree or shrub, move it in early spring. Bare-root plants must be planted in early spring as soon as the soil can be worked. Container

Cornus alternifolia is readily adaptable to landscape use, where it can be used as a large shrub or pruned as an interesting small tree.

plants can be planted any time but the hottest days of summer, during July and August; spring planting is still the best, however.

Before planting, amend the soil with a good amount of organic matter such as compost, peat moss, or well-rotted manure. Mix this organic matter thoroughly with the planting-hole soil. Place the shrub or small tree at the same depth it was growing in the container. Bare-root plants should be planted so that the crown is level with the ground. Newly planted shrubs and small trees should not need additional fertilizer. Do not stake trees unless they are on an extremely windy, open site. It is a good idea to surround all newly planted woody plants with a ring of organic mulch 2 to 4 inches thick. Good mulches are wood chips, shredded bark, and pine needles. Replenish the mulch as needed throughout the growing season.

Care

The first two or three years after planting, make sure the soil is evenly moist, from spring until the ground freezes in fall. Once established, many shrubs can tolerate some dry periods, but don't hesitate to water as needed, especially in sandy soils. Always saturate the soil thoroughly with each watering. Most woody plants will benefit from a spring application of fertilizer. Spread a layer of rotted manure or compost around each plant or use Milorganite or fish emulsion. If possible, allow leaves to fall and decay under shrubs to return nutrients to the soil. Keep weeds pulled or smother them with organic mulch. Do not use rock or black plastic as mulch.

Maintenance needs differ with each species. Most small trees will benefit from some selective pruning while they are young, to develop a good shape. The best time to prune is usually while they are dormant: you can see their silhouette better and reduce the chances of disease and insect problems. Remove branches that have narrow-angled crotches, as these branches are weaker than wide branches and are likely to split as the tree gets older. Shrubs are usually pruned according to their flowering time. In general, spring-flowering shrubs, which set their flower buds in summer, should be pruned right after they have finished flowering. Summer-flowering shrubs, which develop flower buds in spring, are usually best pruned in early spring. Remove any dead, damaged, or diseased parts at any time of year, cutting back to just above a healthy, outfacing bud. Shrubs that have become overgrown will benefit from renewal pruning; cut the plants back to 4 to 6 inches from the ground in early spring. Surround them with a layer of compost or rotted manure and water them well to help them recover.

Possible Problems

Most insect and disease problems are purely cosmetic and don't really threaten the life of shrubs or small trees. The best defense against insect and disease problems is a vigorously growing plant. By choosing the appropriate plant for your site conditions and providing it with the necessary nutrients and ample water, most pest problems will not become serious. Powdery mildew can affect some shrubs, especially when they are growing close together. Snip out the infected areas and dispose of the foliage. Thin out plants to allow for better air circulation and drying of foliage. Leaf spots may leave plants somewhat defoliated by late summer, but this leaf loss is rarely a serious problem. Rake up leaves to reduce the source of inoculum for next year. Aphids often feed on young leaves in hot, dry weather. Dislodge them by spraying the foliage daily with a hard spray from the garden hose. Young trees should be protected from winter rodent feeding, which can kill a tree. The best way is to surround the trunk below the first branch with hardware cloth.

Best Native Deciduous Shrubs and Small Trees for Landscape Use

Amelanchier species (serviceberries)
Ceanothus americanus (New Jersey tea)
Cornus species (dogwoods)
Dirca palustris (leatherwood)
Ilex verticillata (winterberry)
Lindera benzoin (spicebush)
Physocarpus opulifolius cultivars (ninebark)
Potentilla fruticosa cultivars (shrubby cinquefoil)
Prunus nigra 'Princess Kay' (Canada plum)
Ptelea trifoliata (hop-tree)
Staphylea trifolia (bladdernut)
Viburnum species (viburnums)

Amelanchier laevis
Smooth juneberry, Alleghany serviceberry
Zone 3

Native Habitat From dry, sandy, open woodlands to moist riverbanks throughout most of Michigan.

Size 25 to 30 feet tall, 15 to 25 feet wide

Description Juneberry is a single-stemmed or multistemmed small tree or large shrub. Leaves are purple in early spring, turning green in summer and red-orange in fall. The delicate white flowers start blooming in late April with the just-emerging reddish spring foliage. Deep purple-red fruits appear in summer. The bark is silvery gray.

Landscape Use Use this shade-tolerant shrub as an understory plant in deciduous woodland plantings, shade gardens, and shrub borders. The smooth bark is attractive in early spring in wildflower gardens. It can be pruned as a specimen tree near patios and in entry gardens. All *Amelanchier* species are excellent for naturalized settings, where their fruits attract wildlife. The fruits can also be used for jams, jellies, pies, and wine—if you can keep them from the birds.

Site Prefers partial shade to sun and moist, well-drained, slightly acidic soil high in organic matter.

Culture All *Amelanchier* species are easily transplanted and adaptable to culture. Most will tolerate dry, poor conditions once established. Remove some of the older stems each year in late winter to keep plants vigorous and producing more fruits. Renew overgrown shrubs with hard pruning. Prune out suckers if desired; they can be dug up and transplanted in early spring.

Other Species *A. arborea* (downy serviceberry) is a native of swampy to dry soils throughout most of Michigan. It is an understory tree growing 20 to 25 feet tall and 15 to 20 feet wide, with multiple narrow trunks and a rounded crown. Use it in shade gardens and for naturalizing in wet areas. Zone 3.

A. × *grandiflora* (apple serviceberry) is a naturally occurring hybrid of *A. arborea* and *A. laevis*. It is an excellent small clump or single-trunked tree growing to 25 feet. Several cultivars have been selected for their good fall color and interesting growth habit. Good choices for Michigan include 'Autumn Brilliance', 'Robin Hill', 'Princess Diana', and 'Strata'. Zone 4.

A. spicata [*A. stolonifera*] (running serviceberry) is native to acidic, sandy, rocky outcroppings throughout most of Michigan. It grows 1 to 6 feet tall and 3 to 10 feet wide. Its spreading growth habit makes it suitable for drought-tolerant groundcover. Zone 3.

Amelanchier × *grandiflora* 'Autumn Brilliance'

Amorpha canescens
Leadplant
Zone 3

Native Habitat Loamy or sandy, open woods, savannas, and prairies in the far southwestern corner of Michigan.

Size 1¹/₂ to 4 feet tall, 2 to 3 feet wide

Description Leadplant is a semi-woody, loose shrub with numerous spiked clusters of tightly packed, small purple flowers, which bloom from June into August. The pinnately compound leaves and stems are covered in dense, woolly, gray hairs, giving plants a grayish color. It is one of the few woody species common on native prairies. It is especially sensitive to disturbance; hence, its presence indicates that a prairie has not been cultivated.

Landscape Use Use leadplant in prairie gardens, mixed borders, and shrub plantings, where the foliage is attractive all season. It is also good for xeriscaping.

Site Prefers dry, average, well-drained soil in full sun, or light shade at most.

Culture Leadplant requires a nitrogen-fixing soil bacterium. If it is not present, use a commercial soil inoculant when planting. Mulch plants the first winter to prevent frost heaving. Its deep-branching taproot makes leadplant difficult to transplant but helps it survive fire, which improves the growth and bloom of prairie plants. It is a favorite food of deer. Plants can be rejuvenated in spring by cutting them to the ground or pruning out old wood. It is often treated more like an herbaceous perennial, especially when grown in a mixed border. It is on Michigan's special concern list.

Amorpha canescens

Arctostaphylos uva-ursi
Bearberry
Zone 3

Native Habitat Sandy, shallow soils on rocky outcrops, barrens, and dunes in all but the southeastern quarter of Michigan.

Size Stems up to 8 feet long; branches 6 to 12 inches tall

Description Bearberry is a prostrate evergreen shrub with trailing stems. The leaves are dark green and leathery, often turning purplish in fall. Small clusters of tiny, white or pink, urn-shaped flowers appear in late April and May. The showy clusters of bright red berries replace the flowers in fall and persist through winter, even into early spring.

Landscape Use Bearberry is an excellent groundcover for dry sites in sun to partial shade. It will trail over rocks and down banks. The ornamental fruits are showy in fall and winter and

are eventually eaten by songbirds and game birds. It is well suited to coarse-textured soils low in nutrients and can be grown on gentle to steep slopes and dunes for erosion control.

Site Prefers dry, poor, acidic soil in full sun to light shade; grows best in full sun. Does poorly in neutral or slightly alkaline soils.

Culture Acidify and loosen soil before planting, if needed. Bearberry is somewhat difficult to establish, but once it takes hold it is a tough plant. Transplant container-grown plants from a northern seed source in early spring. Pay careful attention to water the first two years or so, until the roots firmly take hold. A 1- to 2-inch layer of compost mulch will help conserve moisture and maintain soil acidity.

Arctostaphylos uva-ursi 'Massachusetts'

Aronia melanocarpa
'Autumn Magic'

Aronia prunifolia [A. melanocarpa]
Black chokeberry
Zone 3

Native Habitat Throughout Michigan in swamps, low areas, or open coniferous woods in acidic soils.

Size 4 to 6 feet tall, 3 to 6 feet wide

Description This upright, mounded shrub has dark green, glossy summer foliage that turns a beautiful red in fall. White flowers produced in early May last for two weeks or more, then are followed by small black fruits that resemble tiny apples.

Landscape Use Black chokeberry is a tough, reliable shrub that offers year-round interest, but it is especially showy in fall. Use it in shrub borders and naturalistic plantings. The lower branches often become sparse; hide them by using low-growing plants in front of black chokeberry. The fruits are low on the list for birds, but they are ornamental enough for use in wreaths and floral arrangements. Although technically edible, the fruits are extremely tart and bitter and are not recommended for eating off the bush.

Site Grows in slightly acidic soil in both wet and dry conditions in full sun to light shade.

Culture Black chokeberry is easy to transplant. Plants do best if left untrimmed. This shrub can be somewhat invasive when the suckers are allowed to remain. Suckers are easily controlled with regular pruning, if desired.

Cultivar 'Autumn Magic' grows upright to 5 feet; it has good flower and fruit production and outstanding fall color. Zone 3.

Asimina triloba
Pawpaw
Zone 5

Native Habitat Found rarely in moist soils in and along the edges of deciduous woods in the southern third of Michigan.

Size 15 to 25 feet tall, 15 to 20 feet wide

Description This shade-tolerant suckering shrub or small pyramidal tree has very large (6- to 12-inch) leaves and large, fleshy, big-seeded fruits. The dark purple, 1- to 2-inch flowers appear in early to mid-May, before leaves are fully expanded. They turn into edible greenish yellow berries that eventually turn brownish black. Leaves have good yellow fall color.

Landscape Use Large droopy leaves and flowers give pawpaw a tropical look. Use it as an understory in large shade gardens, as screening, or for naturalizing along streams. With persistent pruning, it can be trained into a small tree. The edible fruits have a banana-like flavor. They ripen in early autumn and are attractive to wildlife.

Site Prefers moist, fertile, slightly acidic soil in partial shade, but tolerates drier sites in full sun.

Culture Pawpaw can be difficult to transplant because of the taproot. Plant small, bare-root, container-grown, or balled-and-burlapped specimens in spring for best results. Protect young trees from sunburn. Natural compounds in the leaves and bark provide natural insecticidal properties, so trees are rarely bothered by pests.

Cultivars 'Sunflower' was selected for its large fruit. 'Taylor' and 'Taytoo' were originally collected from the wild near Eaton Rapids, Michigan. They both have fruits with light green skin and tasty yellow flesh.

Asimina triloba

Steven Nikkila

Ceanothus americanus
New Jersey tea
Zone 4; trial in zone 3

Native Habitat Well-drained prairies, oak savannas, and woodland edges throughout most of the Lower Peninsula and widely scattered on the Upper Peninsula.

Size 2 to 3 feet tall, 2 to 3 feet wide

Description New Jersey tea is a low-growing, spreading, many-branched shrub. It has dark green leaves with prominent veins. The showy, creamy white flowers appear in upright, umbel-like clusters in midsummer when not many plants are in bloom. The dried seed capsules add interest in late summer. Fall color is an unspectacular yellow-green.

Landscape Use A durable small shrub once established, New Jersey tea can be used in mixed or shrub borders and in foundation plantings. It makes a beautiful small hedge when planted 1 to 2 feet apart. The flowers attract bees, butterflies, and hummingbirds, and birds eat the seeds. It is a good cut or dried flower.

Site A well-drained sandy soil in sun or partial shade; will not tolerate wet soils.

Culture Young plants are easy to move, but older ones are hard to transplant because of the extensive taproot. An occasional hard pruning in late winter will help keep plants looking neat. New Jersey tea is often treated more like an herbaceous perennial, especially when grown in mixed borders. High humidity and heavy summer rainfall can be harmful to plants, especially if they are in heavy soils in partial shade.

Other Species *C. herbaceus* (inland New Jersey tea) is native to open rocky woods in the northern part of the Lower Peninsula and in parts of the Upper Peninsula. Flowering and growth characteristics are similar to *C. americanus*, but it is a nonwoody species. It is often mistakenly sold as *C. ovatus*, a species native farther south and west. Zone 4.

Ceanothus americanus

C. sanguineus (red-stem ceanothus) is native to rocky bluffs and woodland edges in the far northern part of the Keweenaw Peninsula. It has narrower leaves, red twigs, and terminal flower clusters that bloom in late May and early June. It may be difficult to find local sources. Zone 5.

Cephalanthus occidentalis
Buttonbush
Zone 4

Native Habitat In hardwood swamps and along streams and rivers throughout most of the Lower Peninsula.

Size 3 to 8 feet or more tall, 3 to 6 feet wide

Description Buttonbush is a low-branched shrub with smooth, gray-green bark. Its attractive, medium green leaves nicely set off the white flowers, which are borne in a 1-inch globe with protruding pistils. It blooms when few other plants are in flower, from late July into August. Bright red fruits form in autumn.

Landscape Use Plants have an almost tropical look when the interesting flowers appear against the glossy green leaves. The flowers have a musky, sweet scent. The leaves cluster toward the

outside of the canopy, giving an open area underneath for planting. Buttonbush can be grown in standing shallow water and is good for naturalizing alongside ponds. The flowers are a nectar source for butterflies.

Site Moist or wet, fertile soils; intolerant of drought.

Culture Plants can be cut back to 6 inches each winter; they'll grow to 3 feet tall by midsummer and will still flower on the new growth. Buttonbush is often treated more like an herbaceous perennial, especially when grown in mixed borders. It often dies back to the ground after a severe winter. Landscape plants should be well mulched to retain the necessary soil moisture.

Cephalanthus occidentalis

Comptonia peregrina

Comptonia peregrina
Sweet fern
Zone 3

Native Habitat Dry, sandy, acidic soils, scattered throughout the Upper Peninsula and throughout most of the northern half of the Lower Peninsula.
Size 1 to 4 feet tall, 2 to 3 feet wide
Description Sweet fern is not a true fern but rather a low-growing, rhizomatous shrub with dark green, 2- to 6-inch-long, fernlike leaves that have a sweet fragrance.
Landscape Use Sweet fern spreads mainly by rhizomes, forming thickets, and it is effective in controlling erosion on slopes and difficult sites. The fine-textured leaves are aromatic, and the curled, dried foliage remains all winter, adding interest. A carpet of sweet fern will give a landscape a definite woodsy feel. In the wild, it often grows beneath *Pinus banksiana* (jack pine). Flickers eat the small brown fruits, and prairie chickens and sharp-tailed grouse use plants for nesting cover.
Site Prefers dry, acidic, sandy soils, but will survive on most garden soils as long as they are acidic.
Culture Acidify soil before planting, if necessary. Established plants are difficult to move, so start with young container-grown specimens for best success. Sweet fern fixes nitrogen in the soil, which helps it survive tough conditions and eliminates its need for additional fertilizer. It maintains its mature 3- to 4-foot height for a long time without pruning. Remove some of the older canes in spring to keep plants vigorous. It is pest free.

Cornus alternifolia
Pagoda dogwood
Zone 3

Native Habitat Well-drained, moist, open woodlands throughout Michigan.
Size 20 to 25 feet tall, 20 to 25 feet wide
Description This small understory tree or large shrub grows in horizontal tiers of branches, giving it a layered appearance. The deep green leaves are heavily veined and turn reddish in fall. Small, creamy white, musk-scented flowers appear in 3- to 5-inch clusters from late May to early June. The fruit is green and berrylike, turning to white to blue to nearly black on red stalks.
Landscape Use Pagoda dogwood is an excellent landscape plant. It can be grown as a large multistemmed tree or easily pruned to an attractive specimen tree. It has a graceful, tiered branching pattern. Use it as an understory shrub in woodland gardens, in shrub borders, or as an entry or patio tree. Birds love the fruits.
Site Does best in cool, moist, slightly acidic soils in partial shade. It thrives in mulched landscape beds, but will not do well as a lawn specimen.
Culture Acidify soil before planting, if necessary. A little selective pruning in winter to encourage the horizontal branching habit will pay off in a lovely landscape specimen. Plants may self-seed in surrounding garden beds, but the seedlings are easily pulled out or transplanted. Plants grown in full sun should be well mulched and watered. In wet years, dogwoods are susceptible to powdery mildew and leaf spot. These diseases result in unattractive foliage in late summer and early fall, but are not serious enough to kill plants. Reduce chances of infection by keeping plants well watered and pruned to increase air circulation. Cankers causing stem dieback are usually caused by lack of water brought about by improper soil conditions or an incompatible planting site. Prune out infected stems several inches below the canker or at ground level.
Cultivars and Other Species Golden Shadows™ ('W. Stackman') is a new variegated selection. Its leaves display a broad, lime green to chartreuse central zone surrounded by a well-defined, iridescent golden yellow margin. Zone 3.

Cornus florida (flowering dogwood), native to deciduous woods in the southern half of the Lower Peninsula, may well be Michigan's most attractive native small tree. It grows about 25 feet tall and wide and has somewhat horizontal branching that offers winter interest. Leaves are dark green, turning shades of red, orange, or purple in fall. The spring flowers themselves are not very showy, but the white, 2-inch bracts surrounding them are. Glossy red fruits ripen in September and are devoured by birds. Unfortunately, flowering dogwood is susceptible to

Cornus florida

Robert Domm

Cornus racemosa

Cornus stolonifera

several insect and disease problems, including borers and anthracnose, both of which can be serious. To thrive, it requires an acidic, well-drained soil in partial shade. Landscape plants should be mulched, and watered during dry periods. Many cultivars have been selected for disease resistance as well as for flower color and shape, foliage color, fruit color, hardiness, and growth habit. Select plants from a northern seed source for best results. 'Cherokee Princess' is a reliable early flowering selection. 'Cherokee Maiden', also known as 'Ozark Spring', was selected for its winter hardiness. Zone 5.

C. foemina ssp. *racemosa* [*C. racemosa*] (gray dogwood) is native to open woods throughout the Lower Peninsula and is scattered on the Upper Peninsula. It grows 8 to 12 feet tall and up to 10 feet wide. The attractive gray stems support creamy white flowers in May; they are followed by showy white fruits borne on red pedicels in late summer. Birds eat the fruits, but the showy red pedicels persist, contrasting nicely with snow. It grows best in moist, cool soils in full sun, but it is tolerant of dry conditions and partial shade. It spreads slowly by underground stems and is

excellent for naturalizing at the edges of woods or for hedging. It is also successfully grown as a specimen tree with persistent pruning. Zone 4; trial in zone 3.

C. rugosa (round-leaved dogwood) is native to woodlands scattered throughout Michigan. It grows 10 feet tall in dense shade and is useful as an understory shrub in woodland gardens. Plants may be difficult to locate. Zone 2.

C. stolonifera (red-osier dogwood) is native to swamps, low meadows, and forest openings and margins throughout Michigan. An attractive, 10- to 12-foot landscape shrub, it has deep red stems and twigs that are showy in winter; creamy white flowers in spring, followed by attractive white fruits; and maroon-colored fall leaves. Plant it in shrub borders, foundation plantings, or outside a winter window, using evergreens as a backdrop to set off the color. Once established, it is drought tolerant and low on the list of deer favorites. It spreads by layering when the lower stems touch or lie along the ground. It can form dense thickets in the right conditions and can be used as a hedge. Younger stems have the brightest color, so prune out

oldest stems each spring to encourage new growth. Overgrown plants can be cut back to about 6 inches in spring. It is the same plant as *C. sericea*. 'Cardinal' has bright cherry red stems. 'Isanti' has a compact growth habit, growing to about 6 feet tall, and good stem color. Zone 3.

C. amomum (silky dogwood) is native to wet soils throughout the Lower Peninsula and is scattered on the Upper Peninsula. It grows to 10 feet in height and has 2-inch white flower clusters, porcelain blue berries, and purple-red fall color. It is good for areas with poorly drained soils, where it will attract wildlife. Zone 4.

151

Corylus americana
American hazelnut
Zone 3

Corylus americana fruits

Native Habitat Thickets with both dry and moist soils, mainly in the southern half of the Lower Peninsula, but also in a few locations in the southern part of the Upper Peninsula.
Size 10 feet tall, 6 feet wide
Description This multistemmed, rounded shrub has dark green leaves that are slightly hairy above and softly hairy beneath. Fall color is sometimes yellowish. The small but interesting dangling catkins appear in early to mid-April and are followed by edible nuts that mature in fall.
Landscape Use American hazelnut has attractive summer foliage and interesting fall fruits, but its large size and coarse growth habit limit its landscape use to screening, naturalistic plantings, or large shrub borders. The nuts are favorites of squirrels.
Site Well-drained, loamy soil in full sun or light shade.
Culture American hazelnut is easy to transplant and grow. The suckers, which form freely from the base, can be pruned out at any time. Regular pruning helps keep plants neater. It has no serious insect or disease problems.
Other Species *C. cornuta* (beaked filbert) is native to the northern half of the Lower Peninsula and much of the Upper Peninsula. It is similar to *C. americana* except it has a longer beak on its fruits and it is hardier, into zone 2.

Corylus americana

Diervilla lonicera
Bush honeysuckle
Zone 3

Diervilla lonicera

Native Habitat Exposed, rocky sites and dry to mesic, well-drained soils in and along woodlands, all throughout most of Michigan.
Size 2 to 3 feet tall, 2 to 3 feet wide
Description This low, suckering shrub has attractive, glossy, green leaves tinged with red and good orange-to-red fall color. Yellow, trumpet-shaped flowers appear from late June into July and are pretty but not exceptionally showy. The fruit is a dried capsule that is somewhat showy. Plants send up stems from underground rhizomes.
Landscape Use Bush honeysuckle is a rugged, pest-free plant with a long bloom time and attractive foliage. Use it as groundcover or bank cover. It is a good low-maintenance choice for massing and naturalizing on tough sites, and it is one of the few shrubs to tolerate the dry shade under large trees.
Site Adaptable, but prefers organic, well-drained soils in sun or partial shade; tolerates high pH, compacted soils, and windy conditions.
Culture Bush honeysuckle is easy to transplant. Give plants room to expand to their full size. Keep plants in bound by pulling suckers as needed. Plants can be cut back to the ground in spring to improve appearance. Plants rarely require fertilizing.

Dirca palustris
Leatherwood
Zone 2

Native Habitat Rich woodlands and swamp margins throughout most of Michigan.

Size 3 to 6 feet tall, 4 to 6 feet wide

Description This deciduous shrub has attractive, smooth, grayish brown bark and flexible twigs that can become knobby, creating an interesting winter silhouette. Small yellow flowers appear in mid- to late April, just as the leaves are beginning to open. The gray-green leaves turn a soft yellow color in fall.

Landscape Use Leatherwood offers a subtle beauty to the landscape all year round. The early spring blooms and bright green foliage are an especially welcome sight, and the clean summer foliage, fall color, and winter shape add to its list of assets. It can be grown as a specimen, in shrub borders, or naturalized. Its shade tolerance makes it useful in woodland gardens.

Site Prefers moist, slightly acidic soil in partial to heavy shade. Plants in full sun may have bleached-out foliage.

Culture Acidify soil before planting, if necessary. Leatherwood stays dense and symmetrical in full sun, requiring little pruning or shaping. In shade, it is more irregular in shape and may benefit from light pruning after flowering. Plants grown in sun should be well watered and mulched. It has no pest problems.

Dirca palustris

Euonymus atropurpurea
Wahoo
Zone 2

Native Habitat Rich, moist soils, usually along streams, rivers, and floodplains, scattered in the southern half of the Lower Peninsula.

Size 20 to 25 feet tall, 10 to 12 feet wide

Description This large shrub or small tree has an interesting, flat-topped, irregular crown. It is showiest in fall, when the dark green leaves turn a good reddish purple color and the showy pink fruits open to reveal scarlet-orange seed coverings, which ripen over a long period of time.

Landscape Use Wahoo can be pruned to a single- or multiple-trunked tree with an irregular crown and corky stems. With a minimal amount of grooming, it can be used as a specimen tree or as an understory shrub in woodland gardens or shrub borders. Left alone, it is good for naturalizing and for attracting birds. It should be used more often in landscape situations.

Site Prefers a rich, moist, slightly acidic soil high in organic matter, but will tolerate most landscape situations in full sun or partial shade. Fall color is better in full sun, but plants will grow in heavy shade.

Culture Wahoo requires consistent soil moisture. Mulch plants to keep soil moist and acidic. Prune in early spring to shape plants; it tolerates heavy pruning. No serious insect or disease problems, but rabbits and deer may feed on the bark and leaves. It is on Michigan's special concern list and may be difficult to find in the nursery trade.

Other Species *E. obovata* (running strawberry bush) is native to a variety of soils in deciduous forests in the

Euonymus atropurpurea

southern half of the Lower Peninsula. It has a prostrate growth habit, getting about a foot tall. The light green leaves are followed by reddish green flowers and red fruits. It makes a nice groundcover in shade. Zone 3.

Hamamelis virginiana
Witch hazel
Zone 4; trial in zone 3

Hamamelis virginiana

Native Habitat Rich deciduous woods and sandy dry woods throughout the Lower Peninsula and in the western half of the Upper Peninsula.

Size 10 to 12 feet tall, 10 to 12 feet wide

Description This deciduous shrub is the last shrub to bloom in autumn, producing golden yellow flowers that are slightly fragrant. The flowers take a back seat to the wonderful golden yellow fall leaf color. This open, multi-stemmed shrub has a tighter growth habit when grown in more light. Its branches have a zigzag pattern.

Landscape Use Witch hazel's coarse texture limits its formal landscape use, but it's a good choice for the middle layer in woodland gardens. It is also suitable for shrub borders, where other plants can add interest until fall, when witch hazel shines. It can be pruned into a small, wide-spreading tree.

Site Prefers a uniformly moist soil in sun or partial shade, but tolerates dry, shady conditions.

Culture Witch hazel is fast growing when young. Plants grown in full sun may show leaf scorch in summer. Rejuvenate overgrown shrubs with heavy pruning in early spring.

Hypericum prolificum [H. spathulatum]
Shrubby St. John's wort
Zone 4

Hypericum kalmianum

Native Habitat Swamp borders, thickets, and sandy open woods, mainly in the southern half of the Lower Peninsula.

Size 3 to 5 feet tall, 2 to 4 feet wide

Description Shrubby St. John's wort is a dense, upright, branching shrub with dark green leaves. The bright yellow, 1-inch flowers that appear in early to midsummer are followed by showy seed capsules.

Landscape Use This shrub is good for late-summer color in the shrub border. It can also be used as a specimen or in a mass planting. Exfoliating bark and persistent fruit offer winter interest.

Site Tolerates dry, heavy soils in full sun to partial shade.

Culture Shear off old seed heads in spring. Blooms appear on new wood, so plants can be cut back in early spring.

Other Species *H. kalmianum* (Kalm's St. John's wort) is native to sand dunes and some inland soils in all but the far northern part of Michigan. It grows 2 to 3 feet tall and 3 feet wide and has attractive bluish green leaves. Its smaller size and long bloom time make it suitable for use in mixed borders and foundation plantings. It is tolerant of dry soil and will grow in sun to partial shade. Zone 4.

Ilex verticillata
Winterberry
Zone 3

Native Habitat Acidic swamps, bogs, and wet woods throughout most of Michigan.
Size 6 to 10 feet tall, 6 to 10 feet wide
Description Winterberry is deciduous—one of the few hollies to lose its leaves in winter. Its leaves vary from flat to shiny on the upper surface. Its autumn color is not especially showy, but the bright red berries, produced in tight clusters along the stems, are showy after the leaves drop and until winter birds devour them.
Landscape Use From late fall through winter, winterberry steps into the spotlight by producing an outstanding display of bright red berries that persist on the branches even after the leaves have fallen. Plant it in groupings or mix it with other plants that lack winter interest. It can be used for hedging. The red berries are extremely attractive when contrasted by background snow or when reflected in nearby bodies of water.
Site Best performance is in full sun and acidic, organically enriched, moist to wet soils, but it is somewhat adaptable to soils that are occasionally dry. Chlorosis and stunting will occur in alkaline soils.
Culture Berries are only produced on female plants. Plant one male plant in close proximity to three to five female plants to ensure good pollination and subsequent fruit set. Plants in relatively dry soils will have better berry size (and subsequent ornamental appeal) with irrigation during dry periods of July and August. Young plants will grow faster with annual applications of an acidic plant food. Little pruning is needed.
Cultivars Several cultivars have been selected. Most are females that require a male pollinator to set fruit.

Ilex verticillata 'Compacta'

'Afterglow' features smaller, glossy green leaves and large orange-red berries that mature to orange. 'Cacapon' grows to 6 feet and has bright red fruits. 'Red Sprite' (also known as 'Compacta') is a popular dwarf, maturing to only 3 to 4 feet tall. 'Shaver' has large clusters of red-orange berries. Use 'Jim Dandy' or 'Raritan Chief' to pollinate all four cultivars. 'Winter Red' has a good growth habit and profuse bright red fruits that consistently persist into winter; 'Southern Gentleman' is a good pollinator for 'Winter Red'.

Lindera benzoin
Spicebush
Zone 5

Native Habitat Low, rich deciduous woods and swamps, mainly in the southern half of the Lower Peninsula.
Size 6 to 12 feet tall, 6 to 12 feet wide
Description Spicebush is a multi-stemmed understory shrub. In early spring, clusters of small yellow flowers hug the branches before the leaves appear. On female plants, the flowers turn into beautiful bright red fruits. The common name comes from the spicy scent of the twigs.
Landscape Use Grow spicebush where you can enjoy the early spring flowers and bright yellow fall foliage. A dark background of evergreens will set this shrub off nicely. Birds enjoy the red fruits that appear in fall. Spicebush is good for naturalizing or in a shrub border or woodland garden. It enjoys the moist soil found along ponds and can be used in wetland restoration.
Site Prefers moist soil, but will tolerate drier and wetter soils in partial to deep shade. It will tolerate full sun if given adequate water.
Culture Plants can be difficult to transplant and are somewhat slow to establish after planting. Mulch soil to help maintain an even moisture supply. The best fall color comes on plants grown in full sun. Plants are dioecious, so male plants must be nearby for female plants to set fruits. Plants have a nice natural form and require little or no pruning.
Cultivars 'Green Gold' is a nonfruiting form with large yellow blooms. 'Rubra' is also nonfruiting and has deep red-brown blooms. 'Xanthocarpa' has orange-yellow fruits. Zone 5.

Lindera benzoin

Steven Nikkila

Physocarpus opulifolius
Ninebark
Zone 2

Physocarpus opulifolius 'Nugget'

Native Habitat Rocky soils along rivers and lakes throughout Michigan.
Size 6 to 9 feet tall and wide
Description This hardy multistemmed shrub produces fast-growing, arching shoots. The five-petaled, white to pinkish flowers are grouped together in 2-inch flat-topped clusters in June and July and are followed by somewhat showy reddish brown fruits. Older stems are covered with attractive shaggy bark that sloughs off in long fibrous strips, but the foliage usually covers it. The foliage stays clean and attractive throughout the growing season and can be shades of yellow or purple. Dried fruits vary from brown to bright red, depending on soil and weather.

Landscape Use Use ninebark and its cultivars in hedges, foundation plantings, and shrub borders. The foliage adds interest without becoming sickly looking like some other yellow-leaved plants. The species is good for screening and for providing wildlife shelter. The flowers and foliage can be used in cut arrangements.

Site Requires full sun. Tolerates a wide range of well-drained soils.

Culture Space hedge plants 2 to 3 feet apart. Ninebark, especially the cultivars, will benefit from a spring application of an organic fertilizer. Shape plants by pruning as needed immediately after flowering. Overgrown plants can be cut back in late winter, but not every year. Hedges should receive light pruning annually; they will have fewer blooms than unpruned plants. Hedge plants may suffer from powdery mildew in wet years, but otherwise these plants are trouble free.

Cultivars 'Dart's Gold' is a compact, 4- to 6-foot tall and wide selection with good foliage color. Diabolo® has distinctive purple foliage that ages to a bronze shade. It can be pruned harshly each spring to promote vigorous shoots with large leaves. 'Nugget' grows to 6 feet tall and wide and has greenish yellow, textured leaves. 'Snowfall' is free flowering and has medium green leaves.

Potentilla fruticosa
Shrubby cinquefoil
Zone 2

Potentilla fruticosa 'Fargo'

Native Habitat Moist, alkaline soils throughout most of Michigan.
Size 1 to 4 feet tall, 1 to 4 feet wide
Description Shrubby cinquefoil has yellow flowers from June until the first frost. Flowers of the many cultivars come in shades of white, yellow, and gold, which hold up well in summer heat, and orange, pink, and red, which require cooler summer temperatures to hold their color. The grayish green compound leaves are fine textured and attractive. Persistent seed heads offer interest.

Landscape Use This long-blooming, tough shrub is adaptable to landscape use, and in some cases it has been overused. Plant it in groups of three to five in foundation plantings or in shrub borders, or use a single plant in a mixed border or rock garden. It can be used as a low hedge. Its drought tolerance makes it a good choice for waterwise plantings. Plants are also salt tolerant and can be planted along sidewalks and roadways. It can also be used as large-scale groundcover on slopes and in rocky soils.

Site Needs full sun to light shade; thrives in a wide range of soil, but prefers moist and well drained.

Culture Keep soil evenly moist until plants are established; after that, they can tolerate dry periods. A spring fertilizer application is beneficial. Shrubs require regular light pruning in early spring to look their best. Spider mites can be a problem during hot, dry periods. Blast foliage with a garden hose to dislodge these pests.

Cultivars Dakota Sunspot® ('Fargo') grows to only about 2 feet tall and wide and has golden yellow flowers. 'Coronation Triumph' and 'Goldfinger' are compact selections, growing 2 to 3 feet tall and wide and having bright yellow flowers. 'Snowbird' and 'Mount Everest' have white flowers. 'Tangerine' has orange flowers in shade or cool weather, and yellow flowers in full sun and summer heat. Zone 2.

Prunus americana

Prunus nigra 'Princess Kay'

Prunus americana
Wild plum
Zone 3

Native Habitat Moist to moderately dry soils along edges of woodlands, mainly in the southern half of the Lower Peninsula, but also farther north into the Upper Peninsula.

Size 15 to 20 feet tall, 15 to 20 feet wide

Description This single-trunked small tree has twiggy growth and suckers, which lead to large colonies in the wild. It has large, thornlike spur branches. The showy white flowers appear in 3- to 5-inch clusters from April into early May, before the leaves are fully out and fill the air with their perfume. The fruit is a large, fleshy, edible red plum. The dark green leaves turn golden yellow in fall.

Landscape Use The ideal spot for wild plum is a naturalized setting where you can allow it to colonize and where you can enjoy the fragrant spring flowers and fall color. The fruits can be eaten fresh or used in jams, if you can get to them before the birds. With regular pruning of suckers and black-knot infections, it can be used as a specimen tree.

Site Adaptable to a wide range of conditions, but prefers a well-drained soil in full sun.

Culture Prune out root suckers if you don't want thickets to form. Black knot, a fungal disease, can be a problem on all *Prunus* species. It appears as a swollen portion of the stem tissue that matures into a hard, black area on the stem. Remove a knot by cutting off the stem about 4 inches below the knot and destroying the upper portion.

Other Species *P. nigra* (Canada plum) is native to rich, moist soils in scattered spots throughout most of Michigan. It is rarely used as a landscape plant, but the cultivar 'Princess Kay' is an excellent small tree that grows to only about 15 feet. The showy, double, white flowers are among the first blooms to appear in spring, and they are set off nicely by the dark bark. Zone 3.

P. pensylvanica (pin cherry) is native to dry soils and open hillsides throughout most of Michigan. It grows up to 30 feet in height as a single-trunked tree with a narrow crown. Fall foliage color is purplish red. The green cherries turn bright red at maturity and can be used for jams and jellies. The fruits are a food source for wildlife.

P. pumila (sand cherry) is native to dry soils and open hillsides throughout most of Michigan. This shrub grows 1 to 3 feet tall and is covered with white flowers in spring before it leafs out. The plump, roundish cherries turn a deep blackish purple. The astringent fruits can be used for jellies and jams and are a favorite wildlife food. Zone 3.

P. virginiana (chokecherry) is native to a wide variety of soils throughout Michigan. It grows 15 to 35 feet tall and up to 25 feet wide as a thicket-forming shrub or small tree. White flowers appear in 2- to 3-inch racemes in May. Fruits are yellow-to-red cherries, turning nearly black. They are relatively sweet when fully ripe and can be used to make wines, syrups, and jellies. Use chokecherry for naturalizing at wood edges or for bird food. 'Schubert' (also known as 'Canada Red') has leaves that turn coppery red as they mature. It grows to only 20 feet tall and makes a good small tree in a lawn where suckers are mown off regularly. In the garden, these suckers will need to be removed. Zone 3; trial in zone 2.

Ptelea trifoliata var. trifoliata
Hoptree
Zone 4

Native Habitat Wooded to open dunes along Lake Michigan, as well as farther inland on dry-soil prairies in southwestern Michigan.

Size 15 to 20 feet tall, 15 to 20 feet wide

Description Hoptree is a small tree or large shrub with a dense, rounded crown that forms a broad canopy over a slender gray trunk. The 4- to 6-inch leaves are shiny and dark green on top and pale and hairy below, turning yellow in fall. Inconspicuous greenish white flowers appear in terminal clusters in June and have a delicious orange-blossom scent. The fruit is a conspicuous winged samara.

Landscape Use Hoptree is a great understory tree in woodland gardens. It can be used for naturalizing, massing, or in small groups. With regular pruning of suckers, it can be used in a mixed border. The ornamental fruits persist into winter and are enjoyed by wildlife.

Site Thrives in sun or shade; prefers well-drained soils but is adaptable to various soils.

Ptelea trifoliata

Culture Landscape plants will benefit from organic mulch around the roots. Suckers will need to be pruned out to maintain tree form. Avoid overpruning of branches. Plants look best when they have a natural look.

Rhus glabra
Smooth sumac
Zone 3

Native Habitat Dry or poor soils along forested edges, in scattered locations throughout most of Michigan.
Size 10 to 15 feet tall, 10 to 15 feet wide
Description Smooth sumac is a multiple-trunked deciduous shrub with an interesting branching habit. The dark green compound leaves are up to 24 inches long and have a tropical look. They turn a vivid orange, purple, yellow, and red in fall. The greenish flowers appear in dense, upright, 4- to 8-inch-long panicles in July and August. On female plants, the panicles turn into scarlet, cone-shaped clusters in September and October and persist into winter.

Landscape Use Smooth sumac is one of the first plants to change color in fall, sometimes in mid-August, which is its greatest asset. It spreads rapidly by suckers to form large colonies, and it is good for stabilizing slopes to prevent erosion. Suckers are removed by regular mowing, so it can be grown next to lawns. It is tolerant of both salt and drought and can be used along roadsides. Animals and birds eat the fruits.
Site Needs full sun; will take almost any soil except constantly wet or boggy sites.

Culture Smooth sumac spreads quickly by underground roots that send up new trunks. Once established, it is hard to eradicate. Male and female flowers are on separate plants, so not all plants produce showy fruit clusters. Fall color will be poorer on rich sites, so avoid fertilization. Plants can be trained into interesting small trees; choose a plant with a strong, straight leader, and prune it annually to maintain shape. Suckers will need to be removed each spring to keep a small tree from turning into a thicket.

Cultivars and Other Species 'Laciniata' is a female cut-leaf selection. 'Morden Select' is slower growing and reaches only 6 feet in height. Zone 3.

R. aromatica (fragrant sumac) is native to sandy, gravelly soil in oak openings and other forest areas scattered across the eastern half of Michigan. It forms a dense mound of branches covered with glossy leaves. Fuzzy, berry-like fruits form at the tips of some branches when grown in full sun. Fall color varies from red to yellow. It grows in full sun to partial shade, preferring slightly acidic soil. Its suckering growth habit and tolerance of poor soils makes it a good choice for covering slopes and rough terrain, but it is probably too aggressive for formal landscape situations. Zone 3.

R. copallina (winged sumac) is native to sandy hillsides and rocky openings on the edges of woodlands, mainly in the western half of the Lower Peninsula but also in the southeast. It is a colonizing shrub that grows to 20 feet or more and has crooked stems, but it can be pruned to a small tree. Zone 4.

R. typhina (staghorn sumac) is native to dry or poor soils along forest edges throughout most of Michigan. It can grow to 25 feet tall. The dense, velvety hairs on its stems distinguish it from *R. glabra*. Its individual leaves are also narrower and more finely toothed. It has the same great fall color, usually more orange than red, and interesting fruits. It is the same plant as *R. hirta*. 'Laciniata' is a female selection with deeply cut leaves that change color later in the season. Zone 4; trial in zone 3.

Rhus glabra 'Laciniata'

Rhus aromatica 'Gro-low'

Rhus typhina 'Laciniata'

Rosa blanda
Smooth wild rose
Zone 2

Native Habitat Dry to moist woods, prairies, dunes, and outcrops throughout most of Michigan.

Size 2 to 6 feet tall, 4 to 6 feet wide

Description Smooth wild rose forms dense, impenetrable thickets in favorable situations. The stems are thornless or have scattered bristles toward the base of the plant. Its flowers range from rosy pink to white and reach 2 to 3 inches across. They are fragrant and start blooming in June with some repeat bloom throughout the summer. The fruits, called "hips," resemble small apples and are about a half-inch in diameter; they turn a nice red in fall and persist well into winter.

Landscape Use Plants make a nice addition to prairie or wildlife gardens. They can be used for naturalizing, massing, and in shrub borders if there is some control of suckering. The hips are an important winter food source for wildlife.

Site Prefers full sun to light shade and rich soil, but will grow in poorer soils.

Culture Give plants a spring application of fertilizer. Suckers may need to be pruned. Smooth wild rose has no pest problems.

Other Species *R. acicularis* (prickly rose) is native to the sandy soils of coniferous forests and dunes and found mainly in the northern half of Michigan. It is a dense, prickly shrub that grows about 3 feet tall and has dark pink, fragrant flowers in June. It is somewhat shade tolerant and can be used as groundcover in slightly acidic soils that are high in organic matter. Zone 2.

R. arkansana (prairie wild rose) is native in dry to well-drained grassland soils widely scattered in Michigan. It is a spiny shrub, growing about 2 feet tall and spreading 4 to 8 feet wide; it has stiff canes and dark green leaves. The 2-inch, solitary, soft pink flowers appear from late spring to early summer and are slightly fragrant. They are followed by dark red hips. This rapidly spreading plant makes a good tall

groundcover or soil stabilizer. Zone 3.

R. carolina (pasture rose) is native to dry, sandy woods and dunes across the southern half of the Lower Peninsula. It grows 3 to 6 feet tall and freely suckers to form thickets. Its flowers are pink and single, appearing June into July, and are followed by showy red hips. Zone 4.

R. palustris (swamp rose) is native to bogs, swamps, wet thickets, and lake shores throughout most of Michigan. It grows up to 8 feet tall and has large, pink, fragrant flowers starting in late June. Grow it in bog gardens or along ponds. Zone 3.

R. setigera (prairie rose) is native to woods and thickets in the far southern part of Michigan. It is a wide-spreading shrub that grows about 4 feet tall and has arching stems up to 15 feet long. Its flowers start out deep pink then fade to white by the end of their bloom time, and are nearly scentless. The long canes can be trained to "climb." Zone 4.

Rosa blanda

Rosa acicularis

Rosa setigera

Rosa arkansana

Rubus odoratus

Rubus odoratus
Flowering raspberry
Zone 4

Native Habitat Clearings and borders of woodlands, mainly along the eastern edge of the Lower Peninsula.

Size 3 to 6 feet tall, 6 to 12 feet wide

Description This upright, suckering shrub has heart-shaped, lobed leaves that resemble maple leaves. Rich rose-purple, 1- to 2-inch flowers appear in June and last well into August. The fruit is an edible, small, dark red berry. Stems have exfoliating bark and are hairy but thornless.

Landscape Use Flowering raspberry is good for adding color to shade gardens and naturalized plantings. It has interesting exfoliating stems and an arching growth habit. The leaves are attractive all season, and the fragrant flowers last a long time. It will form open colonies if left unpruned. Birds enjoy the fruits.

Site Moist, well-drained soil in sun to shade.

Culture Flowering raspberry likes a moist soil. Mulch and water during dry periods. Prune right after fruiting. Suckers will need regular pruning if you don't want this shrub to travel.

Other Species *R. parviflorus* (thimble-berry) is native to moist soils on wooded hillsides and along stream banks in the northern half of Michigan. It is a scrambling shrub, growing 2 to 8 feet tall. It has attractive, fragrant white flowers and orange to maroon fall foliage. Fruits are red berries that fall to the ground when ripe. It is moderately shade tolerant and can be used as groundcover in most soils. Zone 2.

Salix discolor
Pussy willow
Zone 3

Native Habitat Wet soils of shores, swamps, and wetlands throughout Michigan.

Size 10 to 20 feet tall, 10 to 15 feet wide

Description Pussy willow is a shrub or small tree with multiple trunks and an irregular crown. The narrow leaves are shiny green, turning yellowish in fall. Its most ornamental feature is the 1-inch silvery gray catkins that appear before the leaves in early April. Its twigs are reddish purple to dark brown.

Landscape Use Most people grow this shrub for its charming catkins, which are often part of spring floral arrangements. Although not as large their European cousins, they are still showy and a welcome sign of spring. Pussy willow is good for naturalistic plantings, in wet soils, or in mixed shrub borders, where it can blend in after flowering.

Site Thrives in moist to wet soils in full sun.

Culture This shrub requires little care and is pest free. Soil should be amended with peat moss or compost before planting to ensure adequate moisture retention. Mulch to maintain the necessary soil moisture. Plants can be cut back to the ground in early spring after enjoying the catkins. This pruning keeps plants smaller and encourages growth of long stems with showy catkins that are good for cutting.

Other Species *S. exigua* [*S. interior*] (sandbar willow) is native to dunes and shorelines throughout most of Michigan. The leaves are silky silver-gray. It grows 10 feet tall or more and will form dense thickets. Use it for dune restoration and naturalized plantings. It does well in full sun to partial shade. Zone 2.

S. humilis (prairie willow) is native to drier sites throughout Michigan. The showy catkins are fat and fluffy, and the tiny, bright yellow flowers give the entire shrub a yellow glow in early April. It grows about 8 feet tall. Use it for massing in low areas. Zone 2.

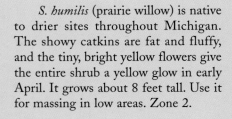

Salix discolor

Salix humilis

Sambucus canadensis
Common elder
Zone 2

Sambucus pubens

Native Habitat Wet to moist soils throughout most of Michigan.

Size 8 to 10 feet tall, 8 to 10 feet wide

Description This large shrub or small tree has an unusually short trunk and multiple stems that are spreading or arching. The compound leaves have five to eleven leaflets, each 2 to 6 inches long. From June to July, small, white flowers are borne in dense, flat-topped clusters, each up to 8 inches across. The flowers are followed in late summer by small, berrylike, purple-black fruits borne in flat-topped clusters.

Landscape Use Even though the foliage, flowers, and fruits are attractive, common elder is difficult to utilize in most formal landscapes because of its unkempt growth habit. It suckers profusely and must be pruned regularly to keep it looking neat. Use it for naturalizing and screening. The fruits are used to make elderberry jam and are favorites of birds.

Site Does best in moist soils, but it will tolerate dry soils, either acidic or alkaline. It grows in full sun to partial shade.

Culture Common elder is drought tolerant once established, but plants will bloom and fruit better if given ample water and a spring application of fertilizer. It can be pruned back hard in spring to keep it in bounds. If you are growing elders for the fruit, you need to plant at least two different cultivars for cross-pollination.

Cultivars and Other Species 'Laciniata' is an attractive cut-leaf selection that does not fruit as well as the species. 'Adams' and 'York' were selected for their larger, more numerous fruits and are often planted by gardeners interested in the edible fruit. 'Aurea' has golden leaves that contrast nicely with its red fruits. It reaches 10 feet tall and wide, but it is often pruned harshly every spring to force fresh foliage. 'Variegata' has narrow leaflets outlined in creamy white. It appreciates some protection from direct sun. Zone 3.

S. pubens [*S. racemosa*] (scarlet elder, red-berried elder) is native to woodlands and woodland edges throughout most of Michigan. This 10-foot-tall shrub is one of the earliest shrubs to leaf out and flower. Tiny greenish flowers and unfurling leaves

Sambucus canadensis 'Laciniata'

appear in early to mid-April and are noticeable because most other shrubs still have bare branches. The small, creamy white flowers are produced in erect pyramidal clusters in late April and early May. They are followed by red fruits that are readily eaten by birds. Scarlet elder is shade tolerant and can be used for naturalizing. Zone 2.

Spiraea alba
White meadowsweet
Zone 2

Native Habitat Moist to wet soils throughout Michigan.

Size 2 to 5 feet tall, 2 to 5 feet wide

Description White meadowsweet has showy, white, branching clusters of numerous tiny flowers, starting in June and continuing into September. These flower clusters give the plants a fuzzy appearance. The twigs are dark brown, and the leaves are blue-green.

Landscape Use This moisture-loving shrub is a good choice for mixed borders or perennial gardens, since it stays small and actually grows more like a perennial. It can be used along water edges and in bog gardens. The flowers are suitable for drying.

Site Prefers moist, fertile soils in full sun, but will tolerate drier landscape conditions.

Culture Keep soil mulched to maintain necessary moisture. Plants will benefit from a spring application of fertilizer. White meadowsweet often dies back over winter and in garden settings is best treated like an herbaceous perennial. Cut plants to the ground in spring to keep them tidy and compact and to give them the new wood necessary for good bloom. This fast-growing plant will recover quickly from being cut back.

Other Species *S. tomentosa* (steeplebush) is a native of moist to moder-

Spiraea alba

ately dry soils. It is found mainly in the southern half of the Lower Peninsula, but also in the Upper Peninsula. It has light pink blooms in mid- to late summer. Use it in the same landscape situations as *S. alba*. Zone 3.

Staphylea trifolia
Bladdernut
Zone 3

Staphylea trifolia

Native Habitat Moist, rich woodlands in the southern half of the Lower Peninsula.

Size 10 to 15 feet tall, 8 to 10 feet wide

Description Bladdernut is an upright, heavily branched, suckering shrub or small tree with attractive striped bark. The leaves have three leaflets and are dark green in summer, turning pale yellow in fall. The interesting flowers appear in nodding panicles in mid-May, turning into light brown capsules in late summer.

Landscape Use Bladdernut makes a good understory shrub in woodland gardens. It can be used in shrub borders or trained as a small, vase-shaped tree. The 3-inch, inflated seedpods add interest in fall and winter and can be used in dried arrangements.

Site Prefers slightly acidic, moist, well-drained, fertile soils in sun or partial shade, but it tolerates heavy shade, dry soils, and a higher pH.

Culture Bladdernut is an attractive shrub that adapts fairly easily to cultivation, and it should be used more often. Maintain soil acidity and moisture by mulching with a 2- to 4-inch layer of shredded pine bark or pine needles. Prune plants in early spring to shape or to maintain the small tree form. No serious insect or disease problems.

Symphoricarpos albus
Snowberry
Zone 2

Native Habitat Dry or rocky woodlands, barrens, and dunes throughout most of Michigan.

Size 3 to 6 feet tall, 3 to 6 feet wide

Description Snowberry's most ornamental feature is its berrylike, white, 1/2-inch fruits, which appear from September into November and persist into winter. Branches often bend to the ground when loaded with fruits. It has bluish green leaves without any significant fall color. Small, pinkish flowers appear in June.

Landscape Use Snowberry's shade tolerance allows it to be planted along the edge of a wood or under tall shade trees in wild gardens. The strong root system suckers freely and forms a thicket, making this shrub good for covering slopes and other tough-to-mow sites. The tangle of dense, twiggy stems has an unkempt look in winter, but these thickets provide excellent cover for wildlife. The berries provide food for birds. Hummingbirds are attracted to the flowers. Fruiting stems are nice additions to autumn cut-flower arrangements.

Site Prefers a well-drained soil in partial shade, but it will grow in almost any light and in any soil. Foliage is denser and the flowering heavier in full sun to partial shade.

Culture Snowberry prefers consistently moist soil, but will survive in moderately dry conditions. Help maintain soil moisture by surrounding plants with organic mulch. Keep these suckering plants in check and control the plants' overall size and shape by cutting out entire stems or portions of stems in early spring. A few leaf diseases, including anthracnose, blights, and powdery mildew, can cause spotting on the fruits and leaves, but they rarely do serious harm to plants.

Symphoricarpos albus

Viburnum trilobum [V. opulus var. americanum]
Highbush cranberry
Zone 2

Native Habitat Moist woods and thickets throughout Michigan.

Size 10 to 12 feet tall, 10 to 12 feet wide

Description Highbush cranberry is a large, rounded shrub with gray, smooth branches. From late May into June, it has lovely, white, lace-cap flowers that grow up to 4 inches across. The indented dark green leaves turn beautiful shades of yellow-orange to red in fall. The edible, showy, deep red fruits appear in August and often persist through winter.

Landscape Use Highbush cranberry has something to offer the landscape all year. Use it in shrub borders, as a specimen plant, in foundation plantings, and for screening. The edible fruits can be used for preserves and are attractive to birds.

Site Prefers a fertile, slightly acidic, well-drained soil in full sun to partial shade, but will tolerate less-than-ideal situations, even drought, when mature. Shrubs will not flower and fruit as well in partial shade.

Culture This shrub readily adapts to landscape situations. Keep the soil evenly moist by mulching plants with wood chips or shredded bark. Plants will benefit from a spring application of fertilizer. Viburnums do not require a lot of pruning, but you can prune right after flowering to improve shape or to reduce height. It is a good idea to remove a few of the older stems every three years or so to encourage new growth from the base.

Cultivars and Other Species 'Compactum' (also known as 'Bailey Compact') grows 6 feet tall and wide and is a good choice for hedging. 'Hahs' has a neat, rounded growth habit and good flower and fruit display. 'Wentworth' and Redwing™ ('J. N. Select') were selected for their heavy fruit production.

V. acerifolium (maple-leaved arrow-wood) is native to deciduous woods throughout the Lower Peninsula and also in the some areas of the Upper Peninsula. It grows about 6 feet tall and wide. The leaves resemble maple leaves and turn interesting shades of soft red to pink in fall. White flowers in June turn into bluish black fruits in late August. Zone 4.

V. cassinoides (wild raisin) is a native of moist to wet soils in the Lower Peninsula and in the eastern half of the Upper Peninsula. It grows 12 feet tall and wide. Dark green leaves turn orange to purple in fall. White flower clusters turn into fruits that start out green, turn pink, and end up bluish black. Zone 3.

V. dentatum var. *lucidum* [*V. recognitum*] (smooth arrow-wood) is native to the southern part of Michigan. It grows about 9 feet tall and wide, spreading by root suckers. Leaves are shiny dark green, turning yellowish to red. White flowers turn into bluish black fruits that really stand out against the leaves in fall. It makes a good informal hedge. It

Viburnum lentago

is salt and drought tolerant, and it is resistant to leaf-spot diseases and stem cankers that can plague other viburnums. Zone 3. Several cultivars of the species have improved leaf color and growth habits. Northern Burgundy® ('Morton') was selected for good leaf color in summer and fall. Chicago Lustre® ('Synnesvedt') has good landscape qualities. 'Ralph Senior' (Autumn Jazz™) has slightly pendulous foliage, colorful red stems, and good fall color. Zone 4.

V. lentago (nannyberry) is native to a wide variety of soils along forest edges, on stream banks, and on hillsides throughout Michigan. It is a 10- to 20-foot upright shrub or a single-stemmed tree with drooping branches and a rounded crown. It grows well in full sun to deep shade, but fall color is best in sun. Leaves are shiny green and crin-

kled; fall color is reddish purple. In late May, creamy white flowers appear in flat clusters that are 3 to 5 inches across. The berrylike fruits start out yellow-green, turn dark purple in September and October, and persist into winter. They turn sweet after a frost and are eaten by birds. Nannyberry is easily pruned into a small tree, or it can be used in shrub borders or for screening. It will sucker and ramble, but not at an aggressive rate, and it is easy to prune. Plants may get powdery mildew, but it is purely an aesthetic problem. Nannyberry is a good choice for places where you want a shade-tolerant specimen tree. Unpruned specimens are good for naturalizing and for use in woodland gardens. Zone 3.

V. prunifolium (black haw) is rare in Michigan, found in deciduous forests

in the far southern part of the state. It grows 12 feet tall and wide and can be pruned as a small tree. Pure white spring flowers turn into blue-black fall fruits. Black haw is useful for shrub borders or screening. It tolerates poor soils and drought but not shade. It is on Michigan's special concern list. Select nursery-propagated plants from a local seed source for best results. Zone 4.

V. rafinesquianum (downy arrow-wood) is native to dry slopes and open woods mainly in southern Michigan, but also in northern areas. It grows 6 feet tall and wide and has white flowers and bluish black fruits. The leaves have an attractive reddish tint when young. Use it as an understory in woodland gardens, as an informal hedge, or in shrub borders. Zone 2.

Viburnum dentatum 'Synnesvedt'

Viburnum trilobum

Viburnum rafinesquianum

Additional Native Shrubs and Small Trees

Alnus rugosa [*A. incana* ssp. *rugosa*] (speckled alder) is native to wet soils in all but the far southeastern corner of Michigan. It is a fast-growing small tree or shrub that grows to 15 to 25 feet tall and has multiple thin trunks. It is shade tolerant and usually grows in dense thickets. Leaves are dull green, turning yellow in fall. The tiny, cone-like seeds, which appear only after plants are eight to ten years old and then only every four years after that, are often used for jewelry or in artwork. Use it for naturalizing on wet sites. Zone 2.

Chamaedaphne calyculata (leather leaf) is native to peaty soils in bogs throughout most of Michigan. It is an evergreen, rhizomatous semi-shrub that grows 1 to 4 feet tall. It has white flowers in April and May. Plants require an acidic peaty or sandy soil that is constantly moist, such as in bog gardens. Zone 2.

Epigaea repens (trailing arbutus) is native to acidic, sandy soils in all but the far southern part of Michigan. It is a creeping shrub, growing less than a foot tall. It has bright green leaves and fragrant, pinkish flowers in April and May. It is difficult to grow but can be tried as groundcover in woodland gardens with acidic soils. Zone 2.

Kalmia polifolia (bog laurel) is native to acidic peat bogs in the northern half of Michigan. It grows 1½ to 2 feet tall and wide, and it has narrow, dark green, evergreen leaves. Rosy red to pink flowers appear in late spring. It requires acidic, boglike conditions, which are difficult to reproduce in landscapes. Consider it for a groundcover if you can provide the moist, acidic conditions it requires. Zone 2.

K. angustifolium (sheep laurel) is native to acidic soils in the northern half of the Lower Peninsula. It blooms about a month later than bog laurel. Both species may be difficult to locate in the nursery trade. Zone 2.

Ledum groenlandicum (Labrador tea) is native to acidic bogs in the northern half of Michigan and a few southeastern locations. It grows to 3 feet tall and wide. It has elongated, evergreen leaves that are wooly underneath. White flowers appear in small, flat-topped clusters in May. You can use it if you have a natural low area with acidic soil or an artificial bog. It needs a soil pH of 4.5 and constant moisture. Zone 3.

Lonicera involucrata (black twinberry) is native to woods and rocky openings on Isle Royale and in the far northern part of the Keweenaw Peninsula. It is an upright shrub that grows to 10 feet. The pale yellow flowers in June are followed by very showy large, glossy, nearly black berries set off by deep red bracts. Black twinberry requires moist or wet soils in partial shade. It is on Michigan's threatened species list. Zone 4.

Shepherdia canadensis (soapberry) is native to dunes, and sandy or rocky soils in open woods, mainly along the Great Lakes but also in scattered inland areas throughout Michigan. It grows 6 to 8 feet tall and wide. It is a loosely branched shrub with leaves that are dark green above and silvery on the lower surface. Yellow-red fruits appear on female plants in summer. The small, yellow-gold flowers that appear in early April are not particularly showy (they are chunky and rough), but they do offer interesting texture to the early spring-landscape. Soapberry's tolerance of wind, drought, salt, and high pH soils makes it useful for tough sites. Use it for screening, naturalizing, and wildlife plantings. It thrives in dry or alkaline soils in full sun. Zone 2.

Vaccinium angustifolium (lowbush blueberry) is native to acidic, sandy soils or bogs throughout Michigan. It grows 20 inches tall and wide. Flowers are white, summer foliage is glossy green, and fall color is an excellent red. It can be used as groundcover in acidic soils or grown for the small edible fruits. Zone 2.

V. macrocarpon (large cranberry) is native to bogs throughout Michigan. It is low growing, spreading up to 3 feet wide. It requires acidic, boglike conditions to do well. The tart fruits can be used in jellies. Zone 2.

V. vitis-idaea (lingonberry, mountain cranberry) is native to acidic bogs on Isle Royale. It grows about 1 foot tall and 3 feet wide. The leathery, dark green leaves set off the white or pink flowers and dark red fruits. It is suitable for bog gardens or as a groundcover on acidic sites; it does not do well on hot, dry sites. The fruits are tart but tasty and can be used in the same ways as large cranberries. Zone 2.

Deciduous Trees

Planting a tree is a long-term investment, but one that returns a great deal of satisfaction and value. Since most trees are not easily moved once established, you should make sure the tree you have selected is a good match for your site. Especially keep in mind the mature size. Don't make the mistake of planting a tiny oak seedling 10 feet from your front door or a basswood under a power line. Also consider hardiness, light requirements, rate of growth, and seasonal aspects like flowers, fruits, fall color, and winter appearance. If you don't want to drastically change the soil, you will probably want to select a tree based on your soil conditions. Consider if you want to attract wildlife and birds. Some trees can be messy, dropping leaves, flowers, fruits, or twigs.

Quercus rubra (red oak) is one of the best native trees for landscape use, offering strong wood and good-colored foliage both in the growing season and in winter.

Planting

You will have the best success planting locally grown nursery trees that have been properly root pruned. They will survive transplanting the best and start growing quickly. If you have the opportunity to move a native tree, stick with one that is 1 or 2 inches in diameter or less, and move it in early spring. Bare-root trees must be planted in spring as soon as the soil can be worked. Balled-and-burlapped, container-grown, and tree-spade trees can be planted any time but the hottest days of summer, during July and August. Spring is still the best time for planting, however.

Before planting, amend the soil with a good amount of organic matter, such as compost, peat moss, or well-rotted manure. Mix this organic matter thoroughly with the planting-hole soil. Place the tree at the same depth it was growing at in the container or the burlap wrap. Bare-root trees should be planted so that the crown is level with the ground level. Newly planted trees should not need additional fertilizer. Do not stake them unless they are on an extremely windy, open site. Any stakes should be removed as soon as the tree has rooted well, usually after the first year. It is a good idea to surround all newly planted trees with a ring of organic mulch 2 to 4 inches thick. Good mulches include wood chips, shredded bark, and pine needles. Replenish the mulch as needed throughout the growing season. Do not use rock or black plastic as mulch.

Care

The first two or three years after planting, make sure the soil is evenly moist from spring until the ground freezes in fall. Once established, most trees can tolerate some dry periods, but don't hesitate to water as needed, especially in sandy soils. Always saturate the soil thoroughly with each watering to encourage deep rooting. Most young trees will also benefit from a spring application of fertilizer. Spread a layer of rotted manure or compost around each tree or use a fertilizer such as Milorganite or fish emulsion. If possible, allow leaves to fall and decay under trees to return nutrients to the soil. Keep weeds pulled or smother them with organic mulch.

Maintenance needs of trees differ with each species. To develop a good shape, most deciduous trees will benefit from some selective pruning while they are young. The best time to prune is usually while they are dormant: you can see their silhouette better, and the chances of disease and insect problems are reduced. Remove branches that have narrow-angled crotches, as these branches are weaker than wide branches and are likely to split as the tree gets older. Remove lower branches only if they interfere with the use of the areas under the tree. Remove any dead, damaged, or diseased parts of trees at any time of year, cutting back to just above a healthy, outfacing bud.

Possible Problems

Some thin-barked trees such as maples and mountain ashes need to be protected from winter sunscald while they are young. Trees are susceptible to sunscald until they have developed a thick, corky trunk. Wrapping trees with a tree wrap made of weather-resistant paper in fall minimizes sunscald. Young trees should also be protected from rodent feeding, which can kill a tree. The best way to keep rodents away is to surround the trunk below the first branch with hardware cloth.

Some native trees are susceptible to insects and diseases, some of which, such as oak wilt and Dutch elm disease, can be fatal. However, most insect and disease problems are purely cosmetic and don't really threaten the tree's life. On large trees, control measures are rarely practical. Some things to watch for on young trees are aphid feeding (spray leaves daily with a strong blast of the hose), iron chlorosis (acidify soil to lower pH), and leaf scorch (water trees well during dry periods and mulch soil). The best defense against insect and disease problems is a vigorously growing tree. By choosing a tree appropriate for your site conditions and providing it with the necessary nutrients and ample water, most pest problems will not become serious.

Best Native Deciduous Trees for Landscape Use

Acer species (maples)
Carpinus caroliniana
    (blue beech)
Celtis occidentalis (hackberry)
Cercis canadensis (redbud)
Crataegus crus-galli var.
    inermis (thornless
    cockspur hawthorn)

Gymnocladus dioica
    (Kentucky coffee tree)
Nyssa sylvatica (black gum)
Ostrya virginiana (ironwood)
Quercus species (oaks)
Tilia americana (basswood)

Acer rubrum
Red maple
Zone 4; most of zone 3

Native Habitat Wet to moist woodland soils throughout Michigan.

Size 40 to 65 feet tall, 45 feet wide

Description Red maple is a medium-sized tree with a broadly rounded symmetrical crown. The smooth, light gray bark on young stems turns dark gray and shaggy on older limbs. Leaves have three- to five-pointed, saw-toothed lobes. The upper surface is light green; the lower surface is whitish and partly covered with pale down. It is the first of the native maples to turn color in fall. Fall color is usually a brilliant red, but it can also be orange or yellow. The small red flowers give the bare branches a red glow for a week or so in early to mid-April, before the leaves appear.

Landscape Use Red maple is a good shade, lawn, or street tree. Its ability to survive in heavy soils means it can tolerate the poorer, compacted soils of streets and parking areas. The red flowers are a welcome sight in early spring when few other trees are showy. All maples have shallow roots and produce deep shade that can make it difficult to grow grass under them.

Site Prefers slightly well-drained, acidic, sandy loam soils in sun to light shade, but tolerates most landscape conditions. It will not grow well in alkaline soils, but it will tolerate moderately moist soils.

Culture This tree is moderately fast growing and tolerant of urban conditions. It has a wide native range; stick with northern seed strains and sources for best results. Wrap young trees during winter to protect them from sunscald. Fall color can be inconsistent; purchase trees in fall if you want good fall color. Avoid pruning trees in late winter when the sap has begun to flow. This "bleeding" sap does not harm the tree, but it is messy and unsightly.

Cultivars and Other Species 'Autumn Spire' was selected for its bright red fall color and columnar form. Zone 3.

Acer rubrum

continued on next page

'Northwood' is fast growing, nicely shaped, and has good fall color. Zone 3.

A. nigrum (black maple) is native to moist, fertile soils; floodplains; and bottomlands in the southern half of the Lower Peninsula. It is similar to *A. saccharum* but the leaves droop at their sides and have yellow fall color. It has greater heat and drought tolerance than sugar maple. Zone 4.

A. pensylvanicum (striped maple) is native to rich woodland soils in the northern third of Michigan. It is a smaller maple, growing to only about 25 to 30 feet tall and wide. It has beautiful, smooth green bark striped with almost white lines. Fall color is a clear yellow. This slow-growing, shade-tolerant species is a good understory plant in woodland gardens. Zone 3.

A. saccharinum (silver maple) is a native of wet to moist soils, mainly in the southern half of Michigan but also farther north. The leaves are deeper cut than those of other maples and are whitish on the undersides. Fall color is usually pale yellow. It grows 80 feet tall or more, so keep it away from small yards and buildings. It produces many seeds, which can become weedy, and the shallow, invasive root system makes it difficult to garden under. It is a fast-growing species with weak wood, which makes it a messy tree after windstorms. It is best used on tough, open sites where quick shade is needed and where other maples won't do as well. Zone 3.

A. saccharum (sugar maple) is native to rich, moist soils throughout Michigan. It is an excellent choice for landscape use where the soil conditions are right. It prefers heavy clay or loam soils that are moisture retentive, and a north-facing slope, but it will tolerate drier, sandier sites. Avoid compacted, alkaline soils. It is larger than red maple, growing 50 to 80 feet, and has a nice round canopy. Its greatest attribute is the brilliant fall color, which ranges from yellow to orange to scarlet. It is slow growing when first trans-planted. It is sensitive to salt damage, so avoid using it as a street tree. It is also susceptible to leaf scorching and tattering when planted on open, exposed sites, which can make the leaves somewhat unattractive in late summer. Zone 4; protected sites in zone 3. 'Legacy' was selected for its good fall color and resistance to leaf tatter. Zone 4.

A. spicatum (mountain maple) is native to woodlands in all but the far southern part of Michigan. It is low branched and grows to only about 25 feet tall and 20 feet wide. Its proportions make it shrublike, but it can be pruned to a small tree. It has a crooked trunk and upright branches. Fall color is a beautiful deep orange to red. It prefers moist, acidic soils in partial shade. Being an understory tree, it doesn't do well on open, exposed sites. If you can provide it with the right conditions, it is a good substitute for the overplanted, nonnative amur maple (*Acer ginnala*). Zone 3.

Acer saccharum

Acer pensylvanicum

Acer spicatum

Aesculus glabra
Ohio buckeye
Zone 4; trial in zone 3

Native Habitat Found rarely in moist soils of deciduous forests in the southern third of Michigan.

Size 30 to 50 feet tall, 20 to 25 feet wide

Description This upright, oval tree has deeply furrowed bark and large leaves made up of five to seven leaflets. Fall color is yellow or orange. Flowers are greenish yellow and appear in upright panicles in April and May. The 1- to 2-inch dark brown fruit is spiny and usually contains one large, smooth, lustrous brown, inedible seed.

Landscape Use Ohio buckeye's large leaves and flowers make it a bold tree in the landscape. Use it as a specimen lawn tree, away from patios and driveways where the fallen fruits can be a problem. The flowers are attractive to hummingbirds. Fruits and bark should be considered toxic.

Site Moist soil in full sun to partial shade.

Culture Trees can suffer from leaf scorch during dry periods. Mulch and water landscape trees. Ohio buckeye reaches the northern edge of its range in southern Michigan, but it is hardy much farther north.

Cultivars 'Autumn Splendor' grows 35

Aesculus glabra

feet tall. It has good dark green foliage color and resists scorch. Fall color is orange red. Zone 4.

Betula papyrifera
Paper birch
Zone 2

Native Habitat Wide variety of habitats throughout most of Michigan.

Size 40 to 70 feet tall, 20 to 30 feet wide

Description Paper birch has attractive bright white bark that peels away in sheets to reveal salmon-colored underbark. Leaves are dark green, turning a nice bright yellow in fall. Slender greenish brown catkins appear in April, before or with the leaves.

Landscape Use Paper birch can be grown as a single-trunk tree, but it is especially attractive in a three-clump form. The peeling, chalky bark adds interest throughout the year. It is a fast-growing but rather short-lived tree, especially in landscape situations.

Site Likes full sun but requires adequate moisture and cool roots—a situation often difficult to find in landscaped yards.

Culture Paper birch is susceptible to cankers, wood rots, leaf miners, birch skeletonizer, and bronze birch borers. To reduce bronze birch borer problems, which can be devastating, plant the tree on cool north-facing sites where the roots are shaded. Spread a wide circle of organic mulch, such as wood chips or shredded bark, under the canopy, and make sure the tree receives adequate water during dry periods. Avoid planting it in a sunny lawn or near hot pavement. Any pruning should be done in late summer to avoid attack by bronze birch borers.

Other Species *B. alleghaniensis* (yellow birch) is native to a wide variety of habitats throughout Michigan. It grows 60 to 80 feet tall, so it is best used in large landscapes. Bark is yellowish or bronze, changing to reddish brown, and it peels off in thin strips, giving the single thick trunk a shaggy appearance. Autumn color is a beautiful golden yellow. It will grow best in moist soils that are not compacted in sun or light shade. It is somewhat resistant to bronze birch borer. Zone 3.

Betula papyrifera

Carpinus
caroliniana fruits

Carpinus
caroliniana

Native Habitat Rich, moist woods, especially along streams, mainly in the Lower Peninsula but also scattered in the western half of the Upper Peninsula.

Carpinus caroliniana
Blue beech
Zone 3

Size 20 to 25 feet tall, 12 to 18 feet wide
Description Blue beech is a bushy small tree or shrub with a spreading irregular crown. The beautiful muscle-like bark is bluish gray, smooth, and sometimes marked with dark brown horizontal bands. Slender brownish catkins dangle from branches in spring. Leaves are dark green in summer, changing to a beautiful orange to reddish purple in autumn. The small nutlets hang in clusters and turn brown, adding interest in fall and winter.
Landscape Use Plant blue beech where you can enjoy the attractive blue-gray

bark in winter. It is good in naturalized plantings and as an understory tree or shrub in woodland gardens. Use it for screening or as a background planting. It can be sheared into a tall hedge or pruned as a single-stemmed small tree. The early spring catkins are a welcome sight, and the nutlets are food for many birds.
Site Prefers a moist, fertile, slightly acidic soil in partial shade or sun; tolerates full shade and drier conditions.
Culture Blue beech is somewhat difficult to transplant. Move balled-and-burlapped or container-grown plants in early spring. Fertilize it lightly when young, and shape it with selective pruning to form a single trunk that will showcase the interesting bark. Without pruning, it will send up suckers from the base and become shrubby in appearance. It has no serious insect or disease problems.

Carya ovata

Carya cordiformis

Native Habitat Rich, damp areas along streams and on upland sites in the southern half of the Lower Peninsula.
Size 60 to 100 feet tall, 40 to 60 feet wide
Description Shagbark hickory is a large, stately tree with a wide-spreading growth habit. It is named for its showy, shaggy bark that flakes off in

Carya ovata
Shagbark hickory
Zone 4

thin plates. It has a narrow, irregular crown. The deep yellow-green summer foliage changes to become rich yellow to golden brown in fall and lasts for a long time.
Landscape Use This slow-growing large tree brings a lot of character to the landscape with its peeling, shaggy bark, especially in winter. It is a good specimen tree, but it requires a large yard or open area. The tough, strong wood is resilient in wind- and snowstorms, making it a good choice for windbreaks and hedgerows. The fruits, which grow up to 1½ inches in diameter, are edible and quite sweet. Squirrels love them, and if you have a shagbark hickory, you will have an abundance of these furry creatures. Shagbark hickory wood chips are used to flavor smoked foods.
Site Prefers well-drained soil in sun; young trees can take some shade. Adaptable to a wide range of soil conditions, including wet sites and acidic soil. The deep taproot allows this tree to survive on dry upland sites.
Culture Shagbark hickory is difficult to transplant because of its taproot.

Move young plants in early spring or plant hickory nuts in fall where you want them to grow. Protect them with some sort of removable wire cage, so rodents don't dig them up before they germinate. The fallen nuts may create a litter problem on the lawn.
Other Species *C. cordiformis* (bitternut hickory) is native to deciduous woodlands in about the same area of Michigan. It has an inedible nut that is not attractive to wildlife, and the bark is smooth and gray. Fall color is a golden yellow. It isn't nearly as ornamental as shagbark hickory, but it is worth preserving if you have one. Zone 4; trial in zone 3.

C. laciniosa (shellbark hickory) is native along riverbanks and in rich woodlands in the far southern areas of Michigan. It is similar to *C. ovata*, but it grows to only about 80 feet in height, the nuts are a little larger, and it is less hardy. Zone 5.

C. glabra (pignut hickory) is native to upland, drier sites in the southern half of the Lower Peninsula. It is a smaller species, usually growing 35 to 60 feet tall, but otherwise is similar to *A. ovata*. It tolerates drier sites. Its fall color is usually outstanding—a rich golden yellow. Zone 4.

Celtis occidentalis
Hackberry
Zone 3

Native Habitat Rich, moist soils and some upland sites, mainly in the southern half of the Lower Peninsula.

Size 40 to 70 feet tall, 20 to 65 feet wide

Description Depending on how much room it has, hackberry varies from a vase-shaped, upright tree to one with an open, wide-spreading crown. The lance-shaped leaves are bright green and rough. Fall color is yellow to greenish yellow. The small fruit turns from orange-red to purple in September and often hangs on for much of the winter, providing food for several wildlife species. Mature trees have deep, corky bark with warty protrusions.

Landscape Use Its adaptability to a wide range of conditions makes hackberry a good tree for shade, windbreaks, street use, and shelterbelts. It can tolerate wind, full sun, and the dirt and grime of city conditions. It should be considered as a replacement for the American elm. Birds and mammals eat the fruits, and leaves are the larval food of many butterflies. The narrow limb crotches and numerous spur branches attract many nesting birds.

Site Prefers moist, well-drained soil, but will tolerate both wet and dry sites and a wide range of soil pH. Grows in full sun or partial shade.

Culture Hackberry transplants easily but sometimes takes up to two years to really start growing after planting. After that, it is moderately fast growing, especially in fertile, moister soils. It is drought tolerant once established. A few cosmetic problems affect hackberry, but none of them are serious. Hackberry nipple gall is a wartlike growth on the lower side of leaves, caused by insects known as psyllids. Clusters of twiggy outgrowth called witches' brooms appear on some branches, caused by feeding mites and a powdery mildew fungus, but this condition is not harmful to the tree. Some people actually find these witches'-broom growths interesting.

Cultivars and Other Species 'Prairie Pride' has thick, leathery, dark green foliage and a nice uniform, compact, oval crown. It does not develop witches' broom. Zone 3.

C. tenuifolia (dwarf hackberry) is native to drier sites, including wooded sand dunes, in a few locations in the far southern part of Michigan. It is more shrublike in its growth habit, reaching only about 20 feet in height, and its leaves are narrower. It can be used as a small tree on dry sites or as an understory shrub at the edge of woodland gardens. It is on Michigan's special concern list and may be difficult to locate in the nursery trade. Zone 5.

Celtis occidentalis

Cercis canadensis
Redbud
Zone 5; protected sites in zone 4

Native Habitat Found rarely in rich woods, especially along rivers and streams in the southern third of Michigan.

Size 15 to 30 feet tall, 20 to 25 feet wide

Description This small, spreading tree has large (4-inch), heart-shaped leaves that start out reddish purple, turn bluish green in summer, and turn yellow in autumn. The attractive purple-pink flowers appear in early spring, before the leaves, and are very showy. Flat, peapod-like fruits appear in early autumn and persist through winter. Bark on mature trees is reddish brown to black and furrowed.

Landscape Use Redbud is an excellent small tree, offering color and interest

all year round. Use it as a specimen or as a grouping of three in a large lawn. It is often grown as a clump tree. It is stunning when grown at the edge of a woodland garden, and it can also be an effective part of a mixed border.

Site Moist, well-drained soil in full sun to light shade.

Culture Redbuds do not do well when stressed. Keep landscape plants mulched and well watered. A spring application of an organic fertilizer may be needed on poorer soils. Canker can be a problem; be sure to protect trunks from lawnmowers and weed whippers. Redbud is sensitive to salt, so keep it away from salted walks and roads. The best flowering occurs on trees four

Cercis canadensis

years old and older. Redbud reaches the northern edge of its range in Michigan and not all redbuds found in the nursery trade are adaptable to Michigan's climate. Select plants that originated from a northern seed source or region for best results.

Crataegus crus-galli 'Inermis'

Native Habitat A wide variety of soils in the southern half of the Lower Peninsula.

Size 18 to 30 feet tall, 20 to 35 feet wide

Description This small, low-branching tree has a wide-spreading crown. It

Crataegus crus-galli var. inermis
Thornless cockspur hawthorn
Zone 4; trial in zone 3

is a thornless variety of the species. Its leaves are dark green and shiny. Showy white flowers appear in clusters in May and are followed by showy red fruits in late summer.

Landscape Use Cockspur hawthorn is a tough, adaptable tree. It can be used as a specimen, in groupings, for screening, and as a barrier plant (consider the thorn-laden species if you really want to keep something out). It tolerates urban conditions, is showy in flower and in fruit, and has an interesting winter silhouette. The apple-like red fruits are eaten by birds and other animals.

Site Well-drained soil in full sun.

Culture Hawthorns are susceptible to several insects and disease problems, the most serious being hawthorn rust, which can severely mar the summer beauty of the leaves. *C. crus-galli* has much greater resistance to hawthorn rust than other species. The thorned types should not be planted in areas where children may play.

Other Species *C. mollis* (downy hawthorn) is native to dry soils mainly in the southwestern corner of Michigan. It is a rounded tree that grows 20 to 30 feet tall. Leaves are thick and shiny dark green; the fragrant flowers are white, sometimes pink, and appear in clusters. Its use is limited by its susceptibility to hawthorn rust and the 2-inch thorns that cover the branches. It can be used in naturalized plantings and shelterbelts. Birds nest in the branches for protection. Zone 3.

Fagus grandifolia

Native Habitat A wide variety of soils, mainly in the Lower Peninsula but also in the eastern half of the Upper Peninsula.

Size 60 to 80 feet tall, 50 to 80 feet wide

Description American beech is a large, stately tree, often with a short,

Fagus grandifolia
American beech
Zone 5; trial in zone 4

crooked trunk and a wide-spreading crown. The attractive bark is thin, smooth, light bluish gray, and often mottled by dark blotches. Leaves are bluish green above and lustrous beneath, turning golden bronze in autumn and often persisting over winter. Two- to four-inch yellowish green inconspicuous flowers appear from April into early May. The fruit is an edible nut enclosed in a bristly bur.

Landscape Use Plant American beech where you can enjoy its smooth bark and spreading form. Choose a site where it will have room to grow without restriction, away from buildings and other large trees. Young trees are very shade tolerant and slow growing. It is difficult to grow grass under mature beech trees.

Site Moist, well-drained, acidic soil in sun or partial shade; will not tolerate wet or compacted soils.

Culture Nursery-grown plants are often slow to start growing after transplanting but will eventually take off. Loosen heavy soils by adding a mixture of sand and organic matter before planting. Young trees may sucker and form colonies if left unpruned. Young trees require adequate water to prevent leaf scorch in dry, hot weather. American beech is susceptible to a few disease problems, including a fungal leaf spot and powdery mildew, neither of which usually does serious damage. It is also susceptible to a bleeding canker and a bark disease, the latter of which is caused by scale insect feeding. Both are serious problems in the eastern United States and may affect Michigan trees. Reduce chances of infection by keeping trees healthy and avoiding injury to the bark.

Fraxinus pennsylvanica
Green ash
Zone 3

Native Habitat Moist to wet soils of deciduous forests throughout most of Michigan.

Size 50 to 65 feet tall, 30 to 50 feet wide

Description Green ash is a round-topped tree with spreading branches. The dark brown or gray bark is strongly furrowed. Leaves are bright green or yellowish green. Fall color is inconsistent, but is usually golden yellow.

Landscape Use This tree's adaptability has made it a widely planted landscape tree, and its overuse has led to many problems. Plant this tree only if there are no other trees suitable for your site and there are not a lot of green ashes in your area. It will grow where many other shade trees won't, offering relatively quick shade. Use it for framing, shelterbelts and windbreaks, shade, and in backyard corner plantings. It tolerates street conditions. Leaves appear late in spring and drop soon after the first fall frost, so it is a good choice where you want sunlight in spring and fall.

Site Grows best in moist, well-drained soils, but also tolerates dry, compacted soils. It is moderately shade tolerant, drought resistant, and alkaline tolerant, making it a good choice for soils with a higher pH.

Culture This large tree is easy to transplant, fairly fast growing, and will withstand severe conditions of both soil and climate. When healthy, it is long lived. In stressful situations, ashes often develop several disease problems collectively called "ash decline." This affliction is thought to be a lethal combination of environmental stresses and insect and disease problems that eventually overwhelm the tree. Afflicted trees have premature leaf and flower drop, creating a mess on lawns, sidewalks, and decks. The emerald ash borer has become a serious pest of ash trees in southeastern Michigan, resulting in the death of millions of trees in the state. The larvae feed on the inner bark, disrupting the tree's ability to transport water and nutrients. This problem makes it unrealistic to recommend ash trees for landscape use in the Lower Peninsula at this time. Female ash trees produce numerous seeds, and the seedlings can become weedy; male seedless cultivars are available. Trees may bleed if pruned in spring.

Cultivars and Other Species 'Bergeson' is a hardy cultivar with an upright, rounded crown. Zone 2. 'Marshall's Seedless' is supposedly seedless and has good green foliage color. 'Prairie Dome' is seedless and has a globe-shaped crown growing to only 40 feet. 'Prairie Spire' was selected for its upright pyramidal shape; it grows 55 feet tall. 'Summit' was selected for its strong central leader. All cultivars zone 3.

F. americana (white ash) is native to well-drained upland soils throughout most of Michigan, but is rare in the western half of the Upper Peninsula. It grows up to 90 feet tall, and fall color ranges from yellow to a distinctive maroon to deep purple. It is not as hardy (zone 4, protected spots in zone 3) or as adaptable as green ash, but it is a handsome tree where its large size can be accommodated. It does best in rich, moist soils and in full sun, though it will suffer during dry periods. 'Autumn Blaze' is a Canadian introduction, hardy into lower portions of zone 3 and growing to only 60 feet tall. 'Autumn Purple' is a male selection with deep purple fall color suitable for zone 4. 'Chicago Regal' has a more upright growth habit and rusty orange to purple fall color. Zone 4.

F. nigra (black ash) is native to moist deciduous and coniferous forests and wetlands throughout most of Michigan. It is slower growing and has an irregular form, sometimes leaning or crooked. It is hardy into zone 2, and it tolerates wet soils. It is not as susceptible to the insect and disease problems that plague green and white ash. 'Fallgold' is a seedless introduction that turns yellow early in fall. It is more adaptable to landscape situations, growing to only about 50 feet in height, but it is hardy only into zone 3.

F. quadrangulata (blue ash) is native to moist, rich deciduous woods only in the southern third of Michigan. It is smaller, growing only 30 to 50 feet tall, and has a spread of about 30 feet. It adapts well to drier soils. It is a good landscape tree but may be difficult to find in the nursery trade. Zone 4.

Fraxinus pennsylvanica

Gleditsia triacanthos var.
inermis 'Imperial'

Gleditsia triacanthos
Honey locust
Zone 4

Native Habitat Moist or rich soils in a few locations in the southern part of Michigan.

Size 35 to 70 feet tall, 25 to 50 feet wide

Description Honey locust is a fine-textured, medium-sized, open-crowned tree with an airy look. The compound leaves are bright green, and their autumn color an inconsistent yellow to yellow-green. Thorns up to 4 inches long appear on one-year-old wood and remain for many years. The fruit is a 10- to 18-inch, flat, dark brown pod that becomes black and twisted as it ripens.

Landscape Use This tree is best used in windbreaks and hedges in southern Michigan. The sharp thorns and large seedpods restrict its use as a landscape plant, but there are several thornless selections that make good specimen and street trees. These selections are good choices where you want light, dappled shade in order to grow other plants beneath the canopy. The small leaflets fall early in autumn and do not require raking. The flowers are a nectar source for bees, and the large seedpods provide food for wildlife.

Site Withstands a wide range of conditions, but does best in rich, moist soils. Tolerates drought, high pH, road salt, and soil compaction. It does require full sun.

Culture Honey locust transplants easily, and its cultivars can be used in many urban situations. It is a thin-barked tree that must be protected while it is young. Surround trees with a circle of organic mulch to keep lawn mowers and weed whippers from damaging the trunks. Trunks of young trees should be wrapped in hardware cloth during winter to prevent damage from rodents. The thornless cultivars have been overplanted in recent years, and several insects and diseases, including a disabling trunk canker, have become serious problems. The seedpods can be messy when they fall, and the main trunk may need some shaping when trees are young to ensure a good mature form.

Cultivars The species is rarely planted because of the thorns and the heavy seed production. Many male seedless cultivars have been selected from the thornless variant, *G. triacanthos* var. *inermis*. 'Imperial' is more spreading than upright, and it often lacks a single central trunk. It grows to about 35 feet tall and produces few, if any, seeds. 'Shademaster' has a strong central trunk and ascending branches. 'Skyline' has a more pyramidal form and bright gold fall color. 'Sunburst' has bright yellow new growth that turns green in summer. All cultivars hardy in zone 4.

Gymnocladus dioica

Native Habitat Deep, rich soils in southern Michigan.

Size 45 to 80 feet tall, 50 feet wide

Description Kentucky coffee tree has a picturesque, open-spreading crown. Its remarkably large, compound, bluish green leaves appear late in spring. The greenish white flowers that also appear in late spring are somewhat fragrant and are attractive to pollinating insects. Fall color is inconsistent, but is sometimes a good yellow. The 6- to 10-inch-long flat

Gymnocladus dioica
Kentucky coffee tree
Zone 4; trial in zone 3

seedpods, deeply furrowed bark, and sparse branching add winter interest.

Landscape Use Kentucky coffee tree is an excellent shade and street tree that deserves to be planted more. It is a good replacement for the disease-prone honey locust. The leaves cast very light shade (also known as filtered shade or dappled shade) that permits shade-tolerant turf grasses and partial-shade perennials to grow underneath. It is tolerant of city conditions and offers good winter interest. Leaves appear late in spring and drop soon after first fall frost, so it's a good choice where you want sunlight in spring and fall.

Site Grows best in evenly moist, rich soil, but tolerates alkaline soils and drought. Needs full sun.

Culture Kentucky coffee tree is slightly difficult to transplant because of the deep taproot. Plant smaller balled-and-burlapped or container-grown specimens in early spring. It is a moderate to slow grower. Encourage faster growth by fertilizing young trees in spring and by providing supplemental water during dry periods. The large seedpods usually fall sporadically over a long period, but some people consider them a litter problem. The seedpods are also poisonous, so children should be discouraged from playing with them. Seed-free male selections are available. It is free of insect and disease problems. It is on Michigan's special concern list.

Cultivars 'Stately Manor' has a more upright growth habit and a narrower crown. It's a male selection that does not produce seeds. 'Espresso' is a fruitless male selection with upward-arching branches in a vaselike form. Prairie Titan® is an upright-spreading male selection with good summer leaf color and interesting winter architecture. All cultivars reliably hardy in zone 4.

Juglans nigra
Black walnut
Zone 4; trial in zone 3

Native Habitat Rich woods and floodplains, as well as drier soils, in the southern half of the Lower Peninsula.

Size 50 to 80 feet tall, 50 feet wide

Description Black walnut has a well-formed trunk devoid of branches halfway to two-thirds from the ground. The bark is thick and dark brown with deep fissures. The pinnately compound leaves have fourteen to twenty-two leaflets and reach up to 24 inches in length, usually turning yellow in autumn. The distinctive, large, round nuts are borne singly or in pairs, enclosed in a solid green husk that does not open even after ripening. The nuts are edible, if you can get the husks open.

Landscape Use Black walnut is most attractive when it is grown as a specimen tree. It is best suited to large sites in southern Michigan. Avoid planting it near sidewalks and streets where falling nuts can be hazardous and messy. The nuts are a popular food source for squirrels and other wildlife, as well as humans.

Site Prefers full sun and deep, neutral to slightly alkaline soils, but tolerates drier soil.

Culture The extensive taproot on older trees makes it difficult to transplant. Plant smaller balled-and-burlapped or container-grown specimens in early spring. Seeds can also be sown in place, provided they are given some protection against hungry squirrels. There are no serious insect or disease problems, but some caterpillars use leaves as a food source. Black walnuts contain a chemical known as juglone, which is toxic to certain plants. The greatest quantities of juglone are found in the area immediately under the walnut tree, where roots are concentrated and where decaying nut hulls and leaves accumulate. Symptoms on affected plants range from stunting, yellowing, and partial to total wilting to complete death. Tomatoes and potatoes are very sensitive to juglone; other plants known to be affected include rhododendrons, white pine, paper birch, eggplants, peppers, lilacs, and cotoneasters. If possible, locate gardens or landscape beds away from the root zone of trees, or grow sensitive plants in containers to avoid root contact with the soil under black walnuts. Native plants usually not affected by juglone include wild bergamot, bloodroot, violets, cinnamon fern, Jacob's ladder, bellworts, trilliums, sensitive fern, and spiderworts.

Cultivars and Other Species 'Laciniata', a rare form, has leaflets that are fernlike and dissected with a fine texture. 'Thomas' and 'Weschcke' are two good nut-bearing cultivars for Michigan. Zone 4.

J. cinerea (butternut) has a native range similar to *J. nigra*. Its susceptibility to butternut canker keeps it from being recommended as a landscape plant. However, this disease has devastated native plants, so a butternut is worth preserving if you have one on your property. It grows 40 to 65 feet tall and has a more rounded crown than black walnut. The nuts are edible. It is hardier, well into zone 3.

Juglans nigra

Juglans nigra nut

Larix laricina

Larix laricina
Tamarack
Zone 2

Description Tamarack is the only deciduous conifer native to Michigan. It has a narrow pyramidal form and short, horizontal branches. The bark is rough with thin, reddish brown scales. The leaves are needles that are flat, soft, slender, about 1 inch long, and borne in clusters on spurlike branches. They are bright green in spring and turn an attractive yellow-gold color from September to October just before falling.

Landscape Use Tamarack's landscape use is limited by its large size, lack of heat tolerance, and falling needles in winter, which causes some people to think the tree has died. It is a good choice for shelterbelts and naturalizing in wet areas, as well as in rural landscapes on a site where the beautiful fall color can be enjoyed.

Site Prefers full sun and moist soils, but is surprisingly tolerant of drier, upland sites. It does not tolerate pollution, heat, or shade.

Culture Transplant tamarack in early spring when it is dormant, putting it into soil with sufficient moisture. Water young trees as needed to maintain soil moisture during the growing season and into early winter. An organic mulch of pine needles or shredded pine bark will help maintain soil moisture and soil acidity. Trees are subject to injury from larch case bearer and larch sawfly, but these are rarely problems in landscape situations.

Cultivars Several rare dwarf cultivars are available from specialty nurseries. They can be used as specimen plants or in the shrub border. 'Deborah Waxman' reaches 4 feet in height. 'Lanark' grows low and wide. 'Newport Beauty' rarely exceeds 2 feet tall and wide. They are all hardy in zone 4, but can be tried in zone 3.

Native Habitat Wet soils of shores, swamps, and bogs throughout Michigan, occasionally on drier sites.
Size 40 to 70 feet tall, 20 to 40 feet wide

Liriodendron tulipifera

Liriodendron tulipifera

Liriodendron tulipifera
Tulip tree
Zone 4

Native Habitat Rich deciduous woods in the southern third of Michigan.
Size 70 to 90 feet tall, 35 to 50 feet wide
Description Tulip tree has a straight trunk with dark gray, deeply furrowed bark. The unique, tuliplike flowers appear very high in the canopy, usually too far up to be enjoyed. They have six yellow petals flushed bright orange at the base, and they appear in late spring. The leaves are also tulip shaped; they are bright green in summer and spectacular golden-yellow in fall.

Landscape Use Tulip tree should be reserved for large sites away from buildings, where it can be allowed to grow unimpeded. The large limbs are susceptible to breaking in windstorms, and roots can be aggressive.

Site Deep, rich, well-drained, acidic soil in full sun.

Culture Plants may be difficult to transplant. Start with smaller trees that have been root pruned or container grown. Young trees will require water during dry periods. An organic mulch will help conserve soil moisture and protect young thin-barked trees from weed-whipper damage. Trees are susceptible to winter sunscald, so apply a tree wrap until the bark is corky. Aphids can build up to large numbers, leaving heavy deposits of honeydew on lower leaves, and eventually a black, sooty mold may grow on the honeydew. Trees that are stressed may be attacked by verticillium, a soil fungus, and by canker diseases. Tulip tree reaches the northern limit of its natural range in southern Michigan, so plant northern strains for best results.

Cultivars 'Aureo-marginatum' ('Majestic Beauty') has leaves edged with yellow. 'Fastigiatum' ('Pyramidale', 'Arnold') is smaller, growing to about 50 feet and having a spread of about 15 feet. It is a good choice for most landscape situations.

Nyssa sylvatica
Black gum
Zone 5; protected sites in zone 4

Native Habitat Mainly in moist woods and swamp borders in the southern half of the Lower Peninsula.
Size 30 to 50 feet tall, 20 to 30 feet wide
Description Black gum has a distinctive silhouette, often with drooping branches that are very crooked toward their ends. Leaves are shiny green in summer, turning an amazing yellow to orange to scarlet to purple in fall. Insignificant flowers in spring turn into bluish black fruits in fall.
Landscape Use Black gum is a good choice for wet sites or for naturalistic plantings. It also makes a nice specimen tree on a lightly shaded lawn. Set off the fall color with a dark background. It is not a good choice as a street tree, since it is intolerant of pollution. The flowers are attractive to bees, and the fruits are eaten by wildlife.
Site Moist, slightly acidic conditions in full sun to partial shade; best form is in full sun.
Culture Plant smaller trees in spring for best results. Trees will develop iron chlorosis (yellow leaves) if the soil is too alkaline. You may need to top-dress soil with acidic fertilizer to maintain the necessary soil pH. Cankers may develop, causing branches to die back; remove infected branches. To emphasize the natural shape, keep pruning to a minimum.

Nyssa sylvatica

Ostrya virginiana
Ironwood
Zone 4; trial in zone 3

Native Habitat A variety of soils throughout Michigan.
Size 20 to 40 feet tall, 20 to 30 feet wide
Description Ironwood is a handsome, small- to medium-sized tree with many horizontal or drooping branches and a rounded outline. The dark green, birchlike leaves turn a mild yellow color in fall. The straight trunk and limbs are covered with interesting, shaggy, gray bark. The seeds ripen in flattened, papery pods that are strung together like fish scales or hops and that turn from light green to gray in late summer.
Landscape Use This tough tree is well suited to smaller city landscapes and tight spaces where most shade trees would grow too large. It can be grown as a clump tree. Its clean, disease-free foliage will provide good summer shade—dense if grown in sun and more open when grown in light shade. The wood is strong and resistant to ice and wind damage. The seedpods are eaten by birds or slowly disintegrate, so there is no litter problem. Its main drawback is its slow growth rate, but this challenge can be somewhat overcome if it's given supplemental water and fertilizer when young. Use it as an understory tree in woodland gardens, where the slow growth is advantageous. Ironwood is not tolerant of salt or compacted soil, so it's not a good street tree.
Site Prefers a cool, moist, well-drained, slightly acidic soil, but adapts to a wide range of landscape situations, provided the soil is acidic and not waterlogged. Tolerates full sun, partial shade, and even heavy shade.
Culture Transplant balled-and-burlapped or container-grown trees in early spring using a northern seed source. Trees are somewhat slow to establish after transplanting. Regular watering and fertilizing when trees are young will help plants come out of transplant shock more quickly and become established. Apply a 2- to 4-inch layer of organic mulch, such as

Ostrya virginiana

pine needles, shredded oak leaves, or shredded pine bark, to keep the soil evenly moist and maintain soil acidity. Prune in winter to remove dead or damaged branches and to shape trees, if needed. Trees may bleed sap in late winter. Ironwood has no serious insect or disease problems.

Platanus occidentalis

Platanus occidentalis
Sycamore
Zone 5; trial in zone 4

Native Habitat Moist soils in the southern half of the Lower Peninsula.
Size 65 to 90 feet tall, 50 to 60 feet wide
Description This large, spreading tree has a tall central trunk and a round or oval crown. The 4- to 9-inch gently lobed leaves are medium to dark green in summer, turning yellow to brown in autumn. Dense heads of inconspicuous flowers appear in May. The fruit is an achene, appearing in fall and persisting into winter. The multicolored bark peels off in patches and is the tree's most ornamental trait.
Landscape Use The large size of the sycamore and its tendency to drop leaves and branches limit its landscape use, but it is effective along the edge of a large lawn area. It makes an impressive specimen planted along a lake or pond. The interesting mottled bark and striking silhouette offer a great deal of winter interest. Native trees are definitely worth preserving if you have one.
Site Moist, rich soil in full sun; tolerates wet, compacted soils.
Culture Anthracnose, a fungal disease that causes leaf spotting and dropping, can be a problem, especially during cool, wet springs. And powdery mildew can mar the beauty of the leaves. Neither disease is usually fatal to the trees. The large leaves, fruits, shredding bark, and twigs can be a litter problem.

Prunus serotina

Prunus serotina
Black cherry
Zone 3

Native Habitat A wide variety of soils throughout most of Michigan.
Size 50 to 75 feet tall, 40 to 50 feet wide
Description Black cherry has a uniformly thick trunk, often tilted or bent, and an open, rounded crown. The narrow, oval, shiny green leaves develop a burgundy-red to yellowish color in fall. The attractive, dark reddish brown bark has long, horizontal lenticels. On older trees, the bark becomes heavily textured, chunky, and beautiful. Attractive 1/2-inch white flowers appear in hanging clusters in May. The fruit is a green cherry, which turns red to dark blue or black and which hangs in pendant clusters.
Landscape Use Although highly ornamental, black cherry is rarely planted in landscape settings because of its susceptibility to black knot. It is definitely worth preserving if you have one on your property, however, and it's a good choice for attracting wildlife and for naturalizing. When it survives in the landscape, it makes a handsome shade or specimen tree. The fruits are tart but edible and are a favorite of birds.
Site Will grow in almost any soil in full sun to partial shade, but best growth is in deep, moist, slightly acidic, fertile soils and full sun.
Culture Black cherry is moderately difficult to transplant because of the taproot. Move it in early spring. Keep trees vigorous with ample water and good soil fertility to help avoid pest problems. The occasional fruits that go uneaten by birds and drop to the ground may sprout new trees that can be weedy. Black knot is a serious fungal problem that can kill trees at a young age. It appears as a swollen black area on the branches. Cut out and destroy infected branches, going back about 4 inches below the knot.

Quercus alba
White oak
Zone 4; southern part of zone 3

Native Habitat Well-drained, acidic soils throughout the Lower Peninsula and the southern part of the Upper Peninsula.

Size 50 to 75 feet tall, 40 to 60 feet wide

Description White oak has a broad, rounded top and irregularly spreading limbs. The leaves, which don't fully unfold until mid-May, are deeply divided into five to nine fingerlike, rounded lobes. They are bright green in summer, turning deep red or violet-purple in fall.

Landscape Use A well-grown oak is an asset in any landscape, usually greatly increasing property value. Its stately presence is felt year-round. The leaves offer summer shade and fall color, and they often persist into winter for added interest. The tree's strong, bold silhouette also offers winter interest. The acorns are a valuable fall food source for many wildlife species. Do not be put off by oaks' reputation for slow growth or their susceptibility to oak wilt, which is not usually a problem in landscape situations.

Site Grows best in fertile, acidic, heavy soil in full sun, but will tolerate lighter, sandier soils and dry conditions.

Culture Oaks are somewhat difficult to transplant, making them hard to find in the nursery trade. Root pruning and container growing have made them more available and easier to transplant. Seedlings are fast growing, so don't hesitate to plant an acorn where you want a tree. Plant it in fall (providing protection from digging squirrels), or store it in moist sand in a cool place over the winter and then plant it in spring. Oak roots are very sensitive to changes in soil levels. Even a small change can kill roots, so avoid adding or removing soil around trees. Oak wilt, a fungal disease, can kill mature oaks; red oaks are more susceptible than white oaks. Insects infect trees with oak wilt when they enter through wounds caused by pruning or by root damage during construction. The fungus can spread to nearby trees by root grafts.

Oak wilt is mainly a problem on native stands; usually landscape specimens are isolated enough not to be at risk. Do not prune oaks while insects are most active, from April 1 to July 1.

Other Species *Q. bicolor* (swamp white oak) is found occasionally on wetter sites in the southern half of the Lower Peninsula. It grows 40 to 65 feet tall and has an open, rounded crown. It is easier to transplant than white oak, and it makes a handsome specimen or shade tree. It is also faster growing and more tolerant of tougher sites. Fall color is brown. Zone 4.

Q. coccinea (scarlet oak) is native to drier sites on the Lower Peninsula. It is a red-oak type, growing 50 to 70 feet tall. It is a good landscape tree and has relatively fast growth, good form, and scarlet fall color. Plant northern strains in acidic soil for best results. Zone 4.

Q. ellipsoidalis (northern pin oak) is found on drier, sandier sites, mainly in the eastern half of Michigan, but there are some scattered populations in the west. It is smaller, growing to only 45 to 65 feet. Fall color is a good deep red to reddish brown. It will suffer from chlorosis in soils with too high of a pH, but this problem is easily corrected by adding iron to the soil, thus lowering the pH. It is susceptible to oak wilt. Zone 3.

Quercus macrocarpa

Q. macrocarpa (bur oak) is native to a wide variety of soils, mainly in the southern half of the Lower Peninsula but also in the Upper Peninsula. The leaves of this white-oak type are shaped like bass fiddles. It grows 50 to 80 feet tall and makes an impressive specimen in a savanna setting. It is adaptable to various soils and more tolerant of city conditions than other oaks, but it can be difficult to transplant. It is too large for most city landscapes, but it is a good choice for rural and large suburban sites. Zone 3.

Q. muehlenbergii (Chinquapin oak) is native to limestone soils in the southern half of the Lower Peninsula. It only grows about 40 to 50 feet tall, making it a good oak for smaller landscapes. It tolerates higher pH soils better than most oaks. Zone 5; trial in zone 4.

Q. palustris (pin oak) is native to moist soils in the southern half of the Lower Peninsula. It grows 65 feet tall and has a spread of up to 50 feet. Easier to transplant than most oaks, it has outstanding fall color and a good pyramidal form. It does suffer from iron chlorosis if the soil pH is too high. Zone 4.

Q. rubra (red oak) is native to a wide variety of soils throughout Michigan. It grows 50 to 80 feet tall and has pointed leaves. It is faster growing than other oaks and easier to transplant. The dark green leaves turn to shades of red in fall and persist into winter. It prefers sandy loam soils that are well drained and acidic; it will get iron chlorosis in high pH soils. It is tolerant of city conditions but is very susceptible to oak wilt. If you have a red oak on your property, it is definitely worth some effort to keep it healthy. Zone 4; trial in zone 3.

Q. velutina (black oak) is native to dry, sandy woods in the southern third of Michigan. It grows about 60 feet tall and has an open crown. Fall color is dull red to orange-brown. It is worth seeking out in the nursery trade. Zone 4.

Quercus bicolor

Quercus rubra

Quercus muehlenbergii

Sorbus americana
American mountain ash
Zone 2

Sorbus decora

Native Habitat Cool, moist sites, mainly on the Upper Peninsula but also into the Lower Peninsula.

Size 20 to 30 feet tall, 15 to 25 feet wide

Description American mountain ash is a small tree, often more shrublike, and has multiple trunks. The spreading, slender branches create a narrow, round-topped crown. Bark is light gray and smooth and has small platelike scales. Leaves are pinnately compound and have thirteen to seventeen leaflets; they are bright green above, turning bright yellow in fall. Creamy white flowers appear in flat clusters in May and early June. The showy scarlet red berries are ornamental in September and October, especially in contrast to the fall leaf color.

Landscape Use American mountain ash is a good single-trunked tree or a multistemmed, vase-shaped shrub. The fine-textured leaves cast light shade. It makes a nice specimen plant on a small site. It can be used as a middle-layer shrub under the canopy of larger trees or massed for screening or a windbreak. Birds love the berries, which are usually stripped from the tree before winter.

Site Does best in acidic, moist locations in full sun, but tolerates drier areas and thinner soils if well mulched and watered. Plant this understory tree where it will be sheltered from afternoon sun in winter.

Culture American mountain ash is hardier and not as susceptible to fire blight as the nonnative European mountain ash (*S. aucuparia*). To reduce chances of infection, avoid wounding the trunk and prune the trees only while they're dormant. Young trees should be protected against sunscald and against rodent feeding in winter. Yellow-bellied sapsuckers often drill rows of horizontal holes to suck the sap, and this damage can be enough to kill trees.

Other Species *S. decora* (showy mountain ash) is native across a wider range farther south in the Lower Peninsula. The leaflets are broader and darker green than *S. americana*. It blooms and fruits a week or two later, and the fruits are slightly larger and deeper red. It is moderately shade tolerant and slow growing. Zone 2.

Tilia americana
Basswood
Zone 3; protected spots in zone 2

Native Habitat Throughout Michigan, usually in rich soils.

Size 50 to 90 feet tall, 40 to 50 feet wide

Description This large tree has a dense, rounded crown and large, heart-shaped, dark green leaves. Autumn color is a dull green to slightly yellow-green. The light gray, smooth bark becomes dark gray with age. The cream-colored flowers appear in June and July; they are fragrant and attractive to bees. The fruit is a rounded nut-like drupe that hangs onto the tree long into winter.

Landscape Use Basswood is a trouble-free, hardy tree that makes a good specimen or shade tree if you have room for its large size. It casts deep shade under which it is difficult to grow other plants. It's not tolerant of soil compaction or air pollution, so it's not well suited as a street tree.

Site Prefers moist, fertile, well-drained soils, but will grow in drier, heavier soils in full sun or partial shade.

Culture Basswood is easily transplanted in early spring. It is moderately fast growing and long lived. Wrap young trees in winter to prevent sunscald. Prune out sprouts that develop at the base of the tree. Few insects or diseases bother it.

Cultivars Several cultivars have been selected for their smaller size. 'Bailyard' (Frontyard®) has a broadly pyramidal shape and good yellow fall color; it grows to 70 feet in height. 'Boulevard' grows 60 feet tall and has a more columnar shape. 'Fastigiata' is more pyramidal; it grows to 50 feet tall and about 35 feet wide. 'Sentry' has an upright-branching habit. The cultivars are hardy in zone 4 and can be tried in zone 3.

Tilia americana 'Fastigiata'

Additional Native Deciduous Trees

Castanea dentata (American chestnut) is native to forests in the southeastern-most part of the Lower Peninsula. It has nearly been exterminated in the state by chestnut blight, a fungal disease first noted in Michigan about 1930. This majestic tree grows to 100 feet in height and has a wide-spreading crown. Flowers are pale yellow. Leaves emerge reddish, changing to dark green in summer and yellow-bronze in fall. The 2-inch husks contain two or three edible nuts. American chestnut is a wonderful tree, and worth preserving if you have one, but no longer realistic for landscape use. It is on Michigan's endangered species list. Zone 4.

Malus coronaria (American crab) is native to rich deciduous woods and borders, mainly in the southern half of the Lower Peninsula. It grows 15 to 30 feet tall, often having a crooked trunk and rounded crown with contorted branches. Fragrant white flowers tinged with rose appear in May and are followed by small green apples, which often hang on trees into winter. The fruits can be used for jelly. It is very susceptible to apple rust, which can greatly mar the beauty of the leaves. It makes a nice small tree at the edges of lawns and could be considered for mixed borders. Zone 4.

Morus rubra (red mulberry) is native to moist soils and floodplains in a few sites in the southern part of Michigan. It grows to 50 feet tall and has a single trunk and spreading branches. The shiny green leaves turn yellow in fall. The prolific fruits are green berries, which turn to red then black. The fruits are a food source for birds and other wildlife, and they can be used in jams, jellies, and pies. Trees often become weedy in the landscape after birds deposit the seeds, and the fruits are messy when they fall. Red mulberry is on Michigan's threatened species list. Protected sites in zone 4.

Populus tremuloides (quaking aspen) inhabits wet or dry soils throughout Michigan. It quickly grows to about 65 feet tall. It has good golden yellow fall color, and the leaves make a wonderful sound when they flutter in the slightest breeze. However, it is short lived, weedy, and has suckers, limiting its landscape use to naturalistic plantings and shelterbelts. Zone 3.

P. grandidentata (big-toothed aspen) is native to moist soils throughout Michigan, but suffers from the same problems as *P. tremuloides*. Zone 3.

P. deltoides (eastern cottonwood) is native to wet soils along streams, rivers, and lakes throughout the Lower Peninsula. It is large, growing 70 to 100 feet tall, and the seeds make a cottony mess in spring. Zone 3.

Salix nigra (black willow) is native to wet soils, stream banks, and wetlands mainly in the southern half of Michigan. It grows 40 to 60 feet tall or more. It has a single, crooked trunk—often forked—and a narrow, irregular crown. Leaves are shiny green, turning light yellow in fall. It is fast growing and short lived, and the brittle wood can become messy. Consider it for use as a lawn tree or for screening in an area with moist soil. Zone 3.

S. amygdaloides (peach-leaved willow) is native a little farther north and is very similar to *S. nigra*. Zone 3.

Sassafras albidum (sassafras) is native to dry, sandy sites in the southern half of the Lower Peninsula. It grows 30 to 60 feet tall and 25 to 40 feet wide and has an irregular shape. The deeply furrowed, reddish brown bark is attractive. Bright green, interestingly shaped leaves turn yellow to orange to scarlet in fall. Yellow flowers appear before the leaves in early spring. Fruits are bluish black with bright red pedicels and appear in early fall. Sassafras is good for naturalized

Populus tremuloides

plantings and can be used as an understory tree in woodland gardens. It is a good landscape tree if you are willing to invest some time in pruning. Birds love the fruits. It requires well-drained, slightly acidic soil in sun to partial shade. It can be difficult to transplant and establish because of the taproot. Plant young trees in early spring for best results. Leaves can get chlorotic if soil is too alkaline. Trees can spread from root suckers and form dense thickets if left to grow. Prune trees in winter to improve their shape. Zone 5; protected sites in zone 4.

Ulmus americana (American elm) is native to moist soils throughout Michigan. It grows 70 to 100 feet tall and 50 to 70 feet wide. The vase-shaped form and arching branches of American elm are quite distinctive, and the dark green leaves turn yellow in fall. Once a favorite because of its urban tolerance, fast growth, and unique vase-shaped silhouette, American elm is not recommended for landscape planting at this time due to widespread Dutch elm disease.

U. rubra (red elm) is native to river bottoms and lowlands, mainly on the Lower Peninsula. It grows 50 to 70 feet tall. It is less susceptible to Dutch elm disease, but it is not nearly as ornamental and becomes weedy in the landscape. It can be used for shelterbelts. Zone 3.

Vines

Vines serve both ornamental and functional roles in the landscape. They are a good way to bring the dimension of height to areas not suitable for trees, such as in tight courtyards or next to buildings. Their verdant covering softens arbors and trellises, often providing shade for areas underneath. They also serve as screening, covering unsightly landscape elements such as chain-link fences or compost and storage structures. There are only a few native vines suitable for landscape use, and most are rampant growers without showy flowers, best suited to covering unsightly objects.

To use vines correctly, you must understand their climbing characteristics. Some, like wild grape, have tendrils that attach the vines to the support. Other vines climb by twining or wrapping themselves around supports; bittersweet is an example. Woodbine sends out sucker-like disks that attach to supports. The support structure should be in place before planting. If you install a fence or trellis after the vine is planted, you run the risk of damaging the roots.

When selecting a vine, consider hardiness, light require-ments, growth rate, and seasonal aspects such as flowers, fruits, fall color, attraction to wildlife, and winter appearance.

Planting

Most vines should be planted in early spring. If you have the opportunity to move a native vine, move it in early spring. Bare-root plants must be planted in spring as soon as the soil can be worked. Container plants can be planted any time but the hottest days of summer, during July and August; spring is still the best time for planting, however.

Before planting, amend the soil with a good amount of organic matter such as compost, peat moss, or well-rotted manure. Mix this matter thoroughly with the planting-hole soil. Place the vine at the same depth it was growing in the container. Bare-root plants should be planted so that the crown is level with the ground. Newly planted vines should not need additional fertilizer. It is a good idea to surround all newly planted woody plants with a ring of organic mulch 2 to 4 inches thick. Good mulches are wood chips, shredded bark, and pine needles. Replenish the mulch as needed throughout the growing season. Once the vines are tall enough, they will probably need to be trained to their support. You can tie them with soft twine or gently wrap the young stems around or through supports.

Care

The first two or three years after planting, make sure the soil is evenly moist from spring until the ground freezes in fall. Once established, most native vines can tolerate some dry periods, but don't hesitate to water as needed, especially in sandy soils. Always saturate the soil thoroughly with each watering. Most vines are rampant growers that need little or no fertilizer once established, but young

Native vines may not always be high on the list for their ornamental value, but they can be functional in the landscape, often used to cover chain-link fencing and other undesirable features.

plants will benefit from a spring application of fertilizer. Spread a layer of rotted manure or compost around each plant or use Milorganite or fish emulsion. Keep weeds pulled or smother them with organic mulch.

Most vines will benefit from some selective pruning while they are young, to develop a good shape. The best time to prune is early spring. Remove any dead, damaged, or diseased parts at any time of year, cutting back to just above a healthy, outfacing bud. Vines that have become overgrown can be renewal pruned by cutting plants back to about 4 inches from the ground in early spring. Surround them with a layer of compost or rotted manure and water them well to help them recover.

Possible Problems

Few insects or diseases bother vines. Powdery mildew can affect some vines, especially when the dense foliage remains wet for long periods of time. Snip out the infected areas and dispose of the foliage. Thin out plants to allow for better air circulation and drying of foliage. Leaf spots may leave plants somewhat defoliated by late summer, but this loss of leaves is rarely a serious problem. Aphids often feed on young leaves in hot, dry weather. Dislodge them by spraying the foliage daily during hot weather with a hard spray from the hose.

Celastrus scandens
American bittersweet
Zone 3

Celastrus scandens

Native Habitat Moist clearings and thickets throughout most of Michigan.
Height Up to 25 feet
Description This vigorous climbing vine's most ornamental feature is its showy fruits, which appear on female plants in fall. The fruit has an outer yellow-orange husk that opens to expose the red aril. Outer husks remain attached to the base of fruits, adding contrast. The fruits hang in 2- to 3-inch-long clusters like small bunches of grapes. American bittersweet has nondescript greenish white flowers in late spring, and wedge-shaped, green summer foliage.
Landscape Use Bittersweet is mainly grown for its showy fall fruits, but it can be used as a screen in difficult sites, to cover a steep bank, or to scramble over stone walls or fences. It is a strong plant that can overtake less vigorous plants growing nearby. The twining,

fast-growing shoots will coil around each other if there is nothing else available. Songbirds eat the fruits.
Site Very adaptable, but prefers moist, well-drained soils. Fruiting is best in full sun, but plants will grow in light shade.
Culture Since plants are dioecious, both male and female forms must be planted to ensure fruit production. It needs a strong trellis or fence to support the prolific growth. Prune this vigorous vine back a bit each spring to allow good sun exposure to all the stems. Harvest branches for use indoors as soon as they reach maturity. American bittersweet has become invasive in warmer areas of the country, but it is pretty well behaved in zone 4 and in colder regions. Be sure you are planting native species and not the more aggressive, introduced *C. orbiculatus* (Asian bittersweet); they look similar.

Clematis virginiana
Virgin's bower
Zone 3

Native Habitat Open or semi-shady, damp woods and thickets throughout Michigan.

Height Up to 20 feet

Description This vigorous vine has compound leaves with three leaflets. The small but numerous creamy white flowers appear in dense panicles in late June and July. The flowers turn to ornamental, fluffy seed clusters in August and September and persist into winter.

Landscape Use Virgin's bower is one of the best native vines for landscape use. It can be grown as a traditional vine, up a trellis or a fence; planted at the base of mailbox posts; or used as groundcover on steep banks or other tough sites. It is a prolific grower that will quickly cover cut stumps or other items that need screening. It will grow up into nearby trees and shrubs, and it is sometimes used this way to bring color to spring-blooming plants that are finished blooming.

Site Adaptable, but prefers well-drained soil in full sun to light shade.

Culture Virgin's bower climbs by twining its stems around its support. Without a support, it will creep along the ground as a groundcover and it can be used this way.

Other Species *C. occidentalis* (western blue virgin's bower) is native to acidic pine forests in scattered locations on the Upper Peninsula. It can grow up to 20 feet long and has blue-to-violet, nodding, 1½-inch flowers from late spring to early summer. It is a nice plant for a shady trellis or along the ground in woodland gardens, if you can provide it with the shady, acidic soil conditions it requires. It is on Michigan's special concern list, and it is difficult to find retail sources. Zone 3.

Clematis virginiana

Menispermum canadense
Moonseed
Zone 4

Native Habitat Moist woods, thickets, and riverbanks, mainly in the southern half of Michigan.

Height Up to 15 feet

Description Moonseed is a semi-woody, deciduous, twining vine with slender stems and no tendrils. The tropical-looking, deep green, nearly round or slightly lobed leaves range from 4 to 8 inches in diameter. Open clusters of white to greenish white flowers appear in June and continue into July. The common name comes from the crescent-shaped seed hidden in the bluish black, ⅓-inch fruits, which grow in clusters resembling wild grape.

Landscape Use Moonseed is grown for its handsome maple-like foliage. The large leaves make this vine effective for screening. It can also be used as a groundcover in woodland gardens. Plants are dioecious, so both a male and a female are needed to produce fruits. The glossy black berries, which are often mistaken for wild grapes, are poisonous.

Site Needs well-drained soil in part to light shade or sun.

Culture Moonseed climbs by twining its stems around its support. Without a support, it will creep along the ground as a groundcover. It often dies back over the winter, but grows back quickly. Suckers may appear. Plants can be difficult to find in the nursery trade.

Menispermum canadense

Parthenocissus quinquefolia
Woodbine, Virginia creeper
Zone 2

Parthenocissus quinquefolia

Native Habitat Moist soil in thickets and upland deciduous forests, mainly in the southern half of Michigan.

Height Up to 30 feet

Description Woodbine has large, palmately compound leaves with five leaflets that turn brilliant red early in fall. Small white flowers appear in inconspicuous panicles in July and August. The bluish black berries are showy after the leaves have fallen. The woody stems are quite large on older plants.

Landscape Use This vine is too aggressive for many landscape situations but is good for covering in less formal situations. Use it for screening fences and other unsightly items. It is the only native vine that will adhere to flat surfaces such as brick walls. It is not a good choice for wood-sided buildings, however, since it can stain the wood. Choose a spot where the showy fall color will stand out. It will grow as groundcover and can be used for screening on tough sites. Birds eat the fruits, and seedlings can appear throughout the landscape.

Site Will grow in almost any soil in sun to shade.

Culture Woodbine is a fast-growing vine that clings by tendrils, which end in sucker-like disks. The tendrils can twine around wire or twigs, and the disks adhere to bark or walls, so it will grow without support. As it becomes established, aerial rootlets grow out of stems to hold it more permanently. It can be cut back to the ground in spring to keep it from developing a thick, woody trunk and from growing out of bounds.

Cultivars 'Engelmannii' and 'Saint-Paulii' have smaller leaflets. 'Saint-Paulii' is best for a brick or stone wall because its sucker-like disks are better developed. 'Variegata' has green-speckled leaves but they often revert to green. Cultivars hardy in zone 3.

Vitis riparia
Wild grape
Zone 2

Vitis riparia

Native Habitat Riverbanks and rich woods throughout most of Michigan.

Height Up to 30 feet

Description This vigorous vine has traditional grape leaves that are 3 to 7 inches long and turn an attractive yellow-gold color in fall. Fragrant flowers appear in panicles in May and June and are followed by showy, purple-black clusters of fruits. Individual grapes are less than half an inch in diameter and have a whitish bloom. Stems of mature plants can be 2 inches or more in diameter and have attractive shredded bark.

Landscape Use Wild grape is one of the more attractive native vines. It can be used for screening or covering a large, sturdy pergola. It needs a substantial structure to support the woody stems. The small fruits can be used for jelly and are a favorite of many wildlife species.

Site Grows well in most soils in full sun to light shade. Fruiting is best in full sun.

Culture The stems of wild grape attach by twining and tendrils. Provide a strong support for the woody stems. Keep stems thinned out to reduce chances of powdery mildew.

Bibliography

Books

Barns, Burton V., and Warren H. Wagner Jr. *Michigan Trees: A Guide to the Trees of the Great Lakes Region.* University of Michigan, 1981.

Boland, Tim, Laura Coit, and Marty Hair. *Michigan Gardener's Guide.* Cool Springs Press, 2002.

Burrell, C. Colston. *A Gardener's Encyclopedia of Wild Flowers.* Rodale Press Inc., 1997.

Cullina, William. *Guide to Growing and Propagating Wildflowers of the United States and Canada.* Houghton Mifflin Co., 2000.

Curtis, John T. *The Vegetation of Wisconsin: An Ordination of Plant Communities.* University of Wisconsin Press, 1971.

Dirr, Michael A. *Manual of Woody Landscape Plants, Their Identification, Ornamental Characteristics, Culture, Propagation, and Uses, Fifth Edition.* Stipes Publishing, 1998.

Leopold, Donald J. *Native Plants of the Northeast, A Guide for Gardening and Conservation.* Timber Press, 2005.

Lund, Harry C. *Michigan Wildflowers in Color.* Thunder Bay Press, 1985.

Michigan State University Extension. *Michigan's Natural Communities: Draft List and Descriptions.* Michigan Natural Features Inventory, 2003.

Michigan State University Extension. *Michigan's Threatened Plants.* Michigan Natural Features Inventory, 2000.

Moyle, John B., and Evelyn W. Moyle. *Northland Wildflowers, The Comprehensive Guide to the Minnesota Region.* University of Minnesota Press, 2001.

Penskar, M. R, A. A. Reznicek, W. W. Brodovich, G. S. Wilhelm, L. A. Masters, K. D. Herman, and K. P. Gardiner. *Floristic Quality Assessment for Michigan.* 2001.

Peterson, Roger Tory, and Margaret McKenny. *A Field Guide to Wildflowers: Northeastern and North-central North America.* Houghton Mifflin Co., 1968.

Sargent, M. S, and Carter, K. S. eds. *Managing Michigan Wildlife: A Landowners Guide.* Michigan United Conservation Clubs, East Lansing, MI, 1999.

Snyder, Leon C. *Trees and Shrubs for Northern Gardens.* Anderson Horticultural Library, 2000.

Szerlag, Nancy, and Alison Beck. *Perennials for Michigan.* Lone Pine Publishing, 2002.

Voss, Edward G. *Michigan Flora, Part I: Gymnosperms and Monocots.* Cranbook Institute of Science, 1972.

———. *Michigan Flora, Part II: Dicots.* Cranbook Institute of Science, 1985.

———. *Michigan Flora, Part III: Dicots Concluded.* Cranbook Institute of Science, 1996.

Wasowski, Sally. *Gardening with Prairie Plants.* University of Minnesota Press, 2002.

Journals

Wild Ones Journal. Several editions.

Websites

Emerald Ash Borer, http://www.emeraldashborer.info/homeownerinfo.cfm

Michigan Department of Natural Resource, www.michigan.gov/dnr.

Michigan Native Plant Producers Association, http://www.nohlc.org/MNPPA.htm.

Michigan Plants Online, http://herbarium.lsa.umich.edu/website/michflora/onlinemaps.html.

Northern Prairie Wildlife Research Center, http://www.npwrc.usgs.gov.

Ornamental Plants plus Version 3.0, Michigan State University Extension & Michigan Nursery and Landscape Assn., http://web1.msue.msu.edu/msue/imp/modzz/modzzc.html.

Plant Conservation Alliance's Alien Plant Working Group, http://www.nps.gov/plants/alien.

United States Department of Agriculture Plants Database, http://plants.usda.gov.

Wisflora Vascular Plants of Wisconsin, http://www.botany.wisc.edu/wisflora/search.asp.

Index

About the Author

Lynn Steiner is one of the Midwest's best-known garden writers. Her enthusiasm for native plants stems from her childhood curiosity about all things natural. She spent many hours hiking near her childhood home in northeastern Wisconsin, camera and notebook in hand, and has traveled extensively throughout Michigan and the Midwest. She is a member of Wild Ones, The Prairie Enthusiasts, and the Minnesota Native Plant Society.

Lynn received a Bachelor of Science in natural resources from the University of Wisconsin. In 1981, she moved to Minnesota and attended the University of Minnesota, where she earned a master's degree in horticulture with a minor in agricultural journalism.

For fifteen years, Lynn was the driving force behind *Northern Gardener*, the official publication of the Minnesota State Horticultural Society. As editor, she took the magazine from a society-based publication to a nationally recognized and respected gardening magazine. Now a freelance writer, editor, and photographer, Lynn is one of the leading authorities on Midwestern plants. She writes a regular column on native plants for *Northern Gardener* magazine, and is also the author of *Landscaping with Native Plants of Minnesota*. Her work has appeared in Better Homes and Gardens *Garden Doctor*, Miracle-Gro *Encyclopedia of Plant Care*, *Sunset Midwest Top 10 Garden Guide*, Better Homes and Gardens *Stone Landscaping*, Miracle-Gro *Guide to Growing Stunning Trees & Shrubs*, *Scott's Lawnscaping*, the *Minneapolis Star Tribune*, and *Gardening How-To* magazine.

Lynn lives with her husband, two teenage sons, a golden retriever, and two cats on a turn-of-the-century farmstead in northern Washington County, Minnesota, where she gets great enjoyment from tending her gardens, watching the progress of her restored prairie, and hunting for native plants in the surrounding countryside.